Praise for a previous edition of

QUICK ESCAPES® FROM
San Francisco

"The itineraries are quite detailed. . . . The presentation is affable, ever helpful, and informative—a fine book for San Franciscans and the rest of us as well."

—*Travelwriter Marketletter*

Help Us Keep This Guide Up-to-Date

We would love to hear from you concerning your experiences with this guide and how you feel it could be improved and kept up to date. Please send your comments and suggestions to:

editorial@GlobePequot.com

Thanks for your input, and happy travels!

QUICK ESCAPES® FROM
San Francisco

The Best Weekend Getaways

SEVENTH EDITION

Karen Misuraca

travel
Guilford, Connecticut

To buy books in quantity for corporate use
or incentives, call **(800) 962-0973**
or e-mail **premiums@GlobePequot.com**.

Quick Escapes is a registered trademark of Morris Book Publishing, LLC.

Editor: Amy Lyons
Project Editor: Lynn Zelem
Layout: Joanna Beyer
Text design: Sheryl P. Kober
Maps: Daniel Lloyd © Morris Book Publishing, LLC.

ISSN 1542-2526
ISBN 978-0-7627-5404-5

Printed in the United States of America
10 9 8 7 6 5 4 3 2 1

Thanks to my traveling partner, golf guru, and tireless Sherpa, Michael, for the best times of my life, on the road in California.

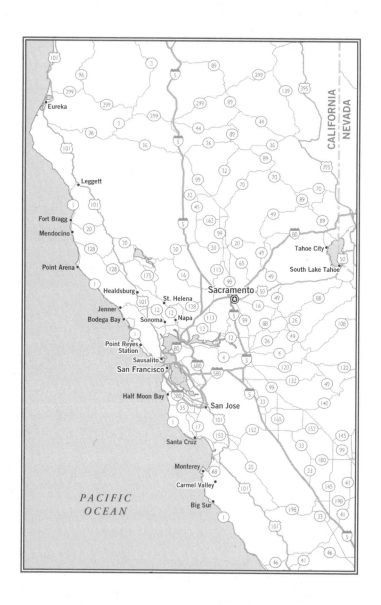

CONTENTS

INTRODUCTION

Thirteen trips are described in this guidebook, with all the details and inside information you will need to know for a perfect weekend getaway from San Francisco. Every escape is a driving tour, with sightseeing, recreation, restaurants, and lodging located and described. To give you a variety of activities from which to choose, each weekend itinerary is quite lively, packed with sights and side trips. Annual special events are listed, as are recommended restaurants and lodgings. There's More gives you reasons to return another time. For advance planning, check out the more than 21 maps and, listed under For More Information, the visitors bureaus.

If you favor getaways tucked away in one peaceful spot, use the chapters to book a quiet bed-and-breakfast inn, choose romantic restaurants, and read about what all the other tourists are doing.

Or, take advantage of the easy accessibility of the Sonoma and Napa Wine Country, of fishing villages by the sea, unique shopping and gallery meccas, and myriad state and regional parks and a National Seashore, all close enough for daytrips and short weekend sojourns. From the shores of the fabled, rocky coastline to honky-tonk beach towns, and wineries, festivals, Victorian-era towns and high-tech museums, ranch resorts and country roads, you can escape every weekend for a year and still have a hundred places to experience.

Keeping California's microclimates in mind, be prepared for weather changes throughout the year, particularly in the coastal and mountain regions. Fog, rain, or snow may not be what you expected, but discoveries made on a wintry weekend could turn you into a California lover, in more ways than one.

If you're looking forward to a particular bed-and-breakfast inn or a restaurant, be sure to call well in advance. And remember that in some resort communities, businesses may not be open every month of the year.

Most restaurants and lodgings listed are in the midrange price-wise; a few special places are expensive. Rates and prices are not noted because they can be counted on to change.

In this seventh edition, you will find more Web site addresses, reflecting the tremendous tide of information now available online, not to mention the benefits of browsing beforehand. Even the tiniest inn is likely to have a Web site, with a virtual tour of each room. Online, you can make restaurant and lodging reservations, get driving instructions, and print out maps to specific street addresses. Not like the old days, when we had to phone and write for brochures and maps!

If you have comments on how the escapes worked out for you, please drop me a note care of The Globe Pequot Press. Thanks to the travelers who made useful suggestions and contributions to this seventh edition of *Quick Escapes® From San Francisco.*

It's a good idea to include the following items in your getaway bag:

- Jacket, long pants, and walking shoes for trail hiking and beachcombing in any weather.
- Binoculars (so as not to miss bald eagles circling and whales spouting).
- Corkscrew, a California necessity.
- Day pack or basket with picnic gear.
- Maps: the directions and maps provided here are meant for general information—you'll want to obtain your own maps.
- Plastic bag for collecting/recycling your trash.
- California State Park Pass: Most state parks charge a day fee of several dollars. Frequent visitors to the state parks will save money by purchasing an annual car pass ($125) and/or boat

launching pass ($75); discounts are available for seniors and those with a limited income). Call (800) 777-0369; www .parks.ca.gov. (Good news! Many state parks now have Wi-Fi at picnic tables, tents, RV spaces, cabins and other sites; see the Web site for the list of participating parks.)

- America the Beautiful National Parks and Federal Recreational Lands Pass, $80: admits the pass holder(s) and passengers in a non-commercial vehicle at per vehicle fee areas and pass holder plus three adults, not to exceed four adults, at per person fee areas (children under 16 are free). Obtain the pass in person at the park, by calling 888-ASK USGS, Ext. 1, or at http://store.usgs.gov/pass.

- America the Beautiful National Parks and Federal Recreational Lands Senior Pass, $10: a lifetime pass for U.S. citizens or permanent residents age 62 and over, providing access to Federal recreation sites that charge an entrance or standard amenity fee. Admits pass holder and passengers in a non-commercial vehicle at per vehicle fee areas and pass holder plus three adults, not to exceed four adults, at per person fee areas (children under 16 are free). Also provides a 50% discount on some Expanded Amenity Fees for such facilities as camping, swimming, boat launch, and specialized interpretive services. In some cases where Expanded Amenity Fees are charged, only the pass holder will be given the 50 percent price reduction. The pass is non-transferable and generally does not cover or reduce special recreation permit fees or fees charged by concessionaires. The pass can only be obtained in person at the park. U.S. citizens or permanent residents with permanent disabilities can obtain this pass at no cost.

If wildlife is your passion, the Web site www.cawatchablewild life.org offers excellent driving itineraries focusing on more than

200 places in the state where you can get up close to birds, mammals, and other wildlife; animal- and bird-related festivals are described, too.

For more information on northern California destinations, write or call the California Travel and Tourism Commission, P.O. Box 1499, Sacramento 94812-1499; (877) 225-4367; www.visit california.com.

NORTHBOUND ESCAPES

NORTHBOUND ESCAPE *One*
Wine Road to the Sea
THE RUSSIAN RIVER ROUTE, HEALDSBURG / 1 NIGHT

Wineries
Farm trails
Antiquing
Redwoods
River rambling
Victorian town

In the mid-1800s tourists from San Francisco rode ferries across the bay and hopped onto a narrow-gauge railroad to reach summer resorts on the Russian River. The arrival of the motorcar and decline of lumbering caused the towns along the river to fall into a deep sleep for a few decades. In the 1970s the tremendous growth of wineries began a new era of tourism. Now more than fifty Sonoma County wineries can be discovered on the back roads of the Russian River and Dry Creek Valleys.

The Russian River winds through redwood canyons—past sandy beaches, orchards, and vineyards—sliding calmly all the way to the Pacific Ocean at Jenner. Rustic inns, casual cafes, leafy walking trails, great fishing holes, and magnificent redwood groves are reason to spend several weekends following its path.

Canoeing, kayaking, and tubing on the Russian are very popular activities. A good paddling route is the scenic 10-mile stretch from Forestville to Guerneville, where you find many beaches and stopping points for fishing and picnicking. It takes a half day, including rest stops. Ospreys, blue herons, deer, and turtles are some of the wildlife that accompany your trek. Bring plenty of water, secure your car keys with a safety pin in your pocket, and beware of sunburn on the top of your legs.

Your weekend begins in the Victorian town of Healdsburg. The westernmost destination of your Russian River Wine Road escape

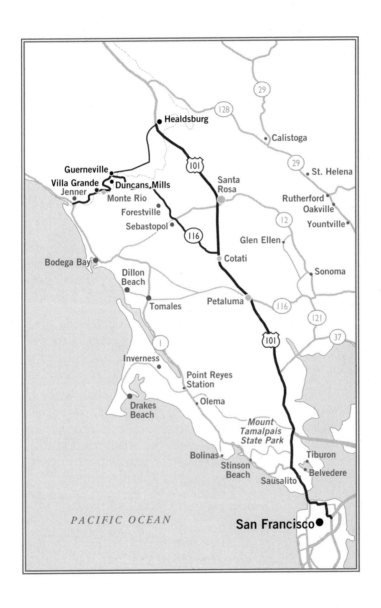

is the tiny town of Jenner, on a high bluff overlooking a marshy bird sanctuary at the mouth of the river.

DAY 1 / MORNING

Head north from the Golden Gate Bridge on US 101 to Healdsburg, about one and a quarter hours, taking the central Healdsburg exit into the center of town, parking on the **Healdsburg Plaza,** a lovely, tree-shaded Spanish-style plaza built when the town was established in 1867. Band concerts and outdoor festivals are held on the plaza green on many weekends.

BREAKFAST   **Downtown Bakery and Creamery,** 308 A Center St., Healdsburg; (707) 431-2719. Dreamy sticky buns, croissants, scones, and muffins, fresh local fruit, espresso drinks, and for lunch: pizza, sandwiches, and luscious cookies, amazing ice cream, tarts, bread pudding, cakes, pies, brownies . . . a reason to come to Healdsburg.

The plaza and surrounding streets are lined with shops, restaurants, bakeries, hotels, bed-and-breakfast inns, and more than a dozen winery tasting rooms, from Gallo of Sonoma to Todd Hollow Vineyards, to Thumbprint Cellars and Lounge. Between the Alexander and Dry Creek Valleys, at the top of the Russian River Valley, Healdsburg is the anchor town for this part of the wine country. On the east side by the river, **Front Street Five** on Front Street is a trendy complex of five separate tasting rooms. Here Camellia Cellars offers samples of reds from the nearby Dry Creek Valley. Sapphire Hill Vineyards features Russian River Valley wines, and Huntington Wine Cellars favors the Alexander Valley wines. Across the street, Davis Family Winery makes a luscious Pinot Noir.

The adjacent Dry Creek Valley is prime wine country, famous for California's finest Zinfandels, a hearty red of Italian heritage. At the **Russian River Wine Company,** 132 Plaza St. (707-433-0490), you can taste and collect wines from more than 60 wineries. Also nearby are the Healdsburg Public Library and the **Sonoma County Wine Library,** 139 Piper at Center St. (707-433-3772), and the **Healdsburg Historical Museum,** 221 Matheson (707-431-3325). Get a walking-tour map at the **Chamber of Commerce,** 217 Healdsburg Ave. (707-433-6935).

Among the shops on and nearby the plaza is **Options Gallery,** 126 Matheson St. (707-431-8861; www.optionsgallery.com), where exceptional ethnic and American crafts are the main attractions. Fifty antiques dealers hold court in the big blue building at **Mill Street Antiques** (44 Mill St.; 707-433-8409). **Artisans and Farmers** displays antique farm and winery implements and agrarian-oriented objects d'art from California and France (Barndiva Building, a half block south of the plaza, 237 Center St.; 707-431-7404; www .artistsandfarmers.com). At **Healdsburg Classics,** 226 Healdsburg Ave. (707-433-4315), are 14 antiques shops selling everything from country pines to garden pieces, estate jewelry, and Native American artifacts. One in a small chain of exceptional stores selling accessories for garden and home, in a garden-surrounded barn, **The Gardener** has plenty of things that a traveler might pick up, from exotic handbags and tote bags to scented gifts, books, sun hats, and wine bottle openers (516 Dry Creek Rd., south of town just off US 101; 707-431-1063; www.thegardener.com).

The **Dry Creek Valley** west of town is top biking and wine tasting territory. A nice 20-mile loop on gently rolling hills starts at the town plaza, heads south to Mill Street, crosses under the highway, and joins Dry Creek Road going north. Endless vineyards and rows of low, forested mountains remain in view throughout the ride. At the old **Dry Creek General Store** (3495 Dry Creek Rd.; 707-433-

4171), buy sandwiches and picnic here or pack provisions into your bike basket.

Ferrari-Carano, at 8761 Dry Creek Rd. (707-433-6700; www .ferrari-carano.com), comes as a surprise in the valley, where most of the wineries are small, country places. Don and Rhonda Carano, second-generation Italian-Americans, re-created Tuscany on their winery estate. Voluptuous gardens surround the Villa Fiore tasting room, where the Mediterranean ambience echoes the character of the wines.

If Zinfandel is your passion, be sure to stop at **Quivira Winery,** 4900 West Dry Creek Rd. (707-431-8333; www.quivirawine.com), where picnic grounds overlook the valley.

Founded in 1876, **Simi Winery** (16275 Healdsburg Ave.; 707-433-6981) offers one of the most comprehensive and enjoyable tours in the valley; the shady terrace here is pleasant on hot days.

On the south end of town on a bend of the Russian River, **Healdsburg Memorial Beach Park** (13839 Old Redwood Hwy.; 707-433-1625) is a popular place to sun and swim; lifeguard on summer weekends.

LUNCH   **Bistro Ralph,** 109 Plaza St., Healdsburg; (707) 433-1380, www.bistroralph.com. Locally raised produce, meats, and poultry are used to create miracles: roasted garlic and polenta with baby lamb, Hog Island oysters, peach shortcake, crème brûlée. Ask for the Local Stash, a special wine list of older vintages from the Dry Creek and Alexander Valley wineries.

AFTERNOON

Proceed southwest out of town on Westside Road, stopping at the sharp left turn and driving through the arch to see **Madrona Manor,** 1001 Westside Rd. (707-433-4231), one of California's largest and finest Victorian masterpieces. Built in 1881, the huge manor is now an inn and restaurant surrounded by magnificent gardens. Walk in and ask for a tour of the museumlike rooms and outbuildings; depending on their bookings, it may or may not be possible but is definitely worth a try.

Mill Creek Vineyards, at 1401 Westside Rd. (707-433-5098), is a small, family-owned winery on a knoll overlooking the valley; it's fun to see their wooden mill wheel turning beside the creek. Two picnic areas offer panoramic views of the valley and beyond. Mill Creek Vineyards makes several wines, from a good "Old Mill Red" table wine to a superb Cabernet Sauvignon.

You'll be following the Russian River now, all the way to the ocean. Valley foothills become mountains, oaks give way to dark redwood and fir forests, and the roadsides become ferny and damp. Along the riverbank in freshwater marshes grow silvery gray-green willows and cottonwoods.

Take a left onto Wohler Road, passing more than a half dozen wineries on your way to River Road, then turn west. Stop at **Korbel Champagne Cellars** (13250 River Rd.; 707-824-7000; www.korbel .com), for a tour of the winery and the gardens. Founded in 1886 by Czech immigrants, the ivy-covered stone winery is a piece of Old Europe tucked into the rolling, vineyard-carpeted hills of the Russian River Valley. The guided winery tour, including museum, film, garden walk, and champagne tasting, is one of the most complete and enjoyable of all California wineries. In-depth garden tours show off antique roses and hundreds of spring bulbs. You can also taste Russian River Brewing Company beer at Korbel and choose from an astonishing variety of gourmet deli items in the market/deli/espresso bar.

You'll follow the river and the redwoods a few minutes farther down the road to the summer-vacation town of **Guerneville,** chockfull of souvenir shops, cafes, and art galleries. Johnson's Beach, below town, is a long stretch of sand with rentals of canoes, kayaks, paddleboats, tubes, umbrellas, and beach chairs; there's also a snack bar (707-869-2022; www.johnsonsbeach.com). You can also launch your own watercraft here.

In the middle of town, turn north onto Armstrong Woods Road a mile or so to **Armstrong Redwoods State Natural Reserve** (707-869-2015), 750 acres of glorious redwood groves along Fife Creek. Easy paths lead to sunny picnic areas and old-growth trees up to 350 feet tall. For a half-day horseback ride into the wilderness bordering Austin Creek State Recreation Area, call the **Armstrong Woods Trail Rides and Pack Station** (707-887-2939). Even beginning riders will love the lunch ride, which meanders gently out of the redwood forest through a variety of wildlife habitats to ridgetops overlooking the Russian River Valley.

Accessed from Armstrong Grove, the **Austin Creek Recreation Area** (707-869-2015) is 4,200 acres of hills, canyons, and river glens that campers, hikers, and horseback riders love to explore. Wildflowers in the spring, deep forests, good birding, bluegill and black bass fishing in Redwood Lake, and primitive camping sites are a few of the attractions. It is hot and dry in summer, glorious in spring with blooming wild azaleas, rushing creeks, and maples, ash, and alder in full leaf.

LODGING **Applewood Inn,** 13555 Highway 116, Guerneville; (707) 869-9093; www.applewoodinn.com. An elegant 1920s California Mission Revival mansion in the redwoods, with a heated swimming pool and acres of glorious gardens and forest, a secluded hideaway. Romantically decorated rooms with garden views, some with fireplaces, Jacuzzis, double showers, and balconies or verandas. You could forget the sightseeing and just settle in here.

DINNER **Applewood Inn.** Candlelight gourmet dinners by the fireplace. Think about sea bass with chive and quinoa crust, and roasted chicken with Bing cherry mustard reduction.

DAY 2 / MORNING

BREAKFAST Brie omelets, eggs Florentine, and more fresh, hot entrees in the beautiful dining room at **Applewood Inn.**

Ten minutes west of Guerneville, bear left across the bridge onto Moscow Road and through the tiny burg of Monte Rio to **Villa Grande,** a small river-bend village that's changed little since the 1920s, when it was built as a summer encampment for vacationers from San Francisco. There is a beach here and a delightful array of early Craftsman-style cottages.

Back on the main road, it's not far to **Duncans Mills,** where a dozen or so shops nestle in a Victorian-era village, another 1880s railroad stop. Take a look at the only remaining North Pacific Coast Railroad station.

The **Duncans Mills General Store** (707-865-1240) stocks fishing gear, groceries, deli items, and antiques. The **Gold Coast Coffee Co. Cafe and Bakery,** Steelhead Boulevard (707-865-1441), offers a selection of freshly baked goods from their wood-fired brick oven. Shops in Duncans Mills sell everything from fishing gear and fine jewelry to top-notch wildlife art. A worldly surprise in this bucolic village, the aromatic, elegant shop (25185 Main St.; 707-865-0900) specializes in beautiful Asian imports.

Farther west, the Russian River meets the sea at Bridgehaven, the junction of CA highways 116 and 1. In winter, ocean waves and the river clash here in a stormy drama. In summer the mouth of the river is cut off from the ocean by temporary dunes.

Fabulous, easily accessible beaches are located just to the north and the south, off Highway 1. Have a picnic on the beach or head back to Duncans Mills for lunch.

LUNCH   **Cape Fear Cafe,** 25191 Highway 116, Duncans Mills; (707) 865-9246. African tribal masks are dramatic accents at this charming little place. The North Carolinian chefs turn out wonderful fresh seafood dishes, homemade pasta, and vegetarian specialties.

AFTERNOON

Drive back on CA 116 to Guerneville, turning south on 116 past Forestville to **Kozlowski Farms** (5566 Gravenstein/CA 116; 707-887-1587; www.kozlowskifarms.com), for luscious berries, jams, fresh fruits, and pies—the ultimate Sonoma County farm store. Pick up a **Sonoma County Farm Trails** map at Kozlowski's to locate the many produce outlets and nurseries in these verdant rolling hills (800-207-9464; www.farmtrails.org). This is Green Valley, a sylvan triangle of the Russian River Valley between Sebastopol, Occidental, and Guerneville. Misted by the nearby Pacific Ocean, gloomy redwood groves live in rocky canyons and creekbeds and march across wild, windy hilltop ridges. Old-time agriculture is celebrated at the annual Apple Blossom Festival in April, when the orchards are floating clouds of white. At the festival and at farmers' markets and roadside stands, apples, berries, artisan cheeses, olive oils, nuts, and other locally produced foodstuffs are for sale, along with pies, ciders, and jams.

On a lovely country lane, Martinelli Road, a redwood, bay, and maple forest is the backdrop for split-rail fences and vintage farmhouses, where the Martinelli family has cultivated vineyards since the late 1800s. **Martinelli Vineyards** welcomes visitors to their historic red hop barn on River Road, where Muscat the cat holds court in a retail shop crowded with old-fashioned china and cottage trinkets (3360 River Rd.; 707-525-0570; www.martinelliwinery.com).

Chardonnay and Pinot Noir are created with Spanish flair at **Marimar Torres Estate Winery** (11400 Graton Rd.; 707-823-4365; www.marimarestate.com). In a tile-roofed, golden-toned hacienda on the hilltop, the winery resembles a Catalan farmhouse—an elegant one—decorated inside with antiques and ceramics from Spain, where the owner's family, the House of Torres, is the largest independent producer of wines in Spain.

A narrow, oak-lined byway, Ross Station Road crosses a bridge and coils up a hill to a spectacular view of the Green Valley. On the grounds of **Iron Horse Ranch and Vineyards,** palm and olive trees and stepped gardens surround the restored 1876 Carpenter Gothic family home of the winery owners (9786 Ross Station Rd., Sebastopol; 707-887-1507). Iron Horse sparkling wines have been served at state dinners in the Reagan, Clinton, and both Bush White Houses.

Developed on an old railroad bed, several miles of the **West County Millennium Community Trail** is paved for walking and bicycle riding. The trail runs through Green Valley from Occidental Road near Graton north to Forestville between farms and vineyards; an unpaved equestrian trail runs alongside.

Between Sebastopol and US 101 are dozens of antiques shops on Gravenstein Highway. Proceed south on US 101 and back to the Golden Gate Bridge.

There's More . . . .

Biking. **Spoke Folk Cyclery,** 201 Center St., Healdsburg; 707-433-7171; www.spokefolk.com. Experienced cyclists who know the area. Ask for free maps and suggested routes for self-guided bike tours.

Wine Country Bikes, 61 Front St., Healdsburg; (707) 473-0610; www.winecountrybikes.com. They will deliver bikes and helmets anywhere in Healdsburg, and they offer guided tours through the Dry Creek Valley including guide, picnic, hybrid bike, and support van. Rentals, maps, showers and changing rooms, cycling clothing, and accessories.

Getaway Adventures, 2228 Northpoint Parkway, Santa Rosa; (800) 499-2453; www.getawayadventures.com. Biking, kayaking, hiking, and van tours throughout Sonoma and Napa counties. "Healdsburg Sip & Cycle" is one of their popular tours.

Canoeing. **River's Edge Kayak & Canoe Trips,** at the Healdsburg Bridge, 13840 Healdsburg Ave.; (707) 433-7247; www.rivers edgekayakandcanoe.com. Canoes, double and single kayaks for self-guided individual and group paddles down the river, with return transportation.

Burke's Canoe Trips, 8600 River Rd., 1 mile north of Forestville; (707) 887-1222; www.burkescanoetrips.com. In business for many years. Ten-mile self-guided canoe and kayaks trips on the Russian River, with return shuttle; riverside camping also available.

Fishing. Pick up a map to fishing access in the Russian River area at the **Russian River Chamber of Commerce & Visitor Center,** 16209 First St., Guerneville; (707) 869-9000.

Shopping. **Jimtown Store,** 6706 Highway 128, a few miles northeast of Geyserville, just north of Healdsburg off US 101; (707) 433-1212; www.jimtown.com. A destination in itself, this is an upscale general store/souvenir and antiques shop/gourmet deli/refreshment stand.

Golf. **Northwood Golf Course,** 19400 Highway 116, Monte Rio; (707) 865-1116; www.northwoodgolf.com. Eighteen holes in a spectacular redwood grove. There is a pleasant cafe here with a shady deck overlooking the fairways.

Spa. **Osmosis Day Spa Sanctuary,** 209 Bohemian Hwy., Freestone; (707) 823-8231; www.osmosis.com. Secluded in a scenic valley between the coast and the Russian River, a Japanese-style retreat with bonsai and bamboo gardens. This is the only day spa in the United States offering the Cedar enzyme bath, a rejuvenating heat treatment, along with massage, facials, and tea service in an idyllic environment.

Park. **Riverfront Regional Park,** 7821 Eastside Rd., Windsor (just south of Healdsburg). A new park with a picnic area in a redwood grove, easy trails and small fishing lakes.

Special Events . . . .

JANUARY
Winter Wineland, Healdsburg; (800) 723-6336; www.wineroad .com. A weekend of tasting, live entertainment, and celebrity events at 100 wineries.

MARCH
Russian River Wine Road Barrel Tasting; (800) 723-6336; www .wineroad.com. More than 100 wineries participate over two weekends.

APRIL
Passport to Dry Creek Valley, Healdsburg; (707) 433-3031; www .wdcv.com. Wine tastings, winery and vineyards tours, food pairings, live entertainment. A huge event—arrive early.

MAY
Memorial Day Weekend Antiques Fair, Healdsburg; (707) 578-7772. An extravaganza of antiques displays and sales, nearly 100 dealers around the leafy plaza.

SEPTEMBER

Russian River Jazz & Blues Festival; (707) 869-1595; www.omega
events.com/russianriverfestivals. Huge crowds at the beach in
Guerneville; big-name performers.

NOVEMBER

Wine & Food Affair "Tasting Along the Wine Road"; (800) 723-
6336; www.wineroad.com. Open houses at about 50 wineries in
the Russian River Valley; wine, food, music, and fun.

Other Recommended Restaurants and Lodgings . . . .

FORESTVILLE

Farmhouse Inn and Restaurant, 7871 River Rd.; (800) 464-6642;
www.farmhouseinn.com. Recently expanded and redecorated,
ultra-luxe interiors in 18 cottages, rooms, and suites, in buildings
reminiscent of barns and water towers; private decks, four-posters,
jetted tubs and saunas or steam showers, fireplaces, living areas,
heated outdoor pool, full-service spa. The award-winning restaurant
has gained a Michelin star with a seasonal menu sourced locally;
i.e., pear and Parmesan ravioli, Niman Ranch rib eye, hearts of
palm and Dungeness crab.

MONTE RIO

Village Inn and Restaurant, 20822 River Blvd. near Guerneville;
(800) 303-2302; www.villageinn-ca.com. A charming, century-
old place with indoor/outdoor river view dining, a popular indoor/
outdoor bar; nice inn rooms with river view decks or balconies,
refrigerators and microwaves, and continental breakfast—hard to
beat the location, the friendliness, the good food, and the lovely
Redwood grove backdrop.

HEALDSBURG

Belle de Jour Inn, 16276 Healdsburg Ave.; (707) 431-9777; www .belledejourinn.com. On a hilltop on six acres, white garden cottages have king or queen beds, fireplaces, big whirlpool tubs, refrigerators, full breakfast, and country charm.

Costeaux French Bakery and Cafe, a block from the plaza, 417 Healdsburg Ave.; (707) 433-1913; www.costeaux.com. Award-winning breads and pastries, scrumptious sandwiches, and picnic items to eat here or take out; breakfast and lunch.

The Haydon Street Inn, 321 Haydon St.; (707) 433-5228; www .haydon.com. A 1912 Queen Anne Victorian on a quiet, tree-shaded street near the plaza, French and American antiques, down comforters, designer touches, gracious veranda and gardens. Clawfoot and Jacuzzi tubs, full breakfasts, air-conditioning. Separate two-room cottage.

Healdsburg Charcuterie, 335 Healdsburg Ave.; (707) 431-7213. An upscale restaurant where locals love the eccentric, pig-inspired decor and the dazzling Provence-inspired food: bouillabaisse, monkfish soup with artichokes, rabbit Provençal, house-cured pork, rib-eye steak in roasted garlic sauce, and more rib-sticking, fabulous food; including the best hamburger in the Wine Country. Lunch and dinner.

Healdsburg Inn on the Plaza, 110 Matheson St.; (707) 433-6991; www.healdsburginn.com. Ca. 1900 bed-and-breakfast with 10 antiques-chocked rooms, private baths, fireplaces, generous afternoon snacks and wine, full breakfast. One of the excellent Four Sisters inns.

Honor Mansion, 14891 Grove St.; (800) 554-4667; www.honor mansion.com. One of the most luxurious and gorgeous small inns on the planet. Each room, cottage, and suite is very private and loaded with romance, from a million pillows to antiques, fireplaces, whirlpool tubs, private gardens, shady porches, sumptuous break-fasts, wine/appetizer service. Tennis, pool, putting green, bocce, PGA putting green, jogging trail, croquet—with a winery down the street, you never need to leave. A place for honeymoons, anniversa-ries, and unforgettable encounters.

Hotel Healdsburg, 25 Matheson St., off Healdsburg Avenue; (707) 431-2800; www.hotelhealdsburg.com. Urban-chic luxury, right on the plaza. Private balconies, high-tech amenities, some rooms and suites with large soaking tubs and fireplaces, full breakfast, courtyard pool. Onsite, the highly rated Charlie Palmer's Dry Creek Kitchen restaurant (yes, that Charlie Palmer) trendy grappa bar, full-service spa.

Madrona Manor, 1001 Westside Rd.; (707) 433-4231 or (800) 258-4003; www.madronamanor.com. California cuisine, French and Italian classic dishes; a much-heralded restaurant in one of the largest and most elegant Victorian mansions in California. Reserva-tions for dinner absolutely necessary. Twenty elaborately decorated inn rooms in the mansion, stunning traditional decor; large rooms and suites in a carriage house, and cottages. Swimming pool, fire-places, private baths, acres of glorious gardens.

Oakville Grocery, 124 Matheson St.; (707) 433-3200; www.oakville grocery.com. In the old city hall, an upscale market and deli with scrumptious food, local wine, and cheese from around the world. Eat here on the patio or take out.

For More Information . . . .

Healdsburg Visitors Bureau, 217 Healdsburg Ave., Healdsburg 95448; (707) 433-6935 or (800) 648-9922; www.healdsburg .com. Wineries, lodging availability, calendar, dining, shopping, and things to do.

Northcoast Authentic California,www.northcoastca.com. Brochures, maps, road trip itineraries, and information on the Wine Country, the North Coast, and Redwood Country. Also, visitor bureaus, attractions, events, weather, California welcome centers, and more.

Russian River Chamber of Commerce and Visitor Center, 16209 First St., Guerneville 95446; (707) 869-9000; www.russianriver .com.

Sonoma County Tourism Bureau, 420 Aviation Blvd., Santa Rosa 95403; (707) 522-5800 or (800) 576-6662; www.sonomacounty .com. Free 65-page visitor guide to the entire county and information online for 250 wineries, lodging, dining, activities, and calendar.

NORTHBOUND ESCAPE *Two*
Sonoma Valley
ON COUNTRY ROADS / 2 NIGHTS

Early California history
Wineries
Shopping
Hiking, biking, golf
Cheese, wine, produce
Mountain and valley parks

Between the rugged Mayacamas Mountains and the Sonoma Mountains, the 17-mile-long Sonoma Valley is a patchwork of vineyards and rich farmlands. Two-lane roads meander along rivers and creeks, through oak-studded meadows and foothills to country villages and to towns with sites on the National Register of Historic Places. The Victorian and early California Mission eras come alive in museums and in hundreds of restored homes, inns, and buildings all over the valley.

Dozens of premium wineries are located here, the birthplace of the California wine industry. Their production facilities and tasting rooms, in many cases, are of significant architectural and historical interest. Thousands of acres of vineyards create a tapestry of seasonal color and texture that cascades across the hills and streams out onto the valley floor.

Moderate climate and rich soil produce world-famous gourmet foods—cheeses, sausages, foie gras, orchard fruits and berries, nuts, and sourdough French bread. California Wine Country cuisine, a gastronomic genre all its own, attracts diners and chefs from afar.

Exploring the Sonoma Valley on quiet back roads by car, foot, or perhaps bike, you'll enjoy the landscape and discover some of old California. After a day of wine tasting, browsing in the shops, gourmet dining, and maybe a round of golf, a cozy bed-and-breakfast inn will be a welcome refuge.

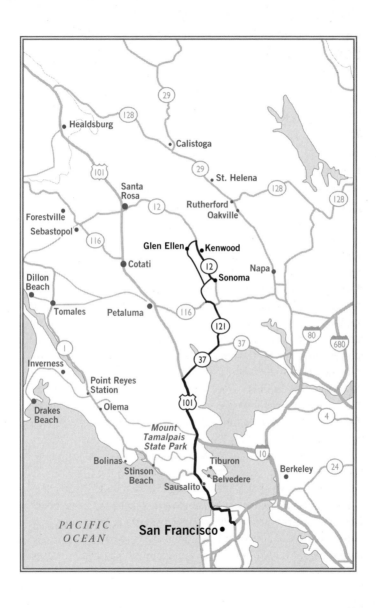

DAY 1 / MORNING

From the Golden Gate Bridge, drive north on US 101 to the CA 37/Napa/Vallejo exit, driving east to the CA 121/Sonoma left turn. Drive north on this road to Schellville (four-way stop) and continue to the Arnold Drive right turn; stay on Arnold for 8 miles to the foresty village of Glen Ellen.

This is the **Valley of the Moon,** named by its most famous (sometimes infamous) resident, Jack London, author of the classic adventure tales *Call of the Wild* and *The Sea Wolf.* Near the gristmill in the rustic Jack London Village complex (http://jacklondonshops.com), you can sip and swirl at **Olive and Vine Café and Wine Bar,** where local wines are poured by the glass, the flight, and the bottle, and you can get tapas and small plate snacks and light meals (707-996-9170; www.oliveandvine.com). Next door, **Figone's of California Olive Oil and Press** sells olive oils that are milled, blended, and bottled onsite; you can taste, tour, and watch the fruit being pressed at harvest time in Nov and Dec (707-938-3164; www.figoneoliveoil.com). The decks and gardens behind the shops overlooking the creek and forested hillside are just what you came to enjoy. Sit on the deck at the **Bluegrass Bar and Grill,** have a beer and dig into barbecue (707-935-4488; www.bluegrassbarandgrill.com). The view from the bar is of the old gristmill, still creaking slowly over a rushing creek.

When you see the large **London Lodge** banner, you've arrived in Glen Ellen, just a few blocks long. Turn left at the lodge, driving 1 mile up into dense oak forests to **Jack London State Historic Park** (707-938-5216; www.jacklondonstatepark.com). Once London's home ranch, the park is 800 magnificent acres of walking trails through groves of oaks, madrones, Douglas fir, redwoods, ferns, and explosions of wildflowers. There are shady picnic sites, mountain and valley views, a romantically spooky ruin, and a museum. Remnants of **Wolf House,** London's gigantic stone mansion, lie deep in a forest glade, at the end of a delightful short path through the trees (wheelchair accessible by golf cart). Only walls and chimneys remain of the elaborately decorated and furnished home, which burned to the ground before London and his wife, Charmian, could enjoy it. Filled with London memorabilia and most of the original furnishings, his smaller home, the **House of Happy Walls,** is open to visitors daily except holidays. Newly restored and loaded with photos and artifacts is the sweet cottage in which London lived and worked in his den, and where he died. **Triple Creek Horse Outfit** offers guided rides in the park, and at Bothe-Napa Valley State Park and Sugarloaf Ridge State Park (707-887-8700; www.triplecreek horseoutfit.com).

On the way back to Glen Ellen, make a wine-tasting and touring stop at **Benziger Family Winery,** 1883 London Ranch Rd. (888-490-2739; www.benziger.com). Beautiful valley oaks and gardens, an art gallery, and picnic grounds are here, in addition to the tasting room. This is the only winery in the valley to offer a motorized tram tour of the vineyards, available by reservation.

In Glen Ellen, cross the stone bridge, bear left, and turn left onto Warm Springs Road for a 6-mile drive. First you'll see **Glenelly Inn,** 5131 Warm Springs Rd. (707-996-6720), a peach-and-white confection built in 1916 as a railroad inn for summer train passengers who came to gambol at nearby mineral springs resorts. Feeling lazy and warm? Stop at **Morton's Sonoma Springs Resort** (707-833-5511; www.mortonswarmsprings.com) for a picnic on sweeping lawns or a swim in one of three heated pools. Just beyond, you'll come into Kenwood, a tiny, overgrown hamlet of cabins and rustic homes. A Southern Pacific train station from 1888 to 1936, the Kenwood Depot is an architectural gem in the Richardsonian Romanesque style. Around the corner, Kenwood Plaza is a nice little park fronting the white-steepled Kenwood Community Church, anchoring the village as it has since 1888.

From here connect with CA 12 and turn left.

LUNCH **Cafe Citti,** 9049 Sonoma Hwy., Kenwood; (707) 833-2690. A deli cafe with tables outdoors under the trees. Fresh, fabulous salads are ready to take out, or you can stay here and enjoy homemade pasta entrees and a glass of wine.

AFTERNOON

Just north on CA 12 is **Sugarloaf Ridge State Park** (707-833-5712), a 3,000-acre green and golden jewel of mountains, redwood groves, creeks, wildflower-strewn meadows, and views. You may take a short walk or a hike, picnic in the pines, park your RV overnight, or camp out in your tent.

Returning toward Kenwood, make a pilgrimage to **Chateau St. Jean** for their highly rated, vineyard-designated wines (707-833-4134; www.chateaustjean.com). Cinq Cépages—"Five Varieties"—has been named as one of the best wines in the world. Surrounding the 1920s-era mansion, formal gardens and a redwood-shaded picnic area make this a nice stop.

Just beyond, at CA 12, watch for the tasting room of **Family Wineries of Sonoma Valley,** staffed primarily by winemakers and owners of five very small premium wineries (9200 Sonoma Hwy.; 707-833-5504; www.familywineries.com). You can taste about three dozen, hard-to-find premium wines, many available only here. Lounge on the grass and have a picnic.

DINNER **Kenwood Restaurant,** 9900 Sonoma Hwy., Kenwood; (707) 833-6326; www.kenwoodrestaurant.com. On the vineyard-surrounded terrace or in the cool, elegant dining room, go for the top-drawer Petaluma duck with brandied cherries, Bodega Bay bouillabaisse, or a hearty Kenwood burger; save room for fresh berry cobbler. The wine list will not disappoint. Reservations absolutely necessary, lunch and dinner.

LODGING Kenwood Inn and Spa, 10400 Sonoma Hwy., Kenwood; (707) 833-1293; www.kenwoodinn.com. A complex of vine-covered, Tuscan-style villas for romantics. Around walled courtyards are gorgeous antiques-filled suites with featherbeds and fireplaces, balconies, and vineyard views; two swimming pools, Jacuzzis, herb and flower gardens. Sumptuous breakfasts, all-day guest-only dining, wine bar, and an in-house Caudalíe® spa with beauty and body treatments—a place for honeymoons and luxurious getaways. Privacy and luxury are to be expected.

DAY 2 / MORNING

BREAKFAST Kenwood Inn and Spa.

CA 12 runs south and becomes West Napa Street, meeting the **Sonoma Plaza,** a typical Spanish town square, the largest and one of the oldest in California, laid out by General Mariano Guadalupe Vallejo in 1834. The site of many annual festivals and historical events, it's a National Historic Landmark, and a beautiful one—huge bay and eucalyptus trees, a meandering stream with chattering ducks, a playground, picnic tables, and the monolithic stone **City Hall,** which houses the **Visitors Bureau,** 453 First St. East (707-996-1090). If you are here on a Tuesday, be sure to take a walk through the plaza during the Farmers' Market in the early evening, when locals get together to picnic and purchase their weekly veggies and fruits, baked goods, cheeses, flowers, honeys, and more, all locally produced.

Surrounding the plaza, and for several blocks around, are many historic buildings, including the **Mission San Francisco Solano de Sonoma,** ca. 1841, the last of the California missions built, with a beautiful small chapel and museum. The commandant who held sway in the Sonoma area when Mexico owned California, Gen. Vallejo constructed a barracks compound for his soldiers, which is now a state park and a museum on the plaza (707-938-1519). Thick-walled adobes, Victorians, and Classic Revival and Mission Revival structures line the plaza and adjacent streets. Park your car, get out your camera, and explore the plaza and the streets and alleyways for a block or so in each direction. The visitors bureau has good walking-tour maps.

Not to be missed on the plaza: **The Wine Exchange of Sonoma,** at 452 First St. (707-938-1794), to taste and buy the wines of almost every winery in the Sonoma and Napa Valleys, and **Kaboodle,** 447 First St. (707-996-9500), a feminine fairyland of country French gifts and accessories.

On the corner, in a historic building topped by a dome, **The Corner Store** is upscale and delightfully crowded with European and Wine Country accessories and gifts, from Italian ceramics and pewter to fine linens, bath products, and French posters. In the store is a popular wine-tasting bar (498 First St. East; 707-996-2211; www.sonomacornerstore.com).

Look for the replica of a San Francisco cable car for a free ride around the plaza and to **Sebastiani Vineyards,** a few blocks away. Behind the winery are shaded picnic tables with vineyard and hillside views (707-933-3230).

The Spirits in Stone Gallery at 452 First St. displays dramatic African Shona stone sculpture, and there are interesting large photographs of Africa and a video to watch (707-935-6254). At **Artifax International,** 450 First St., take a look at African and Asian carvings, masks, jewelry, and doodads of great color and variety in an exotic incensed environment (707-996-9494).

LUNCH **Sunflower Cafe,** 421 First St. West on the plaza; (707) 996-6645; www.sonomasunflower.com. New owners have completely transformed this into a pleasant, leafy spot for all-day refreshments, breakfasts, lunches, and afternoon snacks and wine. Sit at a sidewalk table and people-watch, or head for an umbrella table in the garden patio for luscious sandwiches of roasted pork and smoked salmon (and less exotic choices, too), salads, frittatas, espresso drinks, shakes, smoothies, teas, and chocolates; a popular outdoor wine bar has opened.

AFTERNOON

Even if you're not interested in wine tasting, you'll want to walk, bike, or drive 1.5 miles (take East Napa Street south to Lovall Valley Road, then go left onto Old Winery Road) from the plaza to the **Buena Vista Carneros Winery** (707-265-1472; www.buenavistacarneros.com), an enchanting Wine Country estate with vine-covered stone buildings, ancient trees, and rampant flower gardens. Tasting rooms are stocked with guidebooks, artwork, and museum-quality antiques. Buena Vista's Hungarian founder, Count Agoston Haraszthy, engaged in friendly wine-making competition with General Vallejo in the mid-1800s. The interconnected small roads on this eastern outskirt of town are pretty and quiet for walks, drives, and bike rides to several other wineries.

Also in this area, **Ravenswood** winery is perched above a quiet, winding road that is a perfect 1-mile walking route through vineyard lands. Ravenswood's low-slung, stone tasting room is one of the most interesting for souvenir and wine shopping. They vow, "No wimpy wines allowed," and their famous Zinfandel and spicy Early Harvest Gewürztraminer prove the point (18701 Gehricke Rd.; 888-669-4679; www.ravenswood-wine.com).

Another paved path for walking and biking, accessed near the plaza, winds 1.5 miles, east-west, from Fourth Street East to CA

12, passing by parks, playing fields, and the historic Vallejo Home. A block from the plaza on the walking path, **Depot Park** has a play-ground, barbecue grills, and picnic tables under the trees, a good choice when the plaza is crowded. If you are hooked on local his-tory, visit the small **Depot Park Museum** to see a restored station-master's office, re-creations of Victorian households, and photos of early Sonomans (707-938-1762).

Near the walking path at 315 Second St. East, the **Vella Cheese Company** is one of the best of the great Sonoma County cheese makers (800-848-0505). In this stone building, jack, blue, and cheddar have been made since 1931. Try the pepper jack and the garlic cheddar. Across the street look for **The Patch,** a vegetable stand beside a huge garden, where produce is picked fresh every day.

Accessible by the walking path and by car, the **General M. G. Vallejo Home** is a classic Yankee-style, two-story Gothic Revival shipped around the Horn and erected in 1851 (707-938-1519). You can tour the home, which is called *Lachryma Montis,* meaning "Tears of the Mountain." Original and period furnishings in every room re-create the days when Vallejo and his daughters lived here. The glorious garden has huge magnolia, fig, and oak trees and a fish pond with turtles and koi. The home is part of the state park prop-erty, so one admission ticket is good at the mission, the barracks compound, and the Vallejo home.

DINNER   **Della Santina's,** 133 East Napa St., East Sonoma; (707) 939-1266. The fireplace creates a cozy atmosphere for fancifully prepared fresh sea-food from both coasts; intimate in winter, popular and fun on the patio in summer.

LODGING   **Inn at Sonoma,** 630 Broadway, Sonoma; (707) 939-1340 or (888) 568-9818; www.innatsonoma.com. One of the luxurious Four Sisters inns, a block from the plaza. Eighteen very comfy, plush rooms, each with fireplace, armchair sitting area, high-tech amenities; most have private balconies or patios. Full breakfast, afternoon wine and hors d'oeuvres; complimentary bikes; rooftop hot tub.

DAY 3 / MORNING

BREAKFAST   **Inn at Sonoma.** For a second late breakfast, try the **Basque Boulangerie Cafe** (400 First St. East, Sonoma; 707-935-7687). At a sidewalk table or indoors in the tiny, busy cafe on the plaza, enjoy luscious European pastries, quiche, coffee drinks, and light breakfasts, plus snacks and sandwiches all day.

Leaving Sonoma, head south from the plaza on Broadway/CA 12 for less than 1 mile, then turn left onto Napa Road, another view-filled country byway. If you're extending your trip to the lower Napa Valley (see Northbound Escape Three), turn left at the CA 121 junction; otherwise, turn right at the junction. Go straight on through the Schellville-CA 121 intersection and down the road to **Schug Carneros Estate** (707-939-9363), a winery tucked up against a low range of hills, a lost little corner of the valley. German-owned Schug makes a traditional California Chardonnay, a sparkling red wine, and a German-style Gewürztraminer, unusual for this area.

Continue on CA 121 south at a slow pace along a 10-mile stretch of rolling hills. You can take a scenic ride in an antique biplane at **Aero-Schellville** (707-938-2444). Turn right at the **Gloria Ferrer Champagne Caves** sign and drive up toward the hills to the tile-roofed Spanish hacienda built by the largest sparkling wine company in the world—Freixenet, based in Spain—at 23555 Highway 121 (707-996-7256; www.gloriaferrer.com). Gloria Ferrer has a luxurious tasting salon with a fantastic view. Many annual events are scheduled here, such as Catalan cooking classes and fireside concerts.

Back on CA 121 heading south, a vine-draped arbor leads to **Viansa Village and Winery** (800-995-4740; www.viansa.com), a red-tiled, terra-cotta-colored Italian winery on a hill above the highway. There is much to enjoy at Viansa besides their unusual Italian wine varieties Vernaccia, Nebbiolo, Aleatico, and Trebbiano. At the huge gourmet delicatessen and Italian marketplace you can buy a sandwich, a salad, packaged gourmet foods, cookbooks, ceramics, and waterfowl-related gifts. Barbecues and special events open to the public are held here in the summertime.

You can stroll trails in the 90-acre wetlands below the winery, one of the largest private waterfowl preserves in the state; more than 10,000 birds have been spotted in a single day

At the junction of CA highways 121 and 37, head west toward Marin County and take US 101 south to the Golden Gate.

There's More . . . .

Ballooning. **Balloons Above the Valley,** hot air ballooning over the Sonoma County vineyards; (800) 579-0183; www.balloonrides .com.

Bike rental. **Sonoma Valley Bike Tours,** 520 Broadway, Sonoma; (877) 308-2453; www.sonomavalleybiketours.com. A few steps from the plaza, bike rentals and guided tours of town and wineries.

Cooking. **Ramekins Sonoma Valley Culinary School,** 450 West Spain St., Sonoma; (707) 933-0450; www.ramekins.com. For adventurous home cooks, an annual schedule of more than 300 hands-on classes presented by renowned chefs from around the country, from traditional Provençal recipes to wine and food pairing, Southwestern and California cuisine, artisan bread baking, and much more. Upstairs are six lovely bed-and-breakfast rooms with views of the surrounding hills. This is a beautiful "rammed earth" building with a Spanish adobe look.

Park. **Sonoma Valley Regional Park,** CA 12 between Arnold Drive and Madrone Road, near Glen Ellen; (707) 539-8092. A mostly flat, paved path winding a mile one-way through an oak forest, with a pretty creek along the way. You can bike and picnic; dogs must be leashed.

Hiking. **Sonoma Overlook Trail,** north of the plaza, just as First Street West turns uphill; parking lot next to the cemetery. Wide views of the Sonoma Valley are dazzling from the upper meadows of this 3-mile loop of trails on wooded hillsides. Blue lupine and flax, wild roses, and California poppies are rampant; buckeye, live oak, and manzanita trees create shady hideaways.

Museum. **Sonoma Valley Museum of Art,** 551 Broadway, Sonoma; (707) 939-7862; www.svma.org. Near the plaza, an airy space for a variety of changing exhibitions and events.

Gardens, Shops, and Wine. **Cornerstone Gardens,** 23570 Highway 121; (707) 933-3010; www.cornerstonegardens.com. A quirky complex of garden-related art, from a forest of red bamboo poles to a startling tree made of bright blue balls. A plant nursery, a cafe, and a garden accessory store, wine tasting, and more.

Winery. **Valley of the Moon Winery,** 777 Madrone Rd., Glen Ellen; (707) 996-6941; www.valleyofthemoonwinery.com. Just south of Glen Ellen, award-winning Cabernets, Chardonnays, and more varieties are made in a 19th-century stone building on the creekside. In the visitor center, tall paned windows frame the gardens and an old Zinfandel vineyard, while wine lovers browse the chock-full gift shop and sip wine; a 300-year-old bay tree stands in silent splendor.

Special Events . . . .

JANUARY

Olive Festival, various venues in Sonoma Valley; (707) 996-1090; www.olivefestival.com. Olive harvest events, tastings and tours, restaurant, food and winery events, art shows, music and more, through Feb.

MAY

Passport to Sonoma Valley, at dozens of valley wineries; (707) 935-0803; www.sonomavalleywine.com. Open houses, special tastings and tours, food events, live entertainment.

JUNE

Ox Roast, Sonoma Plaza; (707) 996-1090. Visitors are welcome at this locals' fund-raising event. Scrumptious beef barbecue, wine and beer, live entertainment.

JULY

Fourth of July Parade, Sonoma Plaza; (707) 996-1090. A classic hometown parade, with every kid in town, antique cars, fire engines, the town band, cops on bikes, and more. Food, live music, and art in the plaza all day, and evening fireworks.

JULY THROUGH AUGUST

Jazz Series, Bartholomew Park Winery; (707) 935-9511. At a beautiful outdoor winery site, top-notch jazz performers in concert.

SEPTEMBER

Wine Country Film Festival; (707) 935-FILM; www.winecountry filmfest.com. For nearly two decades, indoor and outdoor venues for film nights, celebrity tributes, food, wine, and entertainment. The celeb events sell out fast.

Valley of the Moon Vintage Festival, Sonoma plaza; (707) 996-1090; http://sonomavinfest.org. For over a century, the harvest is celebrated with three days of food, wine and live entertainment, a grape stomp, historical reenactments, a home-town style parade, and kids' activities.

Sonoma Wine Country Weekend, throughout Sonoma County; (800) 939-7666; www.sonomawinecountryweekend.com. The mother of all wine fests, including a gala wine auction, hundreds of wineries hosting special events, winery lunches and dinners, lodging packages, and the signature Showcase: Taste of Sonoma food and wine extravaganza, held in a gorgeous outdoor setting.

DECEMBER THROUGH FEBRUARY
Sonoma Valley Olive Festival, www.sonomavalley.com/OliveFestival. Blessing of the olives at Sonoma Mission; winery tastings, dinners and luncheons; tours, olive oil production, hikes, classes, art, workshops, food, wine, and music.

Other Recommended Restaurants and Lodgings . . . .

GLEN ELLEN
Fig Cafe and Winebar, 13690 Arnold Dr.; (707) 938-2130; www.thefigcafe.com. To eat here in a casual bistro setting or to take out, thin-crust pizza, pot roast, salads, duck confit, seafood, lavender crème brûlée. Fine cheese plates, risotto, stews, grilled meats and poultry, made with all-local products. Dinner nightly and weekend brunch. No corkage fee.

Gaige House Inn, 1354 Arnold Dr.; (800) 935-0237; www.gaige
.com. An Italianate Victorian on the outside, a mix of styles and
periods within. Gorgeous inn rooms with luxe bedding, some canopy
beds, fireplaces, and whirlpool tubs; big swimming pool, lovely gardens, lots of privacy. Japanese-style spa suites are inspired by the
Ryokan inns of Kyoto, with double soaking tubs above Calabasas
Creek, glass walls, private gardens. Big breakfasts; spa treatments.

SONOMA

Breakaway Cafe, 19101 Highway 12 in the Albertson's shopping
plaza on the west end of Sonoma; (707) 996-5949. Relax in a big
booth and dig into an all-American breakfast of omelets, platter-size
hotcakes, or sausage and eggs. This is a popular locals' place for
breakfast, lunch, and dinner. Come back later for pork chops and
mashed potatoes, roasted chicken, burgers and salads, comforting
soups, veggie specials, luscious desserts, and smoothies; full bar.

Brick House Bungalows, 313 First St. East; (707) 996-8091; www
.brickhousebungalows.com. Five vintage cottages around a private
courtyard, each with garden, kitchen, TV, leather sofas, and luxury
decor. A block to Sonoma Plaza.

Red Grape, 529 First St. West, Sonoma; (707) 996-4103; www
.theredgrape.com. Our favorite pizza place on the planet, specializing in "New Haven" style, thin-crust pies with traditional and
exotic toppings; plus pasta and salads. The light, airy restaurant
and shady patio bustle with families and tourists, just a half-block
from the plaza.

El Dorado Kitchen, 405 First St. West; (707) 996-3030; www
.eldoradokitchen.com. From the owners of Auberge du Soleil in
the Napa Valley, contemporary country-style dining room with bar,

fireplace lounge, and tree-shaded patio featuring seasonal Mediterranean-inspired cuisine. Try the Caesar Provençal and the hearty saddle of lamb; top-notch wine list, including a generous menu of still and sparkling wines by the glass. Be prepared for a high noise level.

El Pueblo Inn, 496 West Napa St.; (707) 996-3651 or (800) 900-8844; www.elpuebloinn.com. In a super-convenient location on CA 12, a motel with heated pool, courtyard garden, and rooftop Jacuzzi; some rooms have fireplaces, mini refrigerators, and two queen beds. Complimentary continental breakfast; rental bicycles. Ask for a room away from the road.

Fairmont Sonoma Mission Inn and Spa, 18140 Highway 12; (888) 270-1118; www.fairmont.com. A pink and white, 1920s style extravaganza guarded by tall palms and surrounded with lush gardens. An elegant lobby and a huge fireplace greets guests. Rooms in the historic building are lovely but small; rooms and suites in the annex buildings are spacious and luxurious, some with fireplaces and terraces. The $20 million spa is world famous, offering exotic and traditional treatments and pampering beauty and health regimes, including weight loss. Ayurvedic "revitalizers," grape seed body polishes, and special couples programs are popular. The glassed-in, elegant Grille dining room overlooks a beautiful swimming pool terrace; the cafe, located on the highway, is a casual place for California cuisine and spa food. Ask about spa and golf packages; hotel guests may play at the private, and top notch, Sonoma Golf Club.

The Girl and the Fig, 110 West Spain St.; (707) 938-3634; www.thegirlandthefig.com. On the plaza, sharing a charming historic building with the Sonoma Hotel; one of the region's most highly rated restaurants. Country French cuisine in a vibrant, artful setting with a garden patio. The menu is always seasonal and local-product based; exceptional cheese and charcuterie platters, Dungeness crab cakes, rabbit pappardelle, morel and spring pea risotto, rib-eyes, pork, creative veggies. Memorable brunches, lunches, and dinners. Sip an aperitif or a local wine at the antique bar.

Hotel Eldorado, 405 First St. West; (800) 289-3031; www.hotelel dorado.com. With French doors and balconies overlooking the plaza or the courtyard, 27 airy, contemporary hotel rooms with four-poster beds, luxe bedding, flat-screen TVs. Two bungalows are wheelchair-accessible. Heated lap pool, health club passes; day spa across the street. Excellent, if noisy, restaurant/bar downstairs.

Lodge at Sonoma, 1325 Broadway; (707) 935-6600; www.the lodgeatsonoma.com. A large luxury hotel with spacious rooms and suites, some with sitting areas, fireplaces, whirlpool tubs. Quite a nice full-service spa with comfy fireplace lounge; fitness facil-ity with outdoor mineral pools; the private Raindance Suite has a fireplace, sauna, shower, and whirlpool tub. Cool, contemporary atmosphere in the award-winning Carneros Bistro; open kitchen, California and Mediterranean cuisine, and a huge wine list. Live music on weekends in the very lively lobby bar.

MacArthur Place, 29 East MacArthur St.; (800) 722-1866; www .macarthurplace.com. Anchored by a smashing 1850s main house and surrounded by gardens and a clutch of large cottages with plush accommodations, MacArthur Place is a full-service spa with bicycles to borrow and a large swimming pool; plus, Saddles, a cowboy-theme steak house and bar.

Schellville Grille, 22900 Broadway; (707) 996-5151. In a "his-toric shack" 3 miles from the plaza on the way to the Bay Area; grilled meats, poultry, and fish; breakfast and lunch; dinner Thurs.

Sonoma Valley

Sonoma Creek Inn, 239 Boyes Blvd.; (888) 712-1289; www
.sonomacreekinn.com. Five minutes from the plaza, an alternative
to pricey accommodations in town. Sixteen sleek, simple rooms
decorated with handcrafted accessories and original artwork; some
rooms with private patios or porches and fountains; all with refrigerators, queen beds, and high ceilings.

Thistle Dew Inn, 171 West Spain St.; (800) 382-7895. Five
antiques-filled rooms and a suite, garden hot tub, fireplaces, private decks and private entrances, lovely gardens, gourmet breakfast, afternoon refreshments; free use of bicycles. Book well in
advance.

Victorian Garden Inn, 316 East Napa St.; (707) 996-5339. A
dream of a century-old home a block from the plaza; pool, fireplaces, and full breakfast.

For More Information . . . .

Bed and Breakfast Association of Sonoma Valley; (800) 969-4667;
www.sonomabb.com.

Sonoma County Tourism Bureau, 420 Aviation Blvd., Santa Rosa
95403; (800) 576-6662, (707) 522-5800; www.sonomacounty
.com. Free 65-page visitors guide to the entire county and information online for 250 wineries, lodging, dining, activities, and
calendar.

Sonoma Valley Visitors Bureau, on the plaza, 453 First St. East,
Sonoma 95476; (707) 996-1090; www.sonomavalley.com.

NORTHBOUND ESCAPE *Three*
Lower Napa Valley
NAPA, YOUNTVILLE, AND RUTHERFORD / 1 NIGHT

Art and architecture
Wineries
Shopping
California cuisine
Vineyard walks
Gourmet picnics
Country lanes

Thirty miles long, just one-sixth the size of Bordeaux, the Napa Valley is home to the densest concentration of wineries in North America and to some of the state's most highly regarded California-cuisine restaurants, championship golf courses, charming bed-and-breakfast inns, and scenery reminiscent of southern Italy and France.

Your escape begins in the town of Napa, with a day in Yountville and a meander down the Silverado Trail. Stretching from Napa 35 miles north to Calistoga, the trail winds along the foot of high mountain ridges. Sprinkled along the way are wineries and champagne cellars, gargantuan mansions, small stone cottages, luxurious hotels, and quaint inns, each in its own idyllic corner of the Wine Country.

DAY 1 / MORNING

From the Oakland Bay Bridge, drive 45 minutes north on I–80, past the Napa/CA 37 exit, to the American Canyon exit a few miles north of Vallejo, turning west and connecting with CA 29 north into Napa; you'll be on Soscol Avenue. From Soscol take a left onto Third Street, crossing the Napa River, and park a few blocks down, across from a bright blue Victorian at 1517 Third St.

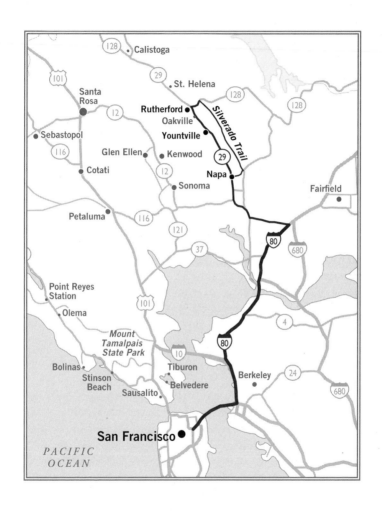

BREAKFAST   **Alexis Baking Company,** 1517 Third St., Napa; (707) 258-1827. Inventive breakfasts, the best pastries and desserts in the county, cappuccino, local color.

Just behind the bakery cafe, charming Victorian neighborhoods are bounded by Franklin, Division, Elm, and Riverside Drives; for just a peek, behind the bakery, drive up Franklin and down Randolph.

If you haven't been to Napa for a couple of years, you will be amazed to see the extensive new development along the river and throughout downtown. A red-and-green trolley trundles along the revitalized Riverfront District at the south end of Main Street, transporting visitors to historic buildings that are now retail and restaurant complexes. Within the Hatt Market and the Napa Mill are cafes, a luxury hotel, a wine bar, a general store, a day spa, a bakery, and an outdoor stage. Rooms at the upscale **Napa River Inn** open onto verandas over the river (877-251-8500; www.napariver inn.com). As fancy as a decorated wedding cake, the 1879 **Napa Opera House** on Main Street, which opened in 1880 with a production of Gilbert and Sullivan's *HMS Pinafore,* is now the venue for a lively schedule of top-notch concerts, drama, jazz, symphony, and cabaret (707-226-7372; www.napavalleyoperahouse.org).

Don't miss **Oxbow Public Market**, an iconic, new food bazaar showcasing everything from the Hog Island Oysters (on the half shell for a buck apiece) to milkshakes at Taylor's Refresher, and two dozen merchants selling local cheeses and charcuterie, gourmet chocolates, Angus beef, cupcakes, cookbooks, breads, pastries and pizza, local olive oils, organic ice cream, spices, culinary gifts and tools, and more, much more. Stop in for a cup of coffee, a snack or a glass of wine, and stroll the aisles of this huge, industrial-chic building; live music on Tues evenings (610 First St., Napa; (707) 226-6529; www.oxbowpublicmarket.com).

Connect again with CA 29 and head north to a left onto Redwood Road, then 6.5 miles through redwood and oak forests to **Hess Collection,** 4411 Redwood Rd., Napa (707-255-1144; www .hesscollection.com). A large and important European and American contemporary art collection resides here in a historic winery building. Take the self-guided tour and enjoy the gardens, the views, and the wine.

Back on CA 29 head north for ten minutes to **Yountville.** Park at V Marketplace. The few streets of this village are lined with vintage cottages in overgrown country gardens. On Washington, the main drag, a blizzard of shops, galleries, restaurants, and nearly a dozen inns makes this a popular Wine Country destination An unbelievable six Michelin stars have been awarded to some of the country's best restaurants, all within two blocks; and, more than two dozen premium wineries lie within a 4-square mile radius. The landmark, 1870-era building, **V Marketplace,** is a huge former winery sheltering import, gift, ice cream, and clothing shops, art galleries, outdoor cafes, and more (707-944-2451; www.vmarketplace .com).

LUNCH   **Bottega,** 6525 Washington St.; (707) 945-1050; www.bot teganapavalley.com. A gorgeous new restaurant owned by the Emmy-winning host of Food Network's *Easy Entertaining,* Michael Chiarello (he was also the creator and formerly the star chef of Tra Vigne in St. Helena). Lounge on a banquette by the fireplace on the covered "terrazzo," enjoying the passing scene around the sprawling V Marketplace and gardens. Yummy seasonal, locally-sourced "*nuovo* Italian" food, from garlic roasted Dungeness crab, wood oven roasted chicken and pizza, to housemade gnocchi, pasta and charcuterie. The rich, warm interior is enhanced by Venetian plaster, Murano glass chandeliers, and old timbers. Across the walkway, step into Chiarello's **NapaStyle Store** (707-945-1229; www.napastyle.com), which is chocked with unique gourmet implements, imported furnishings, gifts and foodstuffs; you can get panini and wine here, too, and sit out on the adjacent patio.

AFTERNOON

Take a rest on a garden bench at V Marketplace, or rush the stores!

Blue Heron Gallery on the second floor (707-944-2044; www .blueheronofnapa.com), has for more than three decades displayed the best of local artists' works. At **Vintage 1870 Wine Cellar,** more than one hundred locally produced wines are available to taste (707-531-7053; www.vwinecellar.com).

Just down the street, the **Overland Sheepskin Company** (707-944-0778) sells sheepskin coats, leather jackets, and Western hats. Across the street, **Raspberry's Art Glass** at Beard Plaza, (6540 Washington; 707-944-9211; www.rasgalleries.com), is one of the loveliest art-glass galleries you will ever see. My favorites are the vibrantly glowing, hand-blown, footlong tropical fish that are "swimming" in the window.

At 6711 Washington in a lovely, ca.-1900 Craftsman-style stone building and in a cloistered garden, Maisonry brings wine, art, and architecturally-oriented accessories and antiques together; wines poured are from limited edition, boutique wineries.

At the north end of town, **Yountville Park** is a grassy, oak-shaded commons with a fantastic children's playground and picnic tables. For a 3-mile round-trip walk or bike ride, go east from the park through the fascinating old cemetery to Yount Mill Road and follow it north to CA 29 and back. Running along a tributary of the Napa River, the road is shady and bedecked with lovely views of the mountains and vineyards. Watch for a plaque about George Calvert Yount, the first white settler in the valley. Yount wangled from Mexico the huge land grant of Rancho Caymus in the 1850s—comprising much of the heart of the valley, including Yountville—and built grist- and sawmills on the river. You will see the remains of one of his large wooden barns.

From the intersection of Yount Mill and Yountville Cross Roads, you can head east a couple of miles to connect with the Silverado Trail. On Yountville Cross Road at the bridge, the **Napa River Ecological Reserve** is a place to walk beside the river under oaks and sycamores. You can wade and fish here, too.

Few people know that you can take an easy, pleasant walk on paved paths around the grounds of the old **Yountville Veterans Home,** on the west side of CA 29 from Yountville (707-944-4600). It's a veritable botanical garden, with magnificent, huge trees that were planted well before the turn of the 20th century.

On the grounds of the Yountville Veterans Home is an architectural surprise, the new **Napa Valley Museum** of contemporary art, winemaking, and the history of the valley, with indoor and outdoor exhibits and a garden terrace (55 Presidents Circle; 707-944-0500; www.napavalleymuseum.org).

Near the museum, **Domaine Chandon** is a French-owned sparkling-wine cellar where you can wander the oak-studded grounds and learn about *méthode champenoise* winemaking (707-944-2280; www.chandon.com). A flute of champagne awaits in the tasting salon; try the Blanc de Noirs, a blossomy pink bubbly. The airy, contemporary-design restaurant here, **Etoile** is headed by a distinguished chef who produces miracles of California and French cuisine (800-736-2892); *Forbes Traveler* says it's "one of the Top Ten Romantic Restaurants in the USA" for 2009.

Arrive at your lodgings in time to enjoy the gardens and perhaps a dip in the pool before dinner.

DINNER For a snazzy, upscale atmosphere and renowned California cuisine, try **Mustard's Grill** (707-944-2424; www.mustardsgrill.com), two minutes north of Yountville on the highway. Go for inventive pastas, grilled and spit-roasted poultry and meats, and the super colossal wine list. Save a few minutes to wander the extensive vegetable and herb gardens. For more than 25 years, this has been a very popular, fun place; you may need to make reservations several days ahead.

LODGING **Villagio Inn and Spa,** 6541 Washington St., Yountville; (800) 351-1133; www.villagio.com. A 112-room luxury garden hotel; elegant, spacious rooms with fireplaces, whirlpool tubs; 60-foot lap pool, tennis, buffet breakfast. Upon the grounds are murals and replicas of ancient Greek and Roman statuary, lush gardens, stone walls, and sunny terraces. Weekends by the pool are lively, with a barbecue and live music; reserve a private cabana. The complimentary hot breakfast buffet is sumptuous, with champagne, smoked salmon, and mountains of fresh fruits, cheeses, egg dishes, and pastries. At the full-service spa, enjoy a grape-seed body polish or a mud wrap, massage, and beauty treatments; relax in the outdoor whirlpool and the sauna; take a yoga, aerobics, or spinning class, a tennis lesson, or a guided walk. Ask for a room away from CA 29—and away from the pool area if you seek privacy; ask about the spa suites. The concierge may be able to snag a reservation for you at Yountville restaurants that are booked up for weeks, if not months, in advance.

DAY 2 / MORNING

BREAKFAST **Villagio Inn.** After breakfast head north on CA 29. Just past Oakville Cross Road, stop at the **Oakville Grocery** (707-944-8802) for the makings of a French country picnic: pâtés, baguettes, quiches, fromages, charcuterie, baby vegetables, salads. There are hundreds of northern California wine selections and specialty foods from this region and around the world; fresh, rustic hearth breads; and the famous oversize cookies.

If you have time for only one winery visit (say it isn't true), this is the one, **Rubicon Estate** (1991 St. Helena Hwy., Rutherford; 707-968-1100; www.rubiconestate.com). Renowned moviemaker Francis Ford Coppola restored one of the oldest winery estates in the valley (Inglenook) to its former glory and had his Hollywood designers create an extravaganza of a winery, gift store, museum, and park. Drive down a long, tree-shaded allée to his spectacular park modeled after the Luxembourg Gardens, complete with bubbling fountains, promenades, and lawns. The elegant Mamarella Cafe is a cozy wine and cigar bar. Walk from the cafe through cool caves, where wine is stored behind iron bars, into high-ceilinged rooms full of Wine Country-style home accessories, clothing, art and books, and the main wine-tasting bar. Notice the gleaming exotic woods and huge stained-glass windows as you listen to Italian opera music. Call ahead about various tours.

Up the road at **St. Supery Vineyards and Winery,** 8440 St. Helena Hwy., Rutherford (707-963-4507; www.stsupery.com), you can walk through a demonstration vineyard, see an art show, tour a lovely Queen Anne Victorian farmhouse, and enjoy elaborate exhibits about grape growing and winemaking. And taste wine, too.

Drive to the Silverado Trail and turn left; then turn right up the hill to **Auberge du Soleil Resort** (180 Rutherford Hill Rd., Rutherford; 707-963-1211 or 800-348-5406; www.aubergedu soleil.com), where you'll feel as though you've dropped suddenly onto the French Riviera. Wisteria-draped arbors and riots of flowers beckon you past fat stucco walls into a tile-floored entry, flooded with light from the terraces where beautiful people dine *al fresco* on California cuisine. Enjoy the heartstopping view, linger with a glass of wine, wander the sculpture garden, and ask to see a villa, for future getaways. This is one of the most luxurious resorts in the Wine Country, if not the world. Rooms and suites have huge, elegant, comfortable furnishings; French doors opening onto private terraces; giant, fabulous bathrooms; and amenities galore. *Travel + Leisure* and *Condé Nast Traveler* have called it one of the world's best and most romantic small resorts.

LUNCH Picnic under the oaks at **Rutherford Hill Winery;** (707) 963-1871; www.rutherfordhill.com. Just up the hill from Auberge du Soleil, with the same panoramic view, this winery has 40,000 square feet of cool, underground caves, seen on 35-minute tours. Enjoy your Oakville Grocery picnic at tables under the oaks or in the olive grove; you will need to purchase your picnic wine here.

A little south of Rutherford Hill, **Mumm Napa Valley,** at 8445 Silverado Trail (707-963-1133; www.mummnapa.com), is a French-American sparkling-wine cellar with a tasting terrace, vineyard views, and a great gift shop. Stop in for a tasting on the terrace, or reserve ahead for a private, two-hour seating on the Oak Terrace, for a library flight tasting and food pairings while you enjoy the spectacular view.

Pine Ridge Winery, at 5901 Silverado Trail (707-253-7500; www.pineridgewinery.com), is a small, top-notch winery where you can tour the caves and barrel-taste (by reservation only), taste medal-winning Chardonnay paired with cheeses, and picnic in a grassy grove under tall pines; cost is $25 per person, no children.

Eighteen-foot-tall, golden columns topped with capital bulls announce **Darioush,** one of the most unusual wineries in the state, if not the country. Inspired by the architecture of Persepolis, the ancient capital of Persia, the Darioush family erected a temple to Persian culture and premium Napa Valley wine (4240 Silverado Trail; 707-257-2345; www.darioush.com). Pale-gold travertine blocks from the Middle East clad the visitor center, where waving palms, formal Mediterranean gardens, and indoor and outdoor water features create a setting fit for a Persian prince. In the sleek tasting room, guests wander the polished floors, sipping Bordeaux varietals such as Viognier, Shiraz, and a luscious late-harvest Sauvignon Blanc; call ahead about private wine and cheese pairings in the caves.

AFTERNOON

Watch for the left turn to the **Silverado Country Club and Resort,** 1600 Atlas Peak Rd., Napa (707-257-0200), a 1,200-acre resort famous for its two 18-hole Robert Trent Jones golf courses. Towering eucalyptus, palm, magnolia, and oak trees line the drive leading to a huge, ca. 1870 mansion. A curving staircase and period chandeliers grace the lobby; a terrace bar overlooks sweeping lawns, waterways, and gardens. Silverado has several restaurants and one of the largest tennis complexes in northern California. Scattered about the lush gardens and quiet courtyards are condominium units and cottages, some with fireplaces; nine swimming pools, and a glamorous, quite large beauty and fitness spa with a lap pool. Take tea in the lounge, then head south to Napa and back to the Bay Area.

There's More . . . .

Ballooning. Floating silently in a hot-air balloon is an unforgettable way to see the Wine Country. Always scheduled for the early morning, balloon trips are usually accompanied by champagne, breakfast, and much revelry. Rates average $185 per person.

Adventures Aloft, P.O. Box 2500, Yountville 94599; (707) 255-8688.

Balloons Above the Valley, P.O. Box 3838, Napa 94558; (707) 253-2222 or (800) 464-6824; www.balloonrides.com. Departs from Domaine Chandon Winery in Yountville.

Bonaventura Balloon Company, P.O. Box 78, Rutherford 94573; (800) FLY-NAPA; www.bonaventuraballoons.com.

Napa Valley Balloons, P.O. Box 2860, Yountville 94599; (707) 253-2228 or (800) 253-2224; www.napavalleyballoons.com. Launches at sunrise from Domaine Chandon Winery.

Biking. The Napa Valley can be divided into three moderately strenuous bike trips: a circle tour around the spa town of Calistoga, a mid-valley tour in and around St. Helena and Yountville, and a third tour in the Carneros region. The mostly flat Silverado Trail, running along the east side of the valley, is a main biker's route. Crisscrossing the valley between CA 29 and the Silverado Trail are myriad leafy country roads. You can arrange to have the bike rental company deliver bikes to your hotel and pick up you and your bikes at a winery or other destination.

Bicycle Trax, 796 Soscol Ave., Napa; (707) 258-8729. You can rent bikes here and start up the Silverado Trail just a few blocks away.

Art. **Di Rosa Preserve,** 5200 Carneros Hwy., Napa; (707) 226-5991; www.dirosapreserve.org. Not your grandfather's art gallery, this is the most significant collection of Bay Area art in the world, more than 2,000 works by a thousand artists on over 200 acres in the idyllic Carneros wine growing area. Besides viewing some of the amusing, flamboyant, and startling art you'll ever see (such as autos hanging from trees, wildly decorated skateboards, the "rhinocar," and more eye-popping sights), enjoy the lovely grounds and the lake. Call ahead for tour reservations and for event dates.

Golf. **Chardonnay Club,** 2555 Jameson Canyon, Napa; (707) 257-8950; www.chardonnayclub.com. On the south end of Napa, 27 semi private holes in a challenging landscape of ravines, hills, and vineyards; predictably windy.

Eagle Vines Golf Club, 580 South Kelly Rd., Napa; (707) 257-4471; www.eaglevinesgolfclub.com. At the south end of the Napa Valley, Johnny Miller's new design is draped over low rolling hills, challenged by prevailing winds off the top of San Francisco Bay, carpets of vineyards, and overhanging oak trees.

J. F. Kennedy Municipal Golf Course, just north of Napa; (707) 255-4333. Eighteen challenging holes, water on 14; reasonable rates.

Vintner's Golf Club, 7901 Solano Ave., Yountville; (707) 944-1992; www.vintnersgolfclub.com. A walkable nine-holer in a beautiful site at the foot of Mount Veeder. Giant redwoods loom along fairways dotted with young trees and watered by a small creek and ponds. Pleasant indoor/outdoor dining.

Special Tour. **Napa Valley Wine Train,** 1275 McKinstry St., Napa; (707) 253-2111 or (800) 427-4124; www.winetrain.com. Elegant restored dining and observation cars, a relaxing way to see the valley; lunch and dinner; no stops on the slow, three-hour chug from Napa to St. Helena and back.

Park. **Skyline Park,** East Imola Avenue, Napa; (707) 252-0481. Hilly woodlands and meadows for hiking, horseback riding, picnicking, and RV and tent camping. Great for winter mushroom expeditions and springtime wildflower walks; find the waterfalls for a summer splash.

Wine education. **Robert Mondavi Winery**'s three-and-a-half-hour tour and wine essence tasting is one of the most comprehensive of the free educational tours offered by wineries. (7801 St. Helena Hwy. [CA 29] in Oakville; 888-766-6328; www.robertmondaviwinery.com).

Merryvale Vineyards holds a beginner's wine-tasting seminar in the cask room on Sat mornings. For reservations call (800) 326-6069. Located at 1000 Main St. in St. Helena.

Franciscan Winery has a hands-on blending seminar; (707) 963-7111.

Camp Napa Culinary, a weeklong, hands-on cooking class with winery tours, by a renowned author/chef (888-999-4844; www.hughcarpenter.com).

Special Events . . . .

JANUARY THROUGH MARCH

Napa Valley Mustard Festival; (707) 944-1133; www.mustardfestival .org. Celebrating the blooming of the mustard in the vineyards, a series of food, art, and wine events that gets bigger every year. Kicks off with a grand event at the Culinary Institute of America (CIA) with auctions, live music, art, food, and wine. Also on the schedule are recipe, art, and photo competitions; a huge showcase and marketplace; and a grand finale party with music and dancing. Special events throughout the valley with celebrity winemakers, chefs, musical performers, and artists.

JUNE

Napa Valley Wine Auction; (707) 963-5246; www.napavintners .com. Wine aficionados from all over the world come for three days of parties, barrel tastings, and events at wineries; auction benefits local hospital.

AUGUST

Music in the Vineyards, Napa Valley wineries; (707) 578-5656. Noted chamber music artists from across the country assemble to play in beautiful winery settings; wine tasting, too.

SEPTEMBER

River Festival, Third Street Bridge, Napa; (707) 226-7459. Napa Valley Symphony performs at the riverside.

OCTOBER

Yountville Days Festival; (707) 944-0904. Parade, music, enter-tainment, food.

NOVEMBER
Napa Valley Wine Fest; (707) 253-3563.

DECEMBER
Napa Valley Jazz Festival, Yountville; (707) 944-0310.

Other Recommended Restaurants and Lodgings . . . .

NAPA

Angele Restaurant and Bar, 540 Main St.; (707) 252-8115; www
.angelerestaurant.com. Classic French and Wine Country cuisine
right on the river, in the cozy dining room or on the patio. Fish stew,
charcuterie, wonderful pâtés, cassoulet, local seafood, nice salads,
and omelettes for brunch and lunch.

Bistro Don Giovanni, 4110 Howard Lane (visible from CA 29), five
minutes north of Napa; (707) 224-3300; www.bistrodongiovanni
.com. Rub elbows with winemakers in a lively, noisy trattoria atmosphere. Country Italian cuisine, pizza, risotto, wood-fire roasted
chicken, suckling pig, steak frites, eclectic pasta, one of the valley's best wine lists.

Blackbird Inn, 1755 First St.; (888) 567-9811; www.foursisters
.com. Built as a private residence in 1910, the inn is a virtual
gallery of California's Arts and Crafts period. Hallways and public
areas are lined with early California landscape art. Guests meet for
wine and hors d'oeuvres, then again for a hearty country breakfast.
Eight rooms with fireplaces and private decks.

The Carneros Inn, 4048 Sonoma Hwy.; (707) 299-4900; www.the
carnerosinn.com. An upscale hostelry on an idyllic site above rolling hills surrounded by vineyards and meadows. Spacious one- and

two-bedroom suites have wood-burning fireplaces, flat-screen TVs; private, heated patios; and gorgeous bathrooms, some with indoor/outdoor showers and soaking tubs; each with a private, fenced patio. On site are two infinity-edge pools, full-service spa, bocce court, fitness classes, and three restaurants. Just down the hill, the casual Boon Fly Cafe serves breakfast and lunch; Farm is an industrial-chic indoor/outdoor restaurant and trendy lounges serving some of the best Wine Country cuisine ever concocted.

La Residence, 4066 St. Helena Hwy., on the north end of Napa; (707) 253-0337. A romantic inn in a French barn and a ca. 1870 mansion surrounded by gardens on two oak- and pine-studded acres. Rooms are elaborately decorated with antiques, designer fabrics and linens, and four-poster beds, and have fireplaces, patios, and verandas. Full breakfast, wine and hors d'oeuvres, swimming pool.

Oak Knoll Inn, 2200 East Oak Knoll Ave.; (707) 255-2200. In the middle of 600 acres of Chardonnay vines, four huge, elegant guest rooms with private entrances, fireplaces, king-size brass beds, hot tub, swimming pool. Full gourmet breakfast, wine and cheese in the evening.

Pasta Prego, 3206 Jefferson St.; (707) 224-9011. A best-kept secret, one of the best casual restaurants in the area: modern Northern Italian cuisine, like polenta with mushroom sauce, smoky grilled veggies, rich risottos, fresh local fish, poultry, meats, and many pastas. Noisy and fun, patronized by the "in crowd" of local winery families. Dining is indoors in the small dining room, at the counter, or on the heated patio.

Ubuntu Restaurant, 1140 Main St.; (707) 251-5656; www.ubuntu napa.com. A "yoga studio-restaurant" (you can see the yoginis practicing behind the opaque glass) that has been lauded by food critics around the country. In a stunning, minimalist-contempo interior, innovative, luscious vegetarian food sourced from the restaurant's biodynamic gardens and from local producers. Rustic stews, chowders, miraculous salads, inventive pizzas, roasted veggies—even if you're a dedicated carnivore, this place will satisfy and delight you. Don't miss the housemade ice creams.

RUTHERFORD

Rutherford Grill, 1880 Rutherford Rd.; (707) 962-1782. Go for the smoky baby back ribs, mountains of feathery onion rings, grilled and spit-roasted poultry and meats, garlic mashed potatoes, and jalapeño corn bread. Big booths inside, umbrella tables and a wine bar outside. The bad news: It is a very popular place, and you may have to wait on weekends. The good news: The attractive patio where you wait has a wine bar and a bubbling fountain.

YOUNTVILLE

Bardessono Napa Valley, 6526 Yount St.; (707) 363-7295; www .bardessono.com. Eco-conscious visitors now have a new, upscale lodge that is already famous for its groundbreaking, LEED-certified (Leadership in Energy and Environmental Design), sustainable design and operation. On-site restaurant headed by a star chef is focused on organic, artisanal, locally-sourced ingredients, some from the hotel's gardens. Sixty-two luxury-level rooms in Tuscan villa style, in a setting dotted with olive trees, stone sculptures. and streams and ponds. Fireplaces, private patios, and balconies, in-room spa treatments, sunken tubs, outdoor showers; separate spa venue and rooftop swimming pool with valley views. Stop in for a glass of wine in the gardens or in the bar by the fireplace. The gift shop is a showcase of artisan crafts from around the world.

Bouchon, 6534 Washington St.; (707) 944-8037; www.bouchon bistro.com. Elegant Parisian brasserie interior with a stunning bar and ceiling fixtures from Grand Central Station. Owned by the legendary Thomas Keller and his brother, this may be the best bistro outside France; it can be quite noisy. Vibrating with freshness, ingredients are from the French Laundry garden and around the valley. Try the classic quiche, steak frites, raw bar, charcuterie, espresso-orange pot de crème. Next door, the incredible breads and pastries made for the French Laundry and Bouchon are available at the Bouchon Bakery, a country-style boulangerie. With your latte, have an apricot spice scone, a pain au chocolat, or a lemon tart.

The French Laundry, 6640 Washington St.; (707) 944-2380; www .frenchlaundry.com. Said to be one of the best restaurants in the world, a veritable temple of country French and California cuisine, so revered and desired it has no sign out front (reserve two months in advance). In a vine-covered stone building in a garden, the food, the service, the wine list and the prices are astounding—for many Wine Country visitors, a once-in-a-lifetime experience.

Hotel Luca, 6774 Washington St., Yountville; (707) 944-8080; http://hotellucanapa.com. A 20-room luxury boutique hotel built of antique stone and hand-hewn timbers, vaulted brick ceilings, and other rustic Italian elements. Dine al fresco at Cantinetta Piero on wood-fired pizza, house-cured salumi and other authentic Italian cuisine. Linger in the Zen garden before a float in the lavender-saltwater soaking pool and a massage. There is a large main pool, too. Rooms have soaking tubs and high-tech amenities, some have fireplaces and balconies; complimentary breakfast.

Maison Fleurie, 6529 Yount St.; (707) 944-1388 or (800) 522-4140; www.foursisters.com. An ivy-covered stone inn with the look of southern France; lush gardens and a swimming pool, bountiful breakfasts, afternoon wine, bikes. Thirteen guest rooms have vineyard views; some have fireplaces and spa tubs.

Napa Valley Lodge, 2230 Madison St.; (707) 944-2468 or (800) 368-2468; www.napavalleylodge.com. In a great location near the city park, with a heated pool on a sunny terrace, this upscale, Mediterranean-style lodge with spacious rooms and suites with balconies or patios in a garden setting; an extravagant champagne breakfast buffet is complimentary. Sauna, fitness center.

For More Information . . . .

Napa Downtown Association, 1310 Napa Town Center, Napa 94559; (707) 226-7459; www.napavalley.com.

Napa Valley Reservations Unlimited, 1819 Tanen, Suite B, Napa 94559; (707) 252-1985 or (800) 251-6272; www.napavalleyres ervations.com.

Yountville Chamber of Commerce, 6484 Washington St., Yountville 94599; (707) 944-0904; www.yountville.com. In Washington Square Center, north end of town.

NORTHBOUND ESCAPE *Four*
Upper Napa Valley
HEART OF THE WINE COUNTRY / 2 NIGHTS

Hot springs
Art galleries
Winery architecture tour
Shopping
Mud baths
Vineyard picnic

"Up valley," as the northern half of the Napa Valley is called, is anchored by Calistoga, a hot springs resort town founded in the 1840s. Steam rises from 200-degree mineral springs at a dozen or so health resorts. Some are scatterings of historic clapboard cottages with simple facilities; others are Roman-style spas with luxurious lodgings. This is the place for rest and rejuvenation, for massages, mud baths, beauty treatments, and slow swims in warm pools. The mud-bath experience must be tried at least once; be warned that après mud bath you won't feel like moving for quite a spell.

As you drive to Calistoga, through the valley bordered by the Mayacamas Range on the west and the Howell Mountain Range on the east, the tremendous variety of Napa Valley soils and microclimates becomes evident. It's fun to try the diverse wines produced from grapes grown on the dry hillsides, those from the valley floor, and especially the wines from grapes grown on the "benches," the alluvial fans of soil and rocks eroded down from the mountainsides into triangles of rich bedding for vineyards whose grapes have produced wines besting the best in France.

Besides wine tasting and hot-bath soaking "up valley," there's tons of shopping to do in St. Helena, plus biking, hiking, golfing, and ballooning; perhaps you'll be forced to return for another weekend or two.

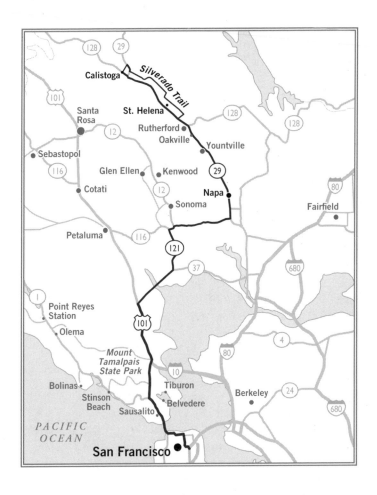

DAY 1 / MORNING

From the Golden Gate Bridge, drive north on US 101 to the Napa/CA 37 exit, connecting with CA 121 east to CA 29 at Napa, then drive 30 minutes north to **St. Helena**—about 90 minutes altogether.

BREAKFAST   **Gillwoods,** 1313 Main St., St. Helena; (707) 963-1788; www .gillwoodscafe.com. Rub elbows with the locals to enjoy unique breakfast special-ties and all-American favorites all day long.

Enjoy the plethora of specialty shops on Main. **Main Street Books,** 1371 Main (707-963-1338), is stocked with regional guidebooks. **Art on Main** shows the best of local artwork and some from around the world, especially vibrant landscapes and whimsical sculptures (1359 Main; 707-963-3350). Assembled by a renowned interior designer for her clientele of the beautiful people of the Napa Valley, **Martin Showroom** is an eclectic emporium of contemporary furnishings, antique architectural fragments, stone sculpture, and one-of-a-kind accessories—come in here for the wow factor and for the stunning mountain views from the garden (1350 Main St., 707-967-8787).

The **St. Helena Wine Center,** 1321 Main (707-963-1313; www .shwc.com), will ship mixed cases of local wines, from Schrams-burg Blanc de Blanc to Marilyn Merlot. They sell fine cigars, too.

Get your pet a rubber frog, a doggie futon, a life jacket, a saddlebag, or some gourmet biscuits at the ultimate dog and cat store, **Fideaux** (1312 Main St.; 707-967-9935).

Anchoring the north end of town on Main Street is tiny Lyman Park, for almost a century a grassy spot for reclining under the oaks, with a gazebo and a stone water fountain for dogs and horses. Across the street at 1429 Main, **Vanderbilt and Company** is a huge store with ceramics, linens, glassware, and myriad accessories from France and Italy (707-963-1010).

If you're a Robert Louis Stevenson aficionado, you'll find 8,000 pieces of his memorabilia at the **Robert Louis Stevenson Museum,** 1490 Library Lane (707-963-3757; http://silveradomuseum.org). Next door, the **Napa Valley Wine Library** (707-963-5145) houses 6,000 books, tapes, and reference materials on the art of wine making and the history of the valley.

A block off the main drag, take a step back in time at the retro **Big Dipper** old-fashioned ice-cream parlor, decorated with old Coke signs and other fun relics. Have a thick shake or a banana split, or some penny candy (1336A Oak Ave.; 707-963-2616).

Driving north from St. Helena, you'll see redwood forests grow darker and deeper. Maples and oaks crowd closer to the roadside, creating canopies of leaves and branches overhead, brilliant canyons of color in the fall. Watch for **Beringer Winery's Rhine House** on the left, built in 1883 as a reminder to the winery founder of his family home in Germany. A recent restoration revived the 40 sparkling stained glass panels, parquet floors, a newly discovered mural, and various Gothic-Victorian elements. This is a good place to take a full winery tour, which includes the huge cellar caves carved into the hillside by Chinese laborers more than a hundred years ago (707-963-8989; www.beringer.com).

LUNCH   **Wine Spectator Greystone Restaurant,** just north of Beringer on CA 29 in St. Helena; (707) 967-1010; www.ciachef.edu/california. A massive stone landmark guarded by towering palms, Greystone was built as a winery in 1889 with 22-inch-thick, hand-cut volcanic stone blocks. Today it houses the West Coast annex of the prestigious culinary college, the Culinary Institute of America (CIA). Visitors interested in fine food and wine history like to browse in the gourmet store and the food and wine museum. You can wander paths through aromatic herb gardens and arrange to tour the state-of-the-art teaching kitchens in the upper reaches of the building. Call ahead to ask about wine seminars.

The stunning Mediterranean (rather noisy) restaurant turns regional cuisine into high art. The outdoor dining terrace overlooks an ancient oak forest and rolling vineyards.

AFTERNOON

Five minutes north of the CIA on CA 29, **Bale Grist Mill State Park** (707-963-2236) is a wooded glade with a 36-foot waterwheel beside a rushing creek. Walk from here into **Bothé-Napa Valley State Park** (707-942-4575) to find a lovely campground in Ritchie Creek canyon, a swimming pool, and shady picnic sites under redwoods and firs along the creek. Both of these parks are home to the endangered spotted owl. You can take a one- or two-hour guided horseback ride along Ritchie Creek and up along the ridges overlooking the valley. **Triple Creek Horse Outfit** offers guided rides here, and at Jack London State Park and Sugarloaf Ridge State Park (707-887-8700; www.triplecreekhorseoutfit.com). Proceed another 10 minutes to Calistoga and have a pre-dinner glass of wine at the trendy **Hydro Bar and Grill,** 1403 Lincoln Ave.; (707) 942-9777. The exotic bistro menu here changes daily and may include red wine-fennel sausage with potato and artichoke hash or roasted mushroom and goat cheese lasagna. The wine and micro-brew list is extensive.

DINNER **All Seasons Cafe,** 1400 Lincoln, Calistoga; (707) 942-9111; www.allseasonsnapavalley.net. A classically trained chef holds forth in the kitchen, inventing American versions of Mediterranean food with all locally grown and produced ingredients. Home-smoked salmon and chicken, grilled Petaluma duck breast, pizzettas, pasta, fresh fish, killer pies. Salads are tops here, such as warm spinach with smoked chicken and lemon dressing. One of the first restaurants in the United States to receive *Wine Spectator's* prestigious "Grand Award."

LODGING **Solage Calistoga,** 755 Silverado Trail, Calistoga; (866) 942-7442; www.solagecalistoga.com. Earning "green design" and sustainability awards, a sleek new urban-chic resort near town, with modernist, light-filled studio accommodations with soaking tubs, adult and children's pools; Solbar, a trendy restaurant/lounge; and two bocce courts. The unique full-service spa features "MudSlide" mud-bath treatments and geothermal pools, and traditional and exotic treatments, plus a fitness venue and daily free yoga and exercise classes. Guests at Solage have the use of spas, restaurants, recreational venues and hiking trails at nearby luxury resorts Auberge du Soleil and Calistoga Ranch.

DAY 2 / MORNING

BREAKFAST **Solage Calistoga.**

Set off on a walking tour of town, a compact grid of tree-shaded streets. The architecture is an eclectic conglomeration of Victorian, Art Deco, 1950s funky, Craftsman, and Greek and Mission Revival. Get a map and some orientation at the **Sharpsteen Museum,** 1311 Washington (707-942-5911; www.sharpsteen-museum.org), where an elaborate diorama re-creates the 1800s resort town. Exhibits are lifelike and colorful, and a huge collection of old photos recalls the people who came here more than a hundred years ago to "take the waters." Ben Sharpsteen was one of Walt Disney's original animators, and you can see his Oscar in the museum.

Just off the main street on Cedar, the green oasis of **Pioneer Park** on the Napa River has lawns, a gazebo, and a great kids' playground. Next door to the park, **The Elms,** 1300 Cedar (707-942-9476), is a bed-and-breakfast inn in a fanciful French Victorian mansion.

Lee Youngman Galleries, at 1316 Lincoln (707-942-0585; www.leeyoungmangalleries.com), displays large collections of well-known California artists' works. The **Evans Ceramics Gallery,** at 1421 Lincoln (707-942-0453), sells one-of-a-kind, fine ceramic art. Don't miss **Ca'Toga Galleria d'Arte,** where a noted Venetian artist and muralist showcases his fabulous glazed ceramics, painted furniture, and garden sculpture, which have been *faux* painted to echo ancient Pompeian, Roman, and 16th-century Venetian originals. The beautiful building itself and the spectacular ceiling mural inside are worth a special visit (1206 Cedar St.; 707-942-3900; www.catoga.com).

The work of some of the best artisans in northern and southern California is shown and sold at the **Artful Eye,** jewelry, wine glasses, ceramics, glass, clothing, and more (1333A Lincoln; 707-942-4743). **Zenobia** (1410 Lincoln Ave.; 707-942-1050) has everything from Z to A: jewelry, glass art, folk art, clothing, and metal artwork—anything that is colorful and bright. If you are a wine aficionado and want to add to your wine book collection or pick up guidebooks to the Wine Country, stop in at the **Calistoga Bookstore,** 1343 Lincoln (707-942-4123). Stop in at **Hurd Beeswax Candle Factory** at 1255 Lincoln Ave. to see wild, weird, and colorful handmade beeswax candles of every description being created for shipment worldwide (707-942-7410).

LUNCH **Wappo Bar and Bistro,** 1226B Washington St., Calistoga; (707) 942-4712; www.wappobar.com. A small cafe with patio tables beside a fountain, serving ethnic-inspired inventions such as Middle Eastern pomegranate-glazed pork, Ecuadorean hornada, Central American duck *carnitas,* Asian noodle salads, and homemade ice cream. Choose from a 600+ label wine list; a wine bar with appetizers is open all day and evening. Try to arrive either before or after the traditional mealtimes, or you may wait for a table.

AFTERNOON

A restored 1868 Southern Pacific train station on Lincoln houses the visitors bureau and the **Calistoga Wine Stop** (1458 Lincoln Ave.; (707) 942-5556; calistogawinestop.net), where you can choose from more than 1,000 Napa and Sonoma Valley wines; taste Thurs through Mon; and arrange for them to be shipped.

Spend the rest of the day at one of Calistoga's health resorts being herbal-wrapped, enzyme-bathed, massaged, and soaked in mineral-rich mud; expect to feel like warm Jell-O when it's over (see Spas in the "There's More" section at the end of this chapter).

Not in the mood for mud and massage? Take a hike in **Robert Louis Stevenson State Park,** 7 miles north of Calistoga on CA 29, or on the **Oat Hill Mine Trail,** a historic landmark that starts at the junction of Lincoln Avenue and the Silverado Trail. Mountain bikers, horseback riders, and hikers like this rocky, rigorous, 5-mile climb to China Camp.

Save a couple of hours to tour **Castello di Amorosa,** a super-colossal, authentic recreation of a medieval Italian castle. You won't believe your eyes as you drive up to the crenellated stone towers and massive walls. Constructed over a decade or so were 100 rooms on eight levels, a moat with a drawbridge, a great hall fit for the Knights of the Round Table, a torture chamber, a chapel, a maze of caves, terraces with valley views, and a cavernous tasting room featuring V. Sattui wines that are produced on-site. This is a prime attraction, so take care to call ahead (4045 St. Helena Hwy., Calistoga; 707-967-6272; www.castellodiamorosa.com). Consider booking a carriage ride on the property, in an 1800s horse-drawn carriage, past historic buildings, vineyards, and winemaking equipment on the way to Lake Mario; wine and chocolates are part of the package. Guided tours are $25–$30 per person, less for children; wine tasting is $10–$15, including entrance fee (without guided tour).

DINNER   **BarVino,** where a cool vibe, cozy booths, live music, and inventive, locally sourced food make this a popular spot (1457 Lincoln Ave. in the Mount View Hotel, Calistoga (707-942-9900; www.bar-vino.com). Rooms at the Mount View Hotel overlook the town or the palm-shaded courtyard; room decor may be Art Deco or Victorian. There is a heated outdoor pool, a whirlpool filled with mineral water from the inn's own hot springs, and an upscale spa facility with beauty and health treatments. Ask about the private spa rooms with double-size Jacuzzis (707-942-6877; www.mountviewhotel.com).

LODGING   Solage Calistoga.

DAY 3 / MORNING

BREAKFAST   Solage Calistoga.

Proceed a few minutes north on the Silverado Trail, north of Calistoga to **Château Montelena,** 1429 Tubbs Lane (707-942-5105; www.montelena.com), at the foot of Mount St. Helena. Secluded in a piney wood, the winery is a spectacular castle built of French limestone brought around the Horn in 1880, poised above a small lake surrounded by gardens and weeping willows, with a vineyard view. A Chinese junk floats serenely, and red-lacquered gazebos provide private places for conversation and sipping of the renowned estate-grown Cabernets and Rieslings, available only here. In 1972 a Château Montelena Chardonnay exploded the myth that French wines are best by winning a blind tasting against France's finest. Tastings are $20, and $40 for private library tastings.

Head south on the Silverado Trail. To commemorate the founding of the Calistoga Mineral Water Company and to have some fun, a larger-than-life sculpture was erected on the roadside near Calistoga—a great photo op. At six tons, 14 feet tall, and 35 feet long, it is an oversized version of the company founder's 1926 truck. Today, Calistoga Water is one of the most popular bottled waters in the world.

Proceed south and turn right onto Dunaweal Lane to **Clos Pegase** (707-942-4982; www.clospegase.com), a russet-colored, postmodern extravaganza of a winery, the result of an international architectural competition. Besides wine tasting here, you'll enjoy the vineyard views, sculpture garden, frescoed murals, about 2,000 works of art, and a slide show about the history of winemaking.

A minute farther on Dunaweal, the sparkling white Moroccan aerie of **Sterling Vineyards** (800-726-6136; www.sterlingvineyards .com) floats like an apparition high on a hilltop. For a small fee, a tram will take you on a gondola ride to a sky-high terrace with valley views. The winery tour is self-guided, and there are outdoor tables up here for picnicking with your own provisions, or you can buy simple deli items onsite.

Back on the Silverado Trail, continue south through the valley to a left onto Meadowood Lane for a stroll on the grounds of the **Meadowood Napa Valley** (707-963-3646), a posh country lodge reminiscent of the 1920s, residing regally on a rise overlooking 250 densely wooded acres, a golf course, and tennis and croquet courts. The full-service health and beauty spa is luxurious, offering traditional and exotic treatments. Spacious, very private cottages and suites nestle in an oak-and-pine forest. The restaurant and bar here are quite pleasant, overlooking a secluded valley. Meadowood is the home of the annual Napa Valley Wine Auction, a spectacular four-day event attended by deep-pocket bidders and wine lovers from all over the world.

In an oak woodland off the Silverado Trail, **Joseph Phelps Vineyards** offers an in-depth, sophisticated wine tasting and educational program (200 Taplin Rd.; 707-963-2745; www.jpvwines .com). Call ahead, and plan to settle in here for an hour or so. An innovator, Joseph Phelps introduced Insignia, the first Bordeaux-style blend produced in California under a proprietary label, and one of the first California-style Syrahs, followed by an entire family of Rhône-style wines. If you decide to picnic under the oaks, a staff member will pair the perfect bottle of wine with your menu.

LUNCH **The Grill,** on the terrace at Meadowood. Or, for a picnic lunch, take a right onto Zinfandel Lane, crossing over to CA 29, and head south a few minutes to Oakville, stopping for gourmet goodies at **Oakville Grocery** (707-944-8802), at Oakville Cross Road. Or try **V. Sattui Winery,** at 111 White Lane south of St. Helena (707-963-7774; www.vsattui.com), which has a pretty, shady picnic grove on two acres of lawn around a stone-walled 1885 winery. The gourmet deli sells hundreds of varieties of cheeses and meats, fresh breads, and juices and drinks. Disadvantages here are the sight of the busy highway and the arrival of tour buses. Don't be concerned if you miss the wine tasting here; there are better choices for wine.

AFTERNOON

Head south to the Bay Area.

There's More

Biking. **Getaway Adventures,** 2228 Northpoint Parkway, Santa Rosa 95407; (707) 568-3040; www.getawayadventures.com. Guided biking and kayaking in the Napa Valley and Sonoma County, with gourmet picnics and wine tasting, from Calistoga "Sip n'Cycle" to Pedal and Paddle in the Alexander Valley, Healdsburg and Jenner kayak tours, and farm tours.

   Las Posadas Bike and Hike Trail: Drive 6 miles up Deer Park Road to Angwin, go right on Cold Spring Road, and take the left onto Las Posadas Road to the parking area. Cruise on your bike or stroll on a leafy trail through dense redwood and oak groves, a cool place to be on a hot day.

Calistoga Bikeshop, 1318 Lincoln Ave., Calistoga 94515; (707) 942-9687; www.calistogabikeshop.com. Ask about the self-guided "Cool Wine Tour," which covers tasting fees and winery bookings, wine pick-up, roadside assistance, concierge service and rentals.

St. Helena Cyclery, 1156 Main St., St. Helena; (707) 963-7736; http://sthelenacyclery.com. From here you can bike out Spring Street to White Sulfur Springs on a level, quiet paved road.

Spring Mountain Road: Bike on Madrona for 3 blocks, west of Main Street in St. Helena; then turn right on (paved) Spring Mountain for a steep ride up (about an hour) and a fast ride down.

Nature. **Old Faithful Geyser of California,** 1299 Tubbs Lane, Calistoga; (707) 942-6463; www.oldfaithfulgeyser.com. Blows its top every 15 minutes. An overrated tourist attraction.

Wildlife Preserve. **Safari West,** 3115 Porter Creek Rd., Santa Rosa; (707) 579-2551 or (800) 616-2695; www.safariwest.com. Giraffes in Napa? Yes, at the far northern end of the valley on open grasslands and rolling hills in a wildlife preserve with more than 400 exotic animals and birds, and African plains animals, including zebras, elands, endangered antelope, giraffe, impala, and Watusi cattle. Private half-day tours in safari vehicles. A once-in-a-lifetime expedition; advance reservations required. Many animals at Safari West are either members of an endangered species or are already extinct in the wild. You can stay overnight here in a nice tent cabin outfitted with two double beds; breakfast is included, and African food is available for dinner in the Savannah Café.

Spas. **Indian Springs Hot Springs Spa and Resort,** at 1712 Lincoln Ave., Calistoga; (707) 942-4913; www.indianspringscalistoga

.com). Founded in 1865, this spa has an old-fashioned ambience, while offering all the treatments that the newer resorts do. The Olympic-size pool is filled with mineral water from three natural geysers, heated to 92 degrees in summer and 101 in winter. From a studio cottage to a large house, the accommodations are simple and comfortable, including gas fireplaces, soft terry robes, and air-conditioning. Amenities include a clay tennis court, bicycles and bike surreys, croquet, hammocks, and barbecue grills.

Lavender Hill Spa, 1015 Foothill Blvd. at Hazel, Calistoga; (707) 942-4495; www.lavenderhillspa.com. This elegant place specializes in couples treatments—everything from massage to acupressure, aromatherapy, and "Vibra Sound" in addition to the traditional mud baths.

Health Spa Napa Valley, 1030 Main St., St. Helena; (707) 967-8800; www.napavalleyspa.com. In the town center, a full-service, pretty day-use beauty and fitness spa offering complete skin and body care, ayurvedic treatments, and massage and couples packages; a lap pool, whirlpool, steam, and more.

Roman Spa, 1300 Washington St., Calistoga; (707) 942-4441; www.romanspahotsprings.com. Mineral pools, beauty treatments, mud baths, enzyme baths, saunas; rooms around a tropical garden. Filled with natural geothermal mineral water, the large outdoor pool is kept at a soothing 92–96 degrees and the large indoor spa at 100 degrees; also, Finnish saunas and hydrojet therapy pools. Some rooms have private mineral water whirlpools and small kitchens.

Special Events

MARCH

Mustard Mud and Music, downtown Calistoga; 707-942-6333. Jazz and wine tasting takes over downtown area. Part of the Napa

Valley Mustard Festival. Some of the Bay Area's best musicians play, two dozen top-notch local wineries are pouring.

SEPTEMBER
Hometown Harvest Festival, Oak Street, St. Helena; (707) 963-4456. Dancing, pet parade, arts and crafts, music, food, wine tasting and wine auction.

NOVEMBER
Calistoga Downtown Jazz Festival and Blues in the Vineyards, (866) 306-5588. A weekend of music, food, and wine throughout the town; shuttle available to wineries.

Other Recommended Restaurants and Lodgings . . . .

CALISTOGA
Cafe Pacifico, 1237 Lincoln Ave.; (707) 942-4400. A Mexican motif is the backdrop for breakfasts, lunches, and dinners. Try the blue-corn buttermilk pancakes and chile rellenos.

Calistoga Inn, Restaurant and Brewery, 1250 Lincoln Ave.; (707) 942-4101; www.calistogainn.com. In a charming ca. 1880 building with a splendid outdoor dining terrace on the Napa River. Breakfast, lunch, and dinner. Hearty country fare: chili, burgers, huevos rancheros, crab cakes, fresh fish, and award-winning home-brewed beers and ales. Also 18 comfortable rooms.

Calistoga Ranch, 580 Lommel Rd.; (800) 942-4220; www.calistogaranch.com. An Auberge Resort, country luxury in a secluded pine and oak forest, 46 spacious, contemporary cedar lodges, each with indoor/outdoor living room, fireplace, outdoor shower. Absolutely beautiful "bathhouse" full-service spa and fitness facility;

bocce, hiking trails, wine cave; dining room and bar; swimming pool, lake.

Carlin Country Cottages, 1623 Lake St.; (707) 942-9102; www .carlincottages.com. Nice, simple cottages in a wide courtyard, with Shaker-style furnishings. Some have Jacuzzi tubs; some have one or two bedrooms. Spring-fed, hot swimming pool.

Cottage Grove Inn, 1711 Lincoln Ave.; (707) 942-8400 or (800) 799-2284; www.cottagegrove.com. One of the most commodious, private, and romantic of Wine Country accommodations; separate cottages with luxurious furnishings, fireplaces, deep whirlpool tubs, front porches with wicker rockers, and perfectly wonderful breakfasts, all within a short stroll of town.

ST. HELENA
Cindy's Backstreet Kitchen, 1327 Railroad Ave.; (707) 963-1200; www.cindysbackstreetkitchen.com. The American-style menu includes meat loaf, chicken pot pie, burgers, lamb shank, tamales, pork chops, and much more, all with Cindy Pawlcyn's signature, surprising, seasonal, locally-sourced ingredients. You're likely to be elbow-to-elbow with local winemakers in the light-filled, casual dining room, at the tiny bar, or on the patio. Portions are generous.

Dean and DeLuca, 601 Highway 29; (707) 967-9980; www.dean deluca.com. Huge gourmet market, wine shop, produce mart, and deli—offshoot of the famous New York store. Incredible variety of cheeses and meats, rotisserie chicken, and wonderful salads and entrees to go, plus packaged foodstuffs of all kinds, from fig balsamic vinegar to olive oil pressed in the most obscure orchard in Tuscany. Enjoy sandwiches, fresh-fruit smoothies, and espresso drinks in the back on the sunny patio. Expensive and worth it.

El Bonita, 195 Main St.; (707) 963-3216 or (800) 541-3284; www.elbonita.com. Hidden behind the original 1930s Art Deco motel are two-story motel units with private balconies looking into the trees and over the gardens. Large, two-room suites have microkitchens. Small pool, sauna; reasonable rates.

Go Fish, 641 Main St.; (707) 963-0700; www.gofishrestaurant .net. Reasonably priced seafood and wine choices make this new, classic West Coast-style fish restaurant a winner from famed restaurateur, Cindy Pawlcyn. Raw bar, sushi, fish and chips, cioppino, tuna Reuben sandwich, shrimp macaroni and cheese, seafood from around the world.

Harvest Inn, 1 Main St., just south of town; (707) 963-9463; www .harvestinn.com. Antiques, four-posters, elaborate furnishings in luxury rooms and suites surrounded by acres of lush English gardens, a labyrinth of shady pathways, lawns, and bowers. Private balconies, fireplaces, two pools. Expanded continental breakfast.

Inn at Southbridge, 1020 Main St.; (800) 520-6800; www.innat southbridge.com. A small inn with spacious, luxurious rooms with fireplaces, sitting areas, private balconies with vineyard views, down comforters, and more amenities.

Pizzeria Tra Vigne, 1016 Main St.; (707) 967-9999. In a charming pizza house with booths, plasma TVs and billiards entertain while you wait for luscious brick-oven-baked, Cal-Ital style pizza. Besides traditional favorites, you can order the Benito (fennel sausage, hot coppa salami, smoked pork), the Ducati (roasted onions, broccoli rabe, smoked mozzarella, and chicken-and-apple sausage), or the Clam Pie (garlic paste and fresh chopped clams); or create your own; no corkage charge.

Taylor's Automatic Refresher, 933 Main St. on the south end of town; (707) 963-3486; www.taylorsautomaticrefresher.com. A roadside stop with picnic tables, serving fabulous burgers and dogs, tacos, fish-and-chips, garlic fries, Mexican food; Double Rainbow ice cream in the shakes, floats, and malts, and good wine.

Tra Vigne, 1050 Charter Oak Ave. at CA 29; (707) 963-4444. At stone-topped tables under the trees and umbrellas, it's easy to imagine you are at a villa in the Italian countryside. Terra-cotta-toned stone walls are rampant with vines, while iron-framed windows disclose a vibrantly painted, high-ceilinged bar and restaurant. A rich balsamic sauce blankets roasted polenta; house-cured prosciutto melts in your mouth, homemade ravioli and roasted poultry rubbed with exotic spices are perfection. Stop in here also at Cantinetta Tra Vigne for luscious gourmet picnic fare, pizzettas and sandwiches in a 19th-century sherry distillery—an Italian deli, market, and wine bar; eat here or take out.

For More Information . . . .

Bed and Breakfast Inns of the Napa Valley, (707) 944-4444; www .bbinv.com.

Calistoga Visitors Bureau, 1506 Lincoln Ave., Calistoga 94515; (707) 942-6333; www.calistogafun.com.

St. Helena Chamber of Commerce, 1080 Main St., St. Helena 94574; (707) 963-6456; www.sthelena.com.

NORTHBOUND ESCAPE *Five*

The Redwood Route

SEACOAST TOWNS, AVENUE OF THE GIANTS / 2 NIGHTS

On your drive up US 101 to the seaside logging town of Eureka, stop along the way to see the redwoods and play on the Eel River. California's coastal redwoods are the world's tallest living things. Walking beneath a 300-foot forest canopy among these silent giants from the age of the dinosaurs is an unforgettable experience.

> Logging towns
> Rivers and seacoast
> Victorian village
> Ancient redwoods
> Seafood cafes
> California history

Eureka and smaller coastal towns look much as they did in their Victorian heyday—streets lined with gracious old homes and elaborate gingerbread-trimmed hotels. Settled during the California gold rush in the mid-1800s, the county's founding coincided with the birth of Victorian architecture, and in every town are glorious examples of the era.

From partaking of bed-and-breakfast inns, fresh seafood, logging and Indian history, wildlife sanctuaries, and sea air to fishing for the mighty salmon, biking on forest paths, and going river rafting or beach-combing, you'll find more than a weekend's worth of enticements here. In addition, Humboldt County is home to nearly 8,000 artists—more artists per capita than any other county in California. Named as one of the "Best Small Art Towns in America," Eureka is a uniquely creative community, as demonstrated in many art-, music-, and culture-related events, festivals, and galleries. Take note of the flamboyant murals around town; ask for a mural walk map at the chamber of commerce.

Expect foggy mornings, even in summer, and winter rains Dec through Mar. These tremendous northern woods are true rain

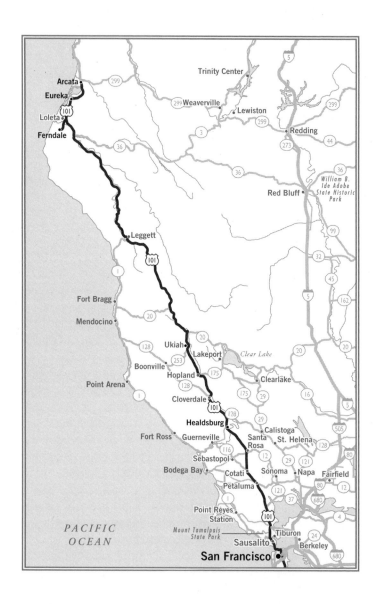

forests, thriving on drizzle and damp. But don't let drippy weather keep you at home. Fishing is best from Oct through Mar; Eureka is misty and romantic then, too.

DAY 1 / MORNING

Begin the 280-mile trip at the Golden Gate Bridge, going north on US 101.

Between Cloverdale and Leggett you'll share the road with logging trucks as the highway winds along the rugged, forested spine of the Coast Range. Above Leggett, watch for the **Tree House,** a fun tourist trap with a good collection of guidebooks and maps. The vestibule is formed from the burned-out shell of a giant sequoia; the tree, however, is still alive and thriving. Ask how long the hanging bulb has been burning.

Twenty-three miles north of Leggett, the four-diamond-rated **Benbow Inn,** built in 1925, is a Tudor-style monolith overlooking a 26-acre summer lake and glorious gardens (445 Lake Benbow Dr., Garberville; 707-923-2124 or 800-355-3301; www.benbowinn .com). You can stay at the historic inn in antiques-filled rooms, some with fireplaces, and have afternoon tea and scones in the parlor. The excellent restaurant overlooks the lake, and there is a nine-hole golf course across the road. Here you can fish and rent a canoe or a kayak; for a refreshing side trip, go with the park rangers (707-923-3238) on a one-hour interpretive canoe tour to absorb some natural history and see ospreys, turtles, herons, and belted kingfishers in the springtime. Take a walk here along a mile of the Eel River.

Now on to the **Avenue of the Giants,** a world-famous 33-mile scenic drive, bypassing the highway. Turnouts and parking areas access short loop trails into spectacular redwood groves along the Eel River in **Humboldt Redwoods State Park** (707-946-2263; www

.humboldtredwoods.org). These are the biggest of the 2,000-year-old beauties remaining in a 30-mile-wide belt of coastal redwoods stretching from Monterey to Oregon.

Pick up picnic goodies at one of the small groceries along the first few miles of the avenue; then begin your tour at the **Humboldt Redwoods Visitor Center** (707-946-2263), about 4 miles from the south end of the avenue. Here you'll get oriented by a movie, exhibits, and trail maps. Ask for advice on the lengths and types of walks and drives you'd like to take in the park. Docents will show you a special binder of trail maps, pointing out new trails and those that may be closed due to weather or maintenance.

Not to be missed is the **Rockefeller Forest** in the **Big Trees** area, a 5-mile drive on Mattole/Honeydew Road. Tiptoeing along boardwalks and spongy pathways in the damp, cool stillness at the foot of these magical giants, you'll hear only the bustle of chipmunks. Under a fragrant green canopy hundreds of feet above your head, the shade on the forest floor is deep, even on a hot summer's day. Wildflowers—trillium, wild iris, and redwood orchid—spring from a carpet of moss and fern, while brilliant blue Steller's jays flash through the branches overhead. A spooky rush of air signals the flight of a black raven; the shiny and silent 2-foot-long ravens are aggressive guardians of their thousand-year-old forest. A short trail leads to a sandy riverbank, for sunbathing, wading, picnicking, and fishing.

LUNCH Have your **picnic** here or at Bull Creek Flats. A flat trail leads along the creek and into redwood groves.

AFTERNOON

Returning toward the highway on the Mattole/Honeydew Road, watch for the sign to **Bull Creek Flats,** a sunny pebbled beach and picnic area at a lovely bend in the river; wild lilacs bloom here in great purple clouds in spring. In the rainy season the river runs with salmon and steelhead. Summer fishing—carp and eels—is for fun, not for food.

One hundred miles of trails in Humboldt Redwoods State Park are for walkers, backpackers, bikers, and horseback riders. Meanderings will turn up old homesteaders' cabins and a plethora of campgrounds. Apple blossoms bloom in orchards planted by early settlers. In the fall big-leaf maples, alders, and buckeyes turn red and gold. In the farthest outback are bobcats, black-tailed deer, foxes, ring-tailed cats, and even black bears.

Reaching Eureka by day's end, you'll be warmly welcomed in the lobby of the Hotel Carter with wine and hors d'oeuvres before the fireplace.

DINNER **Restaurant 301, Hotel Carter,** 301 L St., Eureka; (707) 444-8062 or (800) 404-1390; www.carterhouse.com. At your table beside sky-high windows overlooking Old Town, try fresh Humboldt Bay oysters with teriyaki/wasabi crème fraîche, sesame-seared salmon, portobello chèvre lasagna, or perfectly fresh seafood, local poultry, and game dishes; seasonal produce is featured, including the vast array of veggies from the kitchen gardens. Special dinners with top winemakers are popular occasions booked well in advance. The wine list was chosen by *Wine Spectator* as one of the world's best; oenophiles make pilgrimages here to taste the rare vintages. In spite of it all, the atmosphere is comfortable, welcoming, and understated.

LODGING **Carter House Inns,** 301 L St., Eureka; (707) 444-8062 or (800) 404-1390; www.carterhouse.com. A stunning four-building complex in Old Town: a magnificent replica of a San Francisco Victorian, the Bell Cottage, and the Hotel Carter, each housing plush, ultra-comfortable accommodations. Marble fireplaces, whirlpool tubs, four-poster beds, cushy armchairs and couches, and spacious parlors. No lacy kitsch here, just understated elegance and top personal service, enjoyed by such notables as Steven Spielberg and Rene Russo and their families. Named the "Best B&B/Small Hotel in Northern California," the restaurant and the lodgings here are exceptional in their ambience and comfort.

DAY 2 / MORNING

BREAKFAST A sumptuous breakfast at the Hotel Carter. Take time to browse the kitchen gardens, one of the most extensive at any inn on the West Coast; guests are often invited to join in the daily harvest.

With an architectural/scenic walking-tour map, explore the surrounding Victorian neighborhood, between C and M Streets and about 5 or 6 blocks south of Second Street, ending up under the gaslights in Old Town. For a short waterfront stroll, park at the Carson Mansion (www.eurekaheritage.org) on the north end of town, enjoy glimpses of the mansion gardens, then walk a block south on Second Street and turn right into the Adorni Center parking lot. A paved path extends in both directions along the waterfront for beautiful views of the bay and boats. On the waterfront, home port to more than 500 fishing boats, are several blocks of 1850 to 1904 Queen Anne, Eastlake, and Classic Revival buildings. The Victoriana is enhanced by parks, fountains, playgrounds, and shaded benches for resting between shopping, photo snapping, and museum discoveries along the brand-new Eureka Boardwalk, extending 4 blocks along the bay from G to C Streets.

Not to be missed are the nautical art and artifacts, collectibles, and unique gifts at **Many Hands Gallery,** 438 Second St.; (707-445-0455; www.manyhandsgallery.net). **Gallery Dog** shows and sells work by more than 150 artists, jewelers, furniture makers, and ceramicists (214 E St.; 707-444-3251). The **Humboldt Bay Maritime Museum** displays nautical relics, old navigation equipment, an early radar unit, a lighthouse lens, and fragments of wrecked ships; admission is free (122 First St.; 707-444-9440; www.humboldt baymaritimemuseum.com). The **Clarke Historical Museum,** at Third and E Streets (707-443-1947; www.clarkemuseum.org), a 1920s Italian Renaissance-style former bank with a glazed terra-cotta exterior, houses an extraordinary collection of Indian basketry, antique weapons, maritime artifacts and photos, furniture, and memorabilia of early Humboldt days. **Humboldt's Finest** displays fine art glass, sleek woodwork and furnishings, and a variety of other locally produced home accessories and gifts; not crafty or cute, simply elegant (405 Second St.; 707-443-1258). The **William Carson Mansion,** at Second and M Streets, said to be the most photographed home in America, is a wedding cake of an Italianate/Queen Anne mansion built in the 1880s by a lumber baron; it's a private club, and the interior is off-limits to the public.

LUNCH   **Cafe Waterfront Oyster Bar and Grill,** 102 F St. at First, Eureka; (707) 443-9190. On the waterfront, fresh seafood for breakfast, lunch, and dinner. Fish burgers, clam and oyster specialties, lively bar, casual Victorian decor, and jazz on weekends. Or, for a picnic lunch, go to **Sequoia Park,** Glatt and W Streets, in 52 acres of virgin redwoods with a zoo, a kids' playground, formal gardens, walking paths, and a duck pond.

AFTERNOON

From June through Sept, a 75-minute cruise of the bay, departing from the foot of L Street, can be had on the **MV *Madaket*** (707-1910; www.humboldtbaymaritimemuseum.com), a wooden steamer built in the 1920s. You'll get a narrated tour of historical and natural sights around the bay, passing oyster farms, aquatic birds, and the third largest colony of harbor seals in the West. If it's a clear, mild day, try the cocktail cruise, leaving at 4 p.m. Another choice for touring the bay is at **Hum Boats,** at Woodley Island Marina, where you can rent kayaks and sailboats or go on a guided wildlife ride by water taxi in the bay; also Trinidad Beach whale watching kayak tours (707-443-5157; www.humboats.com).

One of the magical places in Eureka is the **Blue Ox Millworks and Historic Park** (800-248-4259; www.blueoxmill.com), an old mill at the foot of X Street. This museum-like job shop and saw-mill makes custom trim for Victorian buildings, using the same machines that were used to create the originals. Take a self-guided tour on catwalks above the workers, or call ahead for a guided tour. A loggers' camp, a blacksmith shop, a gift shop, a bird sanctuary, and other attractions make this a worthy stop.

DINNER   **Avalon,** corner of 3rd and G Streets; (707) 445-0500; www .avaloneureka.com. Still stacking up the rave reviews, this is the place for a spe-cial, romantic evening. Their specialty is classic French cuisine with locally-sourced ingredients, such as cedar-planked wild salmon, crab cakes, red wine braised lamb shank; crispy duck confit, foie gras with caramelized apple; mouth-watering steak, game, and seafood. Come in early for the cocktail and appetizer menu. For several years, Avalon has received the *Wine Spectator* award of excellence for the wine list; live music some nights.

LODGING   Carter House Inns.

DAY 3 / MORNING

BREAKFAST   **The Samoa Cookhouse,** on the Samoa Peninsula, Eureka; (707) 442-1659; www.samoacookhouse.net. Reached by the CA 255 bridge on the north edge of Old Town, this is the last surviving lumber camp cookhouse in the West. At long oilcloth-covered tables with charmingly mismatched chairs, giant

American breakfasts are served from 6 a.m., including biscuits with sausage gravy, platters of pancakes, and scrambled eggs. Lunch and dinner are served family-style: Huge loaves of bread, cauldrons of soup, big bowls of salad and vegetables, baked ham, and roast beef are followed by wedges of homemade pie. Prices are quite reasonable, and kids four and younger eat free.

Even if you don't eat here, stop in to see the delightful museum of logging equipment, artifacts, and fantastic photos of early days. A short walk from behind the cookhouse is a quiet bayside village and a nice playground. From here you can walk or bike along the edge of Humboldt Bay for 6 miles north to Arcata. Bird life is extraordinary, from marbled godwits to curlews, dowitchers, falcons, and many more.

From the Samoa Cookhouse, drive scenic CA 255 north 15 minutes around Humboldt Bay to **Arcata,** home of Humboldt State University. This is another old logging town with unique attractions, such as the **Historic Logging Trail** in Arcata's 600-acre **Community Forest,** Fourteenth Street and Union (707-822-7091). On foot, take Nature Trail #1 on the west side of the parking lot and follow signs and a map to see logging sites and equipment from a century ago. A new 11.5-mile bike and walking path threads 790 acres of woodlands.

Arcata Marsh and Wildlife Sanctuary, 600 South G St. in Arcata (707-826-2359), is a bird-watcher's mecca. Spend a couple of hours here on 4.5 miles of quiet footpaths in a stunning bayside setting, with freshwater ponds, a salt marsh, tidal mudflats, and winding water channels alive with birds and ducks. This is also a good place to jog or have a picnic; leashed dogs are allowed. You would never guess this is a wastewater reclamation project and, in fact, a model for the nation. Stop at the interpretive center here for maps and information about birding walks throughout the region, and ask about guided walks at the marsh. In April, Godwit Days, the annual spring migration bird festival, is a big event, bringing birders from across the country (800-908-WING; www.godwitdays .com). For daily bird sightings call (707) 822-LOON.

Another area for good walking and biking is **Arcata Bottoms,** just west of town, bordered by Humboldt Bay and Lamphere-Christensen Dunes Preserve.

At the **HSU Natural History Museum and Store** are million-year-old fossils, live tidepools and native animals, and exhibits about the natural history of the region (1315 G St.; 707-826-4479). If you visit Trinidad north of here, stop in at the Humboldt State University Marine Lab and Aquarium (570 Ewing St., Trinidad; 707-826-3671).

Twenty-two miles north of Arcata and stretching for more than 40 miles, **Redwood National Park** is a World Heritage Site encompassing three state parks: **Prairie Creek Redwoods, Del Norte Coast Redwoods,** and **Jedediah Smith Redwoods.** The National Park Visitor Center (707-464-6101; www.nps.gov/redw) is between the park entrance and the town of Orick. You will need to get a (free) permit to drive the steep, 17-mile road to Tall Trees Grove, where a 3-mile round-trip walking trail leads to the world's first-, third-, and fifth-tallest redwoods. There are more than 300 developed campsites in the park, shoreline trails, and swimming beaches in the Smith River and Redwood Creek.

For an afternoon of antiquing and a walk in the country, drive 22 miles south of Eureka and take the Ferndale exit, driving 5 miles west across the Eel River through flat, green dairylands to **Ferndale.** Just two long streets of glorious Victorian buildings, the entire tiny town is a State Historic Landmark. Art galleries, antiques shops, ice-cream parlors, and cafes abound. The **Gingerbread Mansion,** at 400 Berding St. (707-786-4000; www.gingerbread-mansion .com), is one of the premier Victorian masterpieces on the West Coast. Dressed in bright yellow and peach with cascades of lacy white trim and surrounded by whimsical formal gardens, the gigantic hundred-year-old beauty is ½ block long. Nine elaborately decorated rooms have claw-foot tubs (one room has two tubs, toe to toe), and the mansion has four parlors.

It will take a couple of hours to stroll Main Street, take pictures of the old buildings, and browse in the shops. (On the way into town, watch for a large, light green building with striped awnings and a red door: the **Fernbridge Antiques Mall,** a veritable bazaar of 40 dealers selling everything from estate jewelry to Victorian furniture, at 597 Fernbridge Dr.; 707-725-8820).

At **Golden Gait Mercantile** (421 Main St.; 707-786-4891), time is suspended in the 1850s with barrels of penny candy, big-wheeled coffee grinders, and glass cases lined with old-fashioned restoratives and hair pomades. Step into the **Blacksmith Shop** to see the largest collection of modern-day iron accessories in the West, including fanciful chandeliers, lamps, and furnishings (445 Main St.; 707-786-4216; www.ferndaleblacksmith.com).

Take a peek at the **Ferndale Museum** to see a small but mighty exhibit of the history and the agriculture of the "Cream City," with complete room settings, an operating seismograph, and a blacksmith shop (Shaw and Third Streets across from Main; 707-786-4466; www.ferndale-museum.org). Keep up your energy with a shake or an ice-cream soda, or pick up a game of pool, at **Candy Stick Fountain and Grill,** which is also open for lunch and dinner (361 Main St.; 707-786-9373).

At the **Kinetic Sculpture Museum** are strange, handmade, people-powered machines that travel over land, mud, and water (580 Main St. in the **Ferndale Art and Cultural Center** (707-889-3024; www.kineticgrandchampionship.com). These were driven in the World Championship Great Arcata to Ferndale Cross-County Kinetic Sculpture Race, which is held annually in May. Called the "triathlon of the art world," the three-day event is great fun to watch, as the fantastical contrivances are driven, dragged, and floated over roads, sand dunes, Humboldt Bay, and the Eel River. Among the machines in past races were "Nightmare of the Iguana" and "Tyrannosaurus Rust," which was powered by cavemen.

Ferndale sparkles all over and decorates to the max at Christmastime. The lighting of the tallest living Christmas tree in America, a parade, a Dickens Festival, and concerts are among the blizzard of holiday activities.

LUNCH   **Curley's Grill,** 400 Ocean Ave. in the Victorian Inn, Ferndale; (707) 786-9696. California cuisine, homemade soup and focaccia, local fresh fish, grilled sandwiches, and more, indoors in an old-fashioned dining room or on the patio; lunch and dinner.

AFTERNOON

On the south end of Main, go left onto Ocean Street to **Russ Park** to stretch your legs in a 110-acre closed-canopy spruce-and-redwood forest with more than 3 miles of wildflower trails.

On the edge of the Eel River Delta, a resting point on the Pacific Flyway, Ferndale is within minutes of great bird-watching and some nice walks. Running 5 miles west out of town, Centerville Road leads to the beach, where a wide variety of bird life and animals can be seen on walks north and south—swans, geese, sandpipers, pelicans, and cormorants, as well as seals and whales.

On the east side of town are country lanes leading to the Eel River Estuary, great routes for walking and biking, and you can launch canoes and kayaks here in quiet waters. Loons, cormorants, harriers, egrets, and more than 150 feathered species live in or pass through these wetlands. Where the Eel meets the sea, watch for sea lions, seals, and river otters.

Head back to the Bay Area, stopping along the way to walk again under the great redwoods.

There's More . . . .

Beachside Camping. Big Lagoon County Park, off US 101, 34 miles north of Eureka; (707) 445-7651. A 3-mile-long protected lagoon, a popular destination for beachcombing, swimming, sailing, windsurfing, kayaking, parasailing, and boating. Campsites are in a Sitka spruce forest on the lagoon and the shore. Kayak Zak's rents boats here and in Redwood National and State Parks, Trinidad Cove, Humboldt Bay, and other waterways (707-498-1130; www.kayakzak.com). Dogs welcome; no reservations required; no showers or hookups.

Clam Beach County Park, off US 101, 7.5 miles north of Arcata; (707) 445-7652. A long stretch of shoreline for beachcombing, clamming, fishing, picnicking, and surfing. Vehicles, bonfires, leashed dogs and horses are allowed, keeping in mind the posted information about the nesting snowy plover, an endangered shorebird. No reservations.

Gold Bluffs Beach Campground, Prairie Creek Redwoods State Park; (707) 465-7347; www.reserveamerica.com. In the dunes on a stunning 10-mile beach, tent and RV sites (less than 24 feet long); no reservations required; restrooms, solar showers. Exposed to wind, rain, and fog, sites are between the ocean and a forested bluff. Best weather is fall and spring—summer can be cool. Leashed pets allowed. Easy walk to enchanting Fern Canyon.

Patrick's Point State Park, Trinidad, 25 miles north of Eureka; (707) 677-3570; www.parks.ca.gov. On meadow-covered headlands overlooking the ocean, there are more than a hundred sites at Abalone, Penn Creek, and Agate Beach campgrounds, each with table, stove, and cupboard; restrooms, showers (www.reserveamerica.com).

Rafting. **Bigfoot Rafting Company,** P.O. Box 729, Willow Creek 95573; (800) 722-2223; www.bigfootrafting.com. The largest and most experienced white-water outfitter in the Klamath-Trinity region; guided day trips, multiday campouts; Class IV and V wilderness trips; raft and inflatable kayak rentals; steelhead and salmon fishing.

Enjoying the Outdoors. **Humboldt Bay National Wildlife Refuge,** 1020 Ranch Rd., Loleta, just south of Eureka; (707) 733-5406; www.fws.gov/humboldtbay. Take the Hookton Road exit from US 101 and drive 1.2 miles to the Hookton Slough trailhead, a 1.5-mile path along the south edge of Humboldt Bay. Thousands of birds and ducks migrate through these beautiful grasslands, freshwater marshes, and mudflats, including 25,000 black brants that fly from their nesting grounds in the Arctic to Baja. Look for herons, owls, ospreys, mallards, egrets, terns, and more. Restrooms.

Humboldt Lagoons State Park, 40 miles north of Eureka on US 101; (707) 488-2169; www.parks.ca.gov. A marshland habitat for myriad birds and other animals, wonderful for boating, fishing; 6 miles of beach and a 3-mile coastal trail. Picnic areas near the visitor center at the north end of Stone Lagoon on the beach.

Loleta Bottoms. For an easy walk or bike ride on quiet, coastside roads, drive or bike from Loleta (just south of Eureka) west on Cannibal Island Road to Crab Park, at the mouth of an arm of the Eel River. You can scramble around the edge of the estuary and walk back east on the quiet road, watching for plovers, tundra swans, and curlews. Go right on Cock Robin Island Road, where mudflats attract masses of shorebirds. Continue back to your car or on toward Loleta, where the Loleta Cheese Factory (800-995-0453; www.loletacheese.com) is a good place to stop for sandwiches, snacks, and cheese tasting (fabulous organic cheese).

There is a network of two-lane roads in this area, between the highway and the ocean.

Prairie Creek Redwoods, 50 miles north of Eureka on US 101, a World Heritage Site; (707) 465-7354; wwww.parks.ca.gov. A World Heritage Site, 12,000 acres of magnificent coastal redwoods, 70 miles of mountain-biking and hiking trails, herds of Roosevelt elk, a museum, 5-mile-long Gold Bluffs Beach, gorgeous campgrounds, and fabulous Fern Canyon, where lush ferns cover 50-foot rock walls. The visitor center is interesting, with a museum, a natural history bookstore, displays of animals that live in the area— gray fox, great horned owl, elk, mountain beaver, raccoon, black bear—and books. For a drive-through, take the Newton B. Drury Parkway through the redwoods, past walls of ferns and magnificent trees; trails are accessed at the turnouts. Part of the movie, *The Lost World: Jurassic Park* was filmed here. The Gold Bluffs Beach Campground is in the dunes of a stunning 10-mile beach, with tent and RV; no reservations required; restrooms, solar showers; leashed pets allowed. Exposed to wind, rain, and fog, sites are between the ocean and a forested bluff.

Richardson's Grove State Park, 7 miles south of Garberville on US 101; (707) 247-3318. Walk or bike on 10 miles of trails to see old-growth redwoods along the south fork of the Eel River. Swim, fish, picnic, and camp; three leafy, pretty campgrounds are near the river. Wi-Fi near the ranger station.

Hammond Coastal Trail. 2 miles north of Arcata on US 101, take Giuntoli Lane exit, go west on Janes Road; follow signs to Mad River Beach; (707) 445-7651; www.redwoods.info. Residents call this the "best place to walk, jog, or bike" in the county. Five miles of wide, smooth pathway are popular for strollers and Rollerbladers, too. Beaches, bluffs, streamsides and views of the river and the Pacific.

Art. **Morris Graves Museum of Art,** 636 F St., Eureka; (707) 442-0278; www.humboldtarts.org. A restored, stunning library donated to the town by Andrew Carnegie early in the 20th century is now an exceptional art museum showing a wide variety of works in seven galleries. Call ahead for information on musical and theatrical performances held here.

Special Events . . . .

APRIL

Redwood Coast Dixieland Jazz Festival, Eureka; (707) 445-3378; www.redwoodcoastmusicfestivals.org. Put on your zoot suit and kick up your heels to four days of big band, Dixieland, zydeco, and swing music from some of the top bands in the country; all over town and on the waterfront. Arrive a day early for the Taste of Main Street, when 20 area restaurants show off their specialties.

Rhododendron Parade and Festival, Eureka; (707) 834-0278. Home and garden tours, parade, plant show and sale, chicken and polenta feed, and more.

Dolbeer Steam Donkey Days, Fort Humboldt State Historic Park; (707) 445-6567. Logging competition; operation of steam donkeys, locomotives, and equipment; rides.

JUNE

Scandinavian Cultural and Music Festival, Main Street, Ferndale; (707) 444-8444. Dancing, food, a parade, and festivities related to Scandinavian lineage; food, music, and fun.

AUGUST
Humboldt County Fair and Horse Races; (707) 786-9511; www
.humboldtcountyfair.org.

SEPTEMBER
Blues by the Bay, Eureka; (707) 443-7252; www.redwoodcoastmusic
festivals.org. Top notch blues performers, arts and crafts, food,
local breweries.

NOVEMBER
Humboldt County's Coastal Christmas, two months of festivities in
the area finished off with the Truckers' Parade in Dec in downtown
Eureka, when some 150 big rigs and logger-style floats are decorated in Christmas lights; (800) 346-3482.

Other Recommended Restaurants and Lodgings . . . .

ARCATA
Abruzzi's, in historic Jacoby's Storehouse on the town plaza, 780
Seventh St.; (707) 826-2345. Homemade pasta and Italian specialties in an upscale atmosphere; make reservations for lunch and
dinner. Stained-glass glows, and brick and old beams create ambience in a ca. 1850 building. Contemporary and traditional Italian
housemade pasta and veal dishes, steak and wonderful fresh fish;
try the sweet potato crab cakes and the blackened salmon.

Bon Boniere Ice Cream, 215 F St. in the Jacoby Building in Arcata,
and in Old Town Eureka, 215 F St., between 2nd and 3rd; (707)
822-6388. Since 1898, a famous place for homemade ice cream,
caramel popcorn, and other sweets. They also have soup, salad,
and sandwiches.

Cafe Brio, 791 G St.; (707) 822-5922; www.briobaking.com. House-made, European-style pastries; bistro menu for breakfast, lunch, dinner, and snacks daily, ingredients locally sourced. Divine desserts.

Larrupin Cafe, 1658 Patrick's Point Dr., 2 miles north of Trinidad; (707) 677-0230. In a two-story yellow house in the country is an art-filled space with masses of fresh flowers and a fireplace; California cuisine and seafood, barbecued oysters, Cajun ribs; dinner only.

Plaza Grill, 780 Seventh St. in Jacoby's Storehouse; (707) 826-0860; http://abruzziarcata.com. A casual cafe with a fireplace and town views. Terrific burgers, sandwiches, and fish platters; lunch and dinner.

EUREKA

Abigail's Elegant Victorian Mansion, 1406 C St.; (707) 444-3144. Perhaps the finest of Eureka's great treasure trove of Victorian bed-and-breakfast inns, built in 1888, an extravagantly antiques-filled Queen Anne surrounded by a garden of 150 antique roses; there are four large, comfortable rooms, plus croquet, vintage movies, fireplace chats, and a library of guidebooks.

Bayview Motel, 2844 Fairfield; (707) 442-1673; www.bayview motel.com. Spacious, nice motel rooms, reasonably priced and well-managed by the owners, with refrigerators, some with fire-places and large tubs. Pets OK.

Cornelius Daly Inn, 1125 H St.; (707) 445-3638 or (800) 321-9656; www.dalyinn.com. Three-diamond-rates, a bed-and-breakfast inn in a colonial Revival mansion built in 1905, with elegant antiques; three rooms, one with fireplace; and two suites, each very private and very pretty. Full breakfast.

Hurricane Kate's, 511 2nd St.; (707) 444-1405; www.hurricane
kates.com. Cool, casual and hip in Old Town, steel and concrete,
wood-fired pizza, "world fusion" cuisine with lots of luscious small
plates. A wide variety, from barbecued duck to tacos, lumpia and
fresh oysters.

Lost Coast Brewery and Cafe, 617 Fourth St. in the century-old,
three-story "Pythian Castle"; (707) 445-4480; www.lostcoast.com.
At this friendly microbrewpub, try some Alley Cat amber ale or a
rugged glass of Downtown Brown; hearty pub food at lunch and dinner. Owned by a woman who was one of the first females to found
a microbrewery in the United States.

Oberon Grill, 516 2nd St. in Old Town; (707) 443-3663; www
.oberongrill.com. In a fabulous historic building, an upscale saloon
with attitude, open for breakfast (until 2 p.m.), lunch, and dinner.
Big city steaks and prime rib, burgers, pasta, fresh seafood. A real
"dinner house" atmosphere.

FERNDALE
Victorian Inn, 400 Ocean Ave.; (707) 786-4949 or (888) 589-
1808; www.victorianvillageinn.com. The reigning diva of downtown,
built in 1890 of local redwood, a luxurious bed-and-breakfast.
High-ceilinged rooms have antique fixtures and furnishings, sumptuous linens and draperies, private baths; some with fireplaces,
two-person clawfoot tubs. The Victorian Village suite has two fireplaces, dining area, bay window sitting area, two kings and two
twins. Another suite has two bedrooms and two baths. Full hot
breakfast, Wi-Fi. Curley's restaurant and tavern is onsite. Ask about
the new Redwood Suites, a family-oriented annex property.

For More Information . . . .

Arcata Chamber of Commerce, 1635 Heindon Rd., Arcata 95521; (707) 822-3619; www.arcatachamber.com.

Greater Eureka Chamber of Commerce, 2112 Broadway, Eureka 95501; (800) 356-6381; www.eurekachamber.com. Visitor center has an extensive display of local information.

Humboldt County Convention and Visitors Bureau, 1034 Second St., Eureka 95501; (800) 346-3482; www.redwoodvisitor.org. Call for a copy of Destination Redwood Coast, an excellent guide to the area.

Victorian Village of Ferndale, 248 Francis St., Ferndale 95536; (707) 786-4477; www.victorianferndale.com.

NORTHBOUND ESCAPE *Six*

Bodega Bay to Elk
A WEEKEND AT THE COAST / 2 NIGHTS

From the fishing village of Bodega Bay, along the rocky coastline to the tiny burg of Elk, there is much to fill a weekend. Some of the warmest and most beautiful of the northern California beaches are found near Bodega Bay, where sea lions, boats, sailboarders, and birds share a harbor. On up the Sonoma/ Mendocino coast, the wild shoreline is studded with jewel-like beaches, the outlets of several rivers, a harbor or two, and a few old seagoing towns where fishermen and loggers have lived since the 19th century.

> Beachcombing
> Waterfront cafes
> Harbor life
> Whale-watching
> Kite flying
> Fishing
> Bird-watching

Tourism, some agriculture, and the works of resident artists and craftspeople are what fuel the economy today in this magical kingdom between the misty sea and the dark forests. Spring means breezy, clear days; wildflowers and lambs in roadside meadows; and the migration of the great gray whale, easily viewed from the entire coastline. Summers are foggy and busy with visitors, fairs, and festivals. The warm, bright fall is the best time; most tourists are gone and the weather is perfect, each beach a postcard view. Winter is for lovers; magnificent storms turn every sandy cove into a treasure chest of driftwood, shells, and other discoveries washed up the crashing surf, while cozy fireplaces beckon from bed-and-breakfast inns.

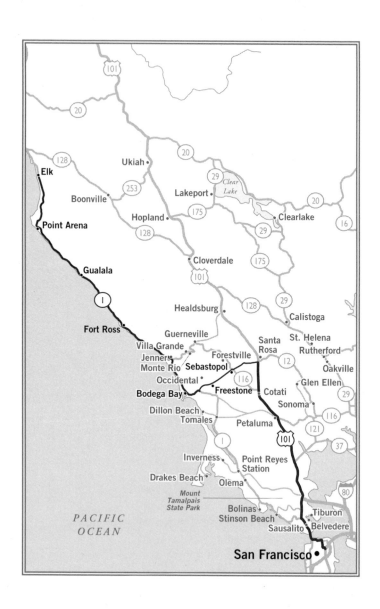

DAY 1 / MORNING

....

Drive north from the Golden Gate on US 101 to Santa Rosa, then head west on CA 12 through Sebastopol, 6 miles farther, to where the Bohemian Highway crosses CA 12 at Freestone. At the roadside store, nip into **Wild Flour Bread** for legendary sticky buns, artisan breads, and other treats made from organic grains and seeds and baked in a eucalyptus-fired oven; pizzas, too (140 Bohemian Hwy., 707-874-2938; open Fri through Mon). They hand-knead everything right in front of your eyes, and the baking goes on all day.

Drive into Freestone, just 0.1 mile, to the **Wishing Well Nursery,** 306 Bohemian Hwy. (707-823-3710), like no other nursery. Surrounding a 200-year-old hotel are acres of fabulous plants and flowers, outdoors and in greenhouses. Exotic birds, fancy chickens, ducks, swans, peacocks, and pheasants twitter in cages, glide on ponds, and strut around as if they owned the place. Decorating the grounds are statuary remnants of the century-old Palace of Fine Arts in San Francisco.

Take a morning walk in **Doran Beach Regional Park** (707-785-3540), a 2-mile curve of beautiful beach separating Bodega Bay and Bodega Harbor. Clamming in the tidal mudflats and sailboarding in the harbor waters are two popular activities. The combination of freshwater wetlands, salt marshes, and the open sea attracts a great variety of shorebirds and waterfowl; you may even see pond turtles, harbor seals, or sea lions. RV and tent camping sites are breezy (707-875-3540).

LUNCH   **The Tides Wharf and Restaurant,** 825 Highway 1, midtown Bodega Bay; (707) 875-2777. Dine at a sunny window table overlooking the action of the wharf and the harbor. Fresh local seafood: clam chowder, Dungeness crab, salmon, mussels, sand dabs—the list goes on. Breakfast, lunch, and dinner; snack bar. Shop for gizmos at the small souvenir shop.

AFTERNOON

Whale-watching cruises and deep-sea fishing party boats leave from the wharf, headquarters for Bodega Bay's harbor and the home port for northern coast fishing vessels. Fishermen unload their catch, and shoppers choose from local and imported fresh seafood. It's crab in fall, herring in spring, salmon in summer—and rock and ling cod all year. Mingled with weathered clapboard houses are a handful of seafood restaurants along with a few shops and motels scattered around the edges of the large, protected harbor where pleasure boats from all over the world come to anchor away from the open sea.

On the north end of town, turn left onto Eastshore Road, then right onto Westshore Road, circling the bay. Fishing boats and sailboats are lined up at **Spud Point Marina** (707-875-3535), and there's a long fishing pier where you can try your luck. Adjacent to the docks, at **Spud Point Crab Company,** (707-875-9472; www.spudpointcrab.com) you can get coffee, breakfast and lunch, chowder and sandwiches, and sit at an outdoor table watching the boating activity; get some home-smoked salmon to take away. At **Westside Park** (707-875-3535), you can picnic, dig for clams and bait, and launch a boat. Most days, sailboarders flit like butterflies in the harbor breezes. Every April, thousands of visitors come to the park for the **Bodega Bay Fisherman's Festival** to see the blessing of the fleet and a decorated boat parade and to enjoy a big outdoor fair with food and entertainment, arts and crafts (707-875-3866; www.bodegabay.com).

At the end of the road, park and get out onto the bluffs of **Bodega Head** (707-875-3483), a prime whale-watching site. Footpaths from here connect to 5 miles of hiking and horseback-riding trails in grassy dunes.

Candy and Kites is a must-stop before you hit the sand, for kites and beach games, air toys, books, saltwater taffy, and chocolates

(1415 Highway 1; 707-875-3777 www.candyandkites.com). Kite festivals in Bodega Bay take place in Apr and July.

The **Ren Brown Collection,** 1781 Highway 1 (707-875-2922; www.renbrown.com), features works from California and Japan— wood blocks, etchings, silkscreens—the largest collection of contemporary Japanese prints in California. The only wine-tasting room on the Sonoma Coast, **Gourmet Au Bay** offers wines by the glass as well as fine crafts and gifts (913 Highway 1; 707-875-9875; www.gourmetaubay.com). The shop is owned by Grammy-winning record producer Ken Mansfield (ask him about the Beatles) and his wife, Connie. You can choose here from more than 1,000 bottles of Sonoma County wines.

The **Bodega Bay Surf Shack** is headquarters for rentals, maps, and advice on biking, beachcombing, kayaking, surfing, and sailboarding, with lessons and guided tours available; plus beachwear. Go to the Web site for fascinating satellite reports, maps, and forecasts about waves and weather (Pelican Plaza; 707-875-3944; www.bodegabaysurf.com).

From Bodega Bay north to Bridgehaven, the **Sonoma Coast State Beach** (707-875-3483) is 13 miles of sandy beaches and coves accessible in a dozen or so places; dramatic rocky promontories and sea stacks, tidepools, and cliffsides make this a thrilling drive. You can camp at **Wright's Beach** or **Bodega Dunes** (800-444-7275). On the north end of the Bodega Bay area, the Bodega Dunes comprise more than 900 acres of huge sand dunes, some as high as 150 feet. There is a 5-mile riding and hiking loop through the dunes and a hiking-only trail to Bodega Head. In a spectacular show of color, thousands of monarch butterflies flock to a grove of cypress and eucalyptus trees adjacent to the dunes every Oct through Feb. There are restrooms here and a campground.

For rock fishing and surf fishing, **Portuguese Beach** is a good choice; for beachcombing and tidepooling, try **Shell Beach.** Across

Highway 1 from Shell Beach, a pretty 0.5-mile trail runs up and over the hills to a small redwood forest. Also from Shell Beach, the **Kortum Trail** winds nearly 5 miles, an easy path through wildflower meadows and gullies along the headlands, north to the beach at Goat Rock.

Surf fishing is good at **Salmon Creek Beach** (campsite reservations: 800-444-7275), a beautiful dune area planted with European grasses. At the north end of the beaches, **Goat Rock,** a notoriously dangerous place to swim, is popular for seashore and freshwater fishing at the mouth of the Russian River; seals like it, too.

DINNER   **Duck Club** at Bodega Bay Lodge, Highway 1 on the south end of Bodega Bay, near Bodega Harbour Golf Links; (707) 875-3525. Fresh Sonoma County seafood, poultry, artisan cheeses, and produce on a California cuisine menu.

LODGING   **Bodega Bay Lodge and Spa,** 103 Highway 1, Bodega Bay; (707) 875-3525 or (800) 875-1007; www.bodegabaylodge.com. Among pines and grassy, landscaped dunes overlooking the Pacific, Doran Beach, bird-filled marshes, and the bluffs of Bodega Head. Spacious, deluxe rooms and luxury suites with views, terraces, or decks; comforters; Jacuzzi tubs; robes; fireplaces. The lobby has a giant stone fireplace and two 500-gallon aquariums filled with tropical fish. Sheltered swimming pool with sea view; spa; fitness center; bikes; golf packages.

Or drive 15 miles north to the **Timber Cove Inn,** on a spectacular point overlooking the craggy shoreline (21780 North Coast Highway 1, Timber Cove; 707-847-3231; www.timbercoveinn.com). The 50 rooms and suites and the public spaces of this inn were recently updated and redecorated, bringing this inn back to its former glory. Accommodations have spectacular views, fireplaces and spa tubs, the lounge has live music on weekends, and the top notch restaurant features weekend wine tastings and winemaker dinners. Sunsets are sensational. Timber Cove is now part of the fine Pacifica Hotel Company of hostelries along the entire California coast (www.pacificahotels.com). While at Timber Cove, linger a while at the new Sonoma Coast Tasting Room, onsite, which features some of the most highly rated boutique wineries in the county; you can purchase a bottle here for your meal in the restaurant, and they will ship.

DAY 2 / MORNING

BREAKFAST Complimentary continental breakfast in the Duck Club restaurant at **Bodega Bay Lodge.** Or enjoy Sunday brunch at Alexander's restaurant at the **Timber Cove Inn.**

Drive north on Highway 1, about 45 minutes, to Fort Ross.

From the parking lot at **Fort Ross State Park,** 19005 Highway 1 (707-847-3286; www.fortrossstatepark.org), walk down to the small, protected beach below the fort. As you breathe in fresh sea air before starting your explorations of the fort, think about the Russians who arrived in 1812, accompanied by Aleut fur hunters. They came to harvest otter and seal pelts and to grow produce for their northern outposts. Their small settlement of hand-hewn log barracks, blockhouses, and homes, together with a jewel of a Russian Orthodox church, was protected with high bastions and a bristling line of cannons, just in case the Spanish decided to pay a call. At the visitor center are exhibits, films, and guidebooks. Inside the restored buildings are perfectly preserved rifles, pistols, tools, furniture, and old photos.

Back on the highway, if you're ready for a snack, stop at the **Fort Ross Store and Deli** (707-847-3221) for an ice-cream cone. Then go on to **Salt Point State Park** (707-847-3221), 6,000 acres of sandy beaches, tidepools, high cliffs, sunny meadows, and hiking and biking trails: a good place to beachcomb, scuba dive, or get a little exercise. Camp with an ocean view (and ocean breezes) at Gerstle Cove Campground; if it's too windy, camp across the highway at tree-sheltered **Woodside Campground** (707-847-3221; www.reserveamerica.com). The dense forestlands of Salt Point are inhabited by gnarly pygmy pines and cypress, their ghostly gray, mossy trunks tickled by maidenhair ferns. Seven miles of coastline are characterized by long, sandy beaches; rocky coves with tidepools rich in wildlife; and many breeding and nesting locations for birds, such as at **Stump Beach,** where a large number of cormorants reside. On both sides of the highway, a wide variety of weather-protected campsites are available: developed and primitive tent sites and biker/hiker sites, RV sites for up to 31-foot vehicles, and walk-in sites (800-444-7275).

Near the park, **Salt Point Lodge Bar and Grill** (23255 Highway 1; 707-847-3234; www.saltpointlodgebarandgrill.com) is a wonderful spot for casual dining, indoors or outdoors, with an ocean view. It specializes in mesquite-grilled fresh fish and a big salad bar. **Salt Point Lodge** here has comfortable rooms, a hot tub, and voluptuous gardens.

Just north of Salt Point, off Highway 1 at Milepost 43, **Kruse Rhododendron State Natural Reserve** (707-847-3221) should not be missed in the months of Apr, May, and June, when wild rhododendron glades up to 15 feet high are brilliant with bloom under redwood, oak, and madrone branches. There is a 1-mile dirt road into the park; a trail sign shows 5 miles of easy and challenging hikes through quiet forest and over picturesque bridges straddling fern canyons and streams.

LUNCH   **Sea Ranch Lodge**, 60 Sea Walk Dr. off Highway 1, Sea Ranch; (707) 785-2371 or (800) 732-7262; www.searanchlodge.com. From your table, enjoy wide ocean views, and the sight of whales in wintertime. Four-star-rated California cuisine and comfort food for breakfast, lunch, and dinner: sandwiches, salads, homemade soups, lots of fresh fish, pasta, pizza and steaks, and an award-winning wine list. The lounge bar has a big fireplace.

Nestled in grassy meadows on headlands above the ocean, the small lodge (now under new ownership) and nearby rentable homes are headquarters for coastal getaways. You can access several beaches (Shell, Pebble, and Black Point Beaches are the best) and walk 8 miles of easy paths on the bluffs. Twenty upscale lodge rooms have ocean views, some have fireplaces and hot tubs; breakfast is complimentary. Two rooms have private garden or patio with hot tub, one with garden view, one with ocean view; each of these has a small refrigerator, sitting area, TV (most rooms do not have TV) and fireplace. The boutique stocks gifts, clothing, and home accessories, toys, games, snacks, logo items, and guidebooks. (The lodge will be closed, except for the restaurant, for more than a year, beginning in early 2010, while a new lodge is under construction.) With an ocean view from 18 holes, the beautiful **Sea Ranch Golf Links** course is laid out on the bluffs and in the meadows and forests above the highway (707-785-2468). Ask about play-and-stay packages.

AFTERNOON

On up Highway 1 about 12 miles, when you see the lace curtains and wooden porches of the century-old **Gualala Hotel,** you are in the village of Gualala, a one-time logging center, now an art colony and fishing headquarters. Shops and several art galleries in the Seacliff Center, on the south end of town, are worth browsing. The **Top of the Cliff** restaurant here serves up gourmet seafood and cocktails with ocean views and legendary sunsets (39140 South Highway 1, 707-884-1539).

The **Dolphin Gallery,** a showplace of local fine arts and crafts (39225 Highway 1; 707-884-3896; http://gualalaarts.org/Exhibits/Dolphin.html), houses the Redwood Coast Visitor Center. Prowl around town a bit to find antiques shops and more art galleries.

At the mouth of the Gualala River, **Gualala Point Regional Park** has a mile-long, driftwood-strewn beach and grasslands, habitat for bird life, including great blue herons, pygmy owls, and seabirds (42401 Coast Highway 1, 707-785-2377). You can camp here and hike on a coastside trail to the Sea Ranch. Stop in the visitor center to view displays of early California, Native American, and logging history and to get trail maps.

DINNER   **Gualala Hotel,** 39301 Highway 1, Gualala; (707) 884-3441. In a landmark 1903 building; family-style Italian dinners, homemade cioppino on Fri night, country-fried chicken with biscuits and gravy, 30-ounce steaks, fresh crab and seafood, all in a lively, friendly, casual environment. Come in early for a tall one at the long bar, where fisherman and tourists rub elbows beneath a museum-like array of photos of early days; or come in late for billiards and jukebox music. Hotel rooms are small, simple, and nicely furnished with antiques; rates for rooms with private or shared bath are reasonable.

LODGING   **Whale Watch Inn,** 35100 Highway 1, 5 miles north of Gualala in Anchor Bay; (800) 942-5342; www.whalewatchinn.com. In contemporary-design buildings on a cliff above the ocean, stained-glass windows, lush gardens, 18 luxurious suites and rooms with whirlpool tubs, fireplaces, and private ocean-view decks. The common lounge has big fireplaces, leather sofas, and a telescope for whale- and sunset watching. Full breakfast, beach with tidepools and a waterfall.

DAY 3 / MORNING

BREAKFAST   Sumptuous breakfast at the **Whale Watch Inn.**

Drive north to **Point Arena.** At the south end of the main street, turn west onto Port Road, following it to the Point Arena Public Fishing Pier, which thrusts 330 feet out into the water from the edge of a cove seemingly protected by high cliffs on either side. The original wooden pier was dramatically smashed to pieces in 1983, along with all of the buildings in the cove. In the **Galley at Point Arena** restaurant, Port Road, Point Arena (707-882-2189), are photos of the storm as it ripped and roared. The Galley serves chowder, snapper sandwiches, homemade pies, salads, and fresh crab in season. This is a good place to watch whales and crusty old salts. Fishing, crabbing, and whale-watching are good from the pier; tidepooling and abalone hunting, from the rocks.

Walk up to the **Wharf Master's Inn,** on the hill behind the pier. Built in the 1870s for wharf masters who watched over the port until the 1920s, this is the town's most elaborate building, a fantasy of turned posts, scroll brackets, and fancy window moldings. Prefabricated in San Francisco, the house was shipped here as a kit.

Rollerville Junction, 3 miles north of Point Arena, is the westernmost point in the continental United States, the site of many a shipwreck; 10 vessels went down on the night of November 20, 1865. The 115-foot **Point Arena Lighthouse** (877-725-4448; www .pointarenalighthouse.com) was erected here in 1870, then re-erected after the 1906 San Francisco earthquake. The lighthouse is the all-time best location for watching California gray whales; Dec through Apr are the prime months. Scramble around in the lighthouse and visit the museum of maritime artifacts below. Vacation house rentals here, too.

Proceed north on the highway to **Elk,** a tiny community perched on cliffs above a spectacular bay. You'll recognize the **Greenwood Pier Inn** complex, 5928 Highway 1 in Elk, by the multitude of blooming flowers and trees. Take your time poking around in the gardens and in the **Country Store and Garden Shop,** 5928 Highway 1, Elk; (707) 877-9997; www.greenwoodpierinn.com. Owners Kendrick and Isabel Petty are artists, cooks, gardeners, and innkeepers, their works found throughout the store, the cafe, and the inn, which is a redwood castle with fabulous ocean views; fireplaces, decks, and romantic privacy.

| LUNCH | **Greenwood Pier Cafe,** (707) 877-9997. Fresh local seafood, greens and vegetables from the inn gardens, sandwiches, salads, breakfast.

Drive back to the Bay Area by way of CA 128 through Boonville and the Anderson Valley wine country, or retrace your Highway 1 route.

There's More . . . .

Rentals. **Adventure Rents,** Cantamare Center, Gualala (888) 881-4386, www.adventurerents.com. Rent canoes or kayaks to explore the Gualala River: transport to and from launch sites included. In the spring, wild azaleas are rampant on the riverbanks.

Golf. **Links at Bodega Harbour,** 21301 Heron, off Highway 1 on the south end of Bodega Bay, Bodega Bay; (707) 875-3538; www .bodegaharbourgolf.com. Newly renovated, a smashingly beautiful links layout, including sand, sea, and breezes. Islands of gorselike scrub and a huge freshwater marsh add challenge.

Park. **Stillwater Cove Regional Park,** 16 miles north of Jenner on Highway 1; (707) 847-3245. A favorite surf-fishing spot, with boat access and picnic area. Five miles of hiking trails in the redwoods, a wheelchair-accessible trail, and a campground.

Special Tours. **UC Davis Marine Laboratory,** open for free drop-in tours on Fri afternoon; call ahead to tour other days. A half mile of coastline and surrounding marine habitat is protected and studied by the university. Exhibits and working research projects such as aqua farming are fascinating (2099 Westside Rd.; 707-875-2211; www.bml.ucdavis.edu).

Special Events . . . .

FEBRUARY THROUGH MAY
Gualala Arts Concert Series; (707) 884-1138; www.gualalaarts .org. Renowned concert artists, bands, and performers at the Dolphin Gallery.

APRIL
Bodega Bay Fisherman's Festival, Bodega Bay; (707) 875-3866; www.bodegabay.com. Thousands come for the blessing of the fleet and boat parade, outdoor fair, food, wine, entertainment, and arts and crafts.

Castles and Kites, Doran Beach; (707) 565-2041. Sand castle building, kite competitions.

JULY
Fort Ross Cultural Heritage Day, Fort Ross State Park; (707) 847-3286. Costumed docents, historic reenactments, demonstrations, and special events.

AUGUST
Art in the Redwoods, Gualala; (707) 884-1138; www.gualalaarts .org. Two days of exhibits by more than 50 artists; live music, food, kids' activities, gourmet gala dinner.

Seafood, Art and Wine Festival, Bodega Bay; (707) 824-8717; www.winecountryfestivals.com. Wine and microbrew tasting, live entertainment, seafood and other local products, art show, kids' zone, carriage rides.

Other Recommended Restaurants and Lodgings . . . .

BODEGA BAY

Bodega Bay and Beyond, (800) 888-3565; www.sonomacoast .com. Home rentals along the coast.

Bodega Coast Inn and Suites, 521 Highway 1; (707) 875-2217; www.bodegacoastinn.com. Forty-four simple, contemporary rooms, each with ocean view and balcony, some with fireplaces and spas.

Claudio's Trattoria, 1400 Highway 1 on the north end of Bodega Bay in Pelican Plaza; (707) 875-2933; www.claudiostrattoria.com. Great sea views from a sunny deck and a sun room, stick-to-the-ribs traditional Italian food for dinner, and weekend lunches.

Inn at the Tides, 800 Highway 1; (800) 541-7788; www.innatthe tides.com. On a hillside above the town and the harbor, two-story buildings on landscaped grounds. Rooms have quite comfortable amenities, like fireplaces, sitting areas, sea views, free breakfast. Completely protected indoor/outdoor pool, spa, sauna. The restaurant here is casual in feel, top-notch in quality—a place to linger when the sun is on the terrace.

Pomo/Miwok Campground, where the Russian River meets the sea at Bridgehaven, 10 minutes off Highway 1; (800) 444-7275. Forty walk-in tent sites in a dense redwood forest at the end of the paved road.

Seaweed Cafe, 1580 East Shore Dr.; (707) 875-2700; www.sea weedcafe.com. Much heralded for Thurs through Sun dinners; a casual, artful little place where the chef concocts creative dishes from local ingredients: urchin fritters, squab salad, crab potpie, and traditional seafood favorites. The Sat and Sun brunches, the desserts, and the wine list are legendary.

Sonoma Coast Villa Inn and Spa, 16702 Coast Highway 1; (707) 876-9818 or (888) 404-2255; www.scvilla.com. On the way to Bodega Bay, a luxurious boutique hotel with 18 romantic, antiques-filled suites, each with private patio, whirlpool tub, wood-burning fireplace, and gracious amenities. Swimming pool, gorgeous gardens, expanded continental breakfast, nine-hole putting green.

GUALALA

Bones Roadhouse, 39350 Highway 1, on the south end of town; (707) 884-1188. With a bank of windows overlooking Gualala Beach and a sheltered dining deck, wood-fired Texas-style barbecue, pulled pork, steak; slow service.

Seacliff on the Bluff, P.O. Box 1317, Gualala 95445; (800) 400-5053; www.seacliffmotel.com. Simple, nice, reasonably priced rooms with private decks and ocean views, fireplaces, large spa tubs, king beds, binoculars, and refrigerators.

JENNER

Fort Ross Lodge, 20705 Highway 1, Jenner; (707) 847-3333; www.fortrosslodge.com. Just north of Fort Ross near the Fort Ross Store, a simple place across the highway from the ocean. Rooms have fireplaces, TV, microwave, refrigerator and small patio with barbecue. On "the hill," one unit has a large in-room Jacuzzi, fireplace, and sauna.

River's End, 11048 Highway 1, just south of Jenner; (707) 865-2484; www.ilovesunsets.com. Sunset and sea views, Hog Island oysters, lots of fresh seafood, a unique wild salmon tasting menu; exotic, eclectic gourmet fare and an award-winning wine list. Stop in for a cocktail on the deck. Cabins here are outdated, pricey.

POINT ARENA
Wharf Master's Inn, 785 Iverson Ave.; (800) 932-4031; www .wharfmasters.com. Garden courtyards surround a fancy landmark Victorian mansion; private decks, fireplaces, spa tubs, ocean or courtyard views, featherbeds; continental breakfast.

For More Information . . . .

Sonoma Coast Visitor Center, 850 Coast Highway 1, Bodega Bay 94923; (707) 875-3866; www.bodegabay.com or www.visitsonoma coast.com.

Sonoma County Tourism Bureau, 420 Aviation Blvd., Santa Rosa 95403; (707) 522-5800 or (800) 576-6662; www.sonomacounty .com. Free 65-page visitors guide to the entire county and information online for 250 wineries, lodging, dining, activities, and calendar. Redwood Coast Chamber of Commerce, P.O. Box 199, Gualala 95445; (800) 778-5252; www.redwoodcoastchamber.com.

California State Park Campground Reservations, (800) 444-7275; www.parks.ca.gov.

NORTHBOUND ESCAPE *Seven*
Mendocino and Fort Bragg
WHERE THE FOREST MEETS THE SEA / 3 NIGHTS

Floating like a mirage on high bluffs above a rocky bay, Mendocino seems lost in another century. The entire town is a California Historical Preservation District of early Cape Cod and Victorian homes and steepled clapboard churches. Though thronged with tourists in summer, the town somehow retains the look and feel of a salty fisherman's and lumberman's village.

Hidden coves

Redwood groves

Art galleries

Harbor views

Fishing, beachcombing, kayaking

Whale-watching

Bed-and-breakfasts

Old-fashioned gardens soften weather-worn mansions and cottages; picket fences need a coat of paint; dark cypress trees lean into the sea breezes. Boutique and art-gallery shopping is legendary, charming bed-and-breakfast inns abound; in fact, there are more bed-and-breakfasts per capita in and around Mendocino than anywhere else in California.

And, this is a major cultural center with dozens of top art galleries, a large art center, and a busy annual schedule of festivals and exhibitions.

A few miles north of Mendocino, Fort Bragg has been a lumbering and commercial fishing town since 1857. Restaurants and accommodations are more reasonably priced here than in Mendocino, and there are several magnificent coastal and forest state parks, and a picturesque fishing port at the mouth of the Noyo River.

DAY 1 / MORNING

Head north from the Golden Gate Bridge on US 101 to Santa Rosa, an hour's drive (it's about three and a half hours from the bridge to Mendocino).

Go west on Guerneville Road to CA 116, heading west toward the coast, then north at the Highway 1 junction at Jenner. On the roller-coaster road from here to Mendocino, make frequent stops to enjoy cliff-hanging views of rocky coves, salt-spray meadows, redwood and pine forests, and a necklace of tiny fishing villages and loggers' towns. For a faster, less curvy route, take US 101 north to CA 128, heading west to Mendocino.

LUNCH   **Salt Point Lodge Bar and Grill,** 23255 Highway 1, Jenner, just north of Timber Cove; (707) 847-3234; www.saltpointlodgebarandgrill.com. Solarium windows overlooking gardens and Ocean Cove; mesquite-grilled specialties, fresh fish, salad bar, barbecue. Also an updated, reasonably priced 1950s-style motel.

AFTERNOON

After you arrive in Mendocino, revive yourself with a bracing walk along the bluffs, the grassy headlands that surround the town. From the bluffs are views of a deep river valley as it meets the sea at **Big River Beach.** Looking back at the town's skyline, you can imagine when horse-drawn carriages were parked in front of the Mendocino Hotel and ladies with parasols swept along the boardwalk in their long gowns. Restrooms and a picnic area are located on the north end of the park along Heeser Drive.

At the foot of the bluffs on the south side of Mendocino, **Big River State Park** combines the gorgeous sandy, driftwood beach and tidepools at the foot of the cliffs with the river running inland

lined with pristine forest and wildlife habitat. The park now con-
nects by old logging roads two adjacent state parks and a state
forest (707-937-5804). Harbor seals, river otters, and great blue
herons are among the inhabitants. Access the beach by a steep
stairway from the headlands trail or from a small parking area off
the highway, just south of town.

Kayaking and canoeing are popular on the river (see Catch a
Canoe, page 114). You can hike into Jackson Demonstration State
Forest and Mendocino Woodlands State Park on the north and to
Van Damme State Park to the south.

Good old days in mind, now is the time to visit the **Kelley
House Museum on Albion Street** (707-937-5791; www.mendocino
history.org). A sunny yellow house built in 1852, it's set back from
the street next to a huge water tower and a pond surrounded by an
old garden. Among the historical photos are those of burly loggers
hand-sawing ancient redwoods. Lumber for shipbuilding and for
construction of the gold rush city of San Francisco brought Eastern-
ers here in the mid-1800s; it took them six months by ship from
the East Coast to reach this wilderness of mighty river valleys and
seacoast.

On Main Street's headlands is the **Ford House** museum (707-
937-5397; www.mendoparks.org), built in 1854. A scale model of
Mendocino in the 1890s shows the dozens of tall water towers that
existed at that time; more than 30 towers, some double- and triple-
deckers, are distinctive features of today's skyline. Here you can
purchase guidebooks and history books, tide tables, and maps. The
picnic tables in the meadow out back are delightful perches from
which to watch the whales, which cruise close to the shoreline in
the wintertime. During the Whale Festival in March, special exhibits are held here, and guided whale walks are offered.

Step into **Out of This World** at the corner of Main and Kasten
to get up-close views of the crashing surf through high-powered

telescopes that are trained on the coastline. This unusual store specializes in premium optics, binoculars and scopes, and space and science kits (707-937-3324).

Have a sunset cocktail at the **Mendocino Hotel,** a gloriously overdecorated gathering place since 1878.

DINNER **MacCallum House Restaurant** and **Grey Whale Bar & Cafe,** 45020 Albion St., Mendocino; (707) 937-0289; www.maccallumhousedining.com. Haute cuisine in a rambling Victorian mansion: oysters, gnocchi, sesame-encrusted ahi tuna, duck in blackberry sauce, fresh salmon, and Meyers lemon curd Napoleons. Sophisticated wine list. This long-established and beloved bed-and-breakfast inn has remodeled and refurbished its rooms and suites. American Historic Inns calls this one of the top 10 most romantic inns in the United States.

LODGING **Whitegate Inn,** 499 Howard, Mendocino; (707) 937-4892; www.whitegateinn.com. A dream of a Victorian mansion in the heart of town. Behind a pristine white picket fence, a lush English garden and huge old cypress trees hint at the luxury within six inn rooms and a cottage. High-ceilinged and airy, all rooms have European featherbeds and down comforters, fireplaces, garden or sea views, gorgeous antique beds, and a romantic, but not fussy, aura. A full breakfast is served in the truly spectacular dining room, which looks onto the garden and the coastline 2 blocks away. Think about evening wine parties, a bottomless cookie jar, a concierge to make your local arrangements, sunny afternoons in a lounge chair on the garden terrace, caramel apple French toast, and a long soak in a claw-foot tub.

Next door, a sister property, Abigail's is a charming 1906 house with five suites with small kitchens; child and pet friendly. A few blocks away is a lovely three-bedroom vacation rental house, managed by Whitegate.

DAY 2 / MORNING

BREAKFAST Whitegate Inn.

Set out from the inn to explore on foot. Browsing the boutiques and galleries in Mendocino village can take an hour or a week, depending on your love of discovery. Many Mendocino artists are renowned not only throughout the state but also internationally, and you will find galleries on every street of the town. At **Creative Hands of Mendocino,** 45170 Main (707-937-2914), look for handcrafted gifts for children and adults. The **Artists' Co-op,** upstairs at 45270 Main is operated by artists who show and sell primarily landscape works in a variety of media (707-937-2217; www.artgallerymendocino.com).

At 10481 Lansing St. is the exceptional **William Zimmer Gallery,** showing fine jewelry, handcrafted furniture, paintings, and more (707-937-5121; www.williamzimmergallery.com). Some of the gallery's sculpture collection is displayed at Stevenswood Lodge, just south of Mendocino in a gorgeous forest and garden setting. Look for miraculous wood sculptures of wheeled vehicles. Hub of the artistic community, the **Mendocino Art Center** offers classes, seminars, and special events related to countywide arts all year. **The Gallery** and **The Showcase** here exhibit and sell the fine work of member artists (45200 Little Lake St. between Williams and Kasten Streets; 707-937-5818; www.mendocinoartcenter.org).

Music lovers stop in at **Lark in the Morning Musique Shoppe** to see and try out ethnic musical instruments, from harps to African percussion, guitars, whistles, drums, bagpipes, instruments for youngsters; books, recordings, videos, and more (45011 Ukiah St.; 707-937-5275; www.larkinthemorning.com).

Main Street shops of note include the **Golden Goose** (707-937-4655), two floors of European antiques, country-luxe bed and table linens, and a children's boutique for heirs and heiresses. For nearly 30 years, **Highlight Gallery** has specialized in fine crafts, hand-crafted furniture, wooden boxes and cutting boards; blown glass, and the best works of local painters (three levels of galleries at 45052 Main St.; 707-937-3132; www.thehighlightgallery.com). On the west end of Main, at **Mendocino Sandpiper,** take a look at gorgeous, unusual jewelry, much of it created locally, and Art Nouveau, Art Deco and Egyptian-theme sculpture (707-937-3102; http://mendocinosandpiper.com).

Overgrown country gardens will draw you up and down the side streets and alleys; look for the two old cemeteries, where headstones are fascinating relics of the days when European sailors, Russian soldiers, and Chinese workers lived here.

LUNCH **The Moosse Cafe,** on the southwest corner of Kasten and Albion Streets, Mendocino; (707) 937-4323; www.themoosse.com. This restaurant in the Blue Heron Inn features Asian-style gourmet fish and seafood dishes as well as pasta, pork, and fancy desserts. Daily lunch and dinner, indoors or on the deck.

AFTERNOON

Three miles south of Mendocino on Highway 1, the beach, campground, and hiking trails at **Van Damme State Park** are popular weekend destinations (707-937-5804). This is the home of the uniquely beautiful **Pygmy Forest,** where an easy 0.3-mile trail takes you through a lush fern canyon and spooky woods of dwarf cypress, rhododendrons, and other bonsai-like plants and trees. A 50-year-old cypress, for instance, may be only 8 inches tall and have a trunk less than 1 inch in diameter. To reach the Discovery Trail and other trails, stop at the ranger station or take Little River Airport Road off Highway 1 and go 2.7 miles to the Pygmy Forest parking lot.

There are 74 developed campsites at Van Damme and sites for RVs up to 21 feet long. A few hike-in campsites are accessed by a 2-mile scenic trail.

A unique way to explore the coastline here is with **Kayak Mendocino,** whose experienced guides conduct sea kayak tours from Van Damme beach (707-964-7480; www.kayakmendocino.com). For both beginners and experienced kayakers, in boats that are easy to maneuver, two-hour tours explore the rocky edges of coves and tidepools, accompanied by shorebirds, seabirds, and harbor seals.

If you crave a little more strenuous outdoor adventure for the afternoon, call **Catch a Canoe and Bicycles, Too!** (707-937-0273; www.catchacanoe.com) to ask about paddling the **Big River** (on your own or with a guide), which runs into the sea below the high bluffs on the south side of Mendocino. Along banks lush with fir and redwood groves, wildflowers, and wild rhododendrons, you can paddle a canoe or a kayak from the mouth of the river 7 or 8 miles upstream on an estuary—the longest unchanged and undeveloped estuary in northern California—stopping at a tiny beach or a meadow for a picnic. You will undoubtedly see ospreys, wood ducks, and blue herons, probably harbor seals and deer, too.

Catch a Canoe and Bicycles, Too! is located at the wondrous, four-diamond-rated **Stanford Inn by the Sea** on a hillside above the river across from Mendocino. The luxurious, 26-room country inn is surrounded by spectacular gardens. Herds of llamas and horses graze in the meadows. Guests enjoy a spa, a sauna, and an Olympic-size swimming pool enclosed in a greenhouse crowded with tropical plants.

If you stay at the Stanford Inn (Highway 1 and Comptche-Ukiah Road, Mendocino; 800-331-8884; www.stanfordinn.com), you will enjoy a fireplace or wood-burning stove in your sitting area, a down comforter on your four-poster or sleigh bed, a private deck from which to watch the sun set over the sea, complimentary wine, and a bountiful buffet breakfast.

DINNER **Cafe Beaujolais,** 961 Ukiah St., Mendocino; (707) 937-5614; www.cafebeaujolais.com. A 1910, sunny yellow Victorian house is surrounded by lush gardens, so exceptional they are toured at special events. Organically produced local products supply ingredients for the inventive menu of seasonal delights. Don't miss the award-winning crab cakes, and save room for French bittersweet chocolate and sour cherry cake, and passion fruit crème brûlée; 60 wines by the glass on an exceptional wine list. The wood-floored dining room is homey, with flowery wallpaper and lace curtains; a sunny, glass-enclosed deck floats in the garden; and the wood-fired oven in The Brickery produces take-out breads to dream about. Reserve well ahead for lunch and dinner.

LODGING Whitegate Inn.

DAY 3 / MORNING

BREAKFAST Whitegate Inn.

On a drive north on Highway 1, on the way to the lumbering and fishing town of Fort Bragg, stop at a beach, forest parks, and a botanical garden.

Two miles north of Mendocino on Highway 1, **Russian Gulch State Park** (707-937-5804) is known for sea caves, a waterfall, and a beach popular for rock fishing, scuba diving, and swimming in chilly waters. From the headlands, you can see the Devil's Punch Bowl, a 200-foot-long tunnel with a blowhole. Inland, the park includes 3 miles of Russian Gulch Creek Canyon, with trails in dense forest and stream canyons. A hiking trail leads to a 36-foot waterfall and to high ridges where views are breathtaking. A small campground here is particularly lovely, and there is an equestrian campground with riding trails into Jackson State Forest. RVs up to 27 feet are allowed (www.reserveamerica.com).

One mile north of Russian Gulch State Park, turn west into **Jug Handle State Reserve** (707-937-5804), a 700-acre park notable for an "ecological staircase" marine terrace rising from sea level to 500 feet. Each terrace is 100,000 years older than the one above, a unique opportunity to see geologic evolution. The plants and trees change from terrace to terrace, too, from wildflowers and grasses to wind-strafed spruce, redwood, and pygmy forests of cypress and pine.

Six miles south of Fort Bragg, **Point Cabrillo Light Station** lies on a spectacular headland, a photogenic, restored, century-old lighthouse with a museum and tide pool aquarium. The lighthouse is open year-round on weekends, and the nature preserve is open for wandering every day (707-937-6122; www.pointcabrillo.org).

Save at least two hours for the **Mendocino Coast Botanical Gardens** (18220 Highway 1, 2 miles south of Fort Bragg; 707-964-4352; www.gardenbythesea.org), with 47 acres of plantings, forest, and fern canyons on a bluff overlooking the ocean—the only coastal botanical gardens in the West. Easy paths lead through perennial and native-plant gardens, forests, a marsh, and organic vegetable gardens, and to a new sculpture garden. From late Apr through early June, hundreds of rhododendrons, azaleas, and spring bulbs are in bloom. From Nov through Jan, Japanese maples and winter heathers are aflame. One of the loveliest walks is along a creek in a mossy fern canyon. On the coastal bluff are wildflower meadows above a dramatic, rocky shoreline with waves crashing in the coves below. The garden paths are primarily wheelchair-accessible; two electric carts are available at no charge. You can buy super-healthy plants here at reasonable prices, as well as garden accessories and books. Bring a picnic lunch or snacks and enjoy the garden benches and picnic tables.

LUNCH **Silver's at the Wharf** bar and restaurant at 32260 North Harbor Dr., Fort Bragg (707-964-4283; www.silversatthewharf.com), overlooking the harbor, is a great place for lunch. Try the grilled fresh fish, grilled eggplant salad, mushroom crepe torte, or the apple-wood rotisseried game hen.

Just south of Fort Bragg, at the mouth of the **Noyo River, Noyo Harbor** is headquarters for a large fleet of fishing trawlers and canneries. Barking and posing, sea lions lounge on the wooden piers, waiting for the return of the boats at day's end.

This is the best place on the coast from which to take a whale-watching cruise—the boats usually find the whales within 15 or 20 minutes. Thousands of majestic gray whales parade off the North Coast each winter on their annual 12,000-mile round-trip migration from the Arctic Circle to Baja California. On the 80-mile Mendocino coastline, they are spotted in late Nov through Dec, and they head north again in Feb and Mar. Some of the best whale-watching sites on the North Coast are MacKerricher State Park, Mendocino Headlands State Park, and Point Cabrillo Light Station. Whale-watching cruise companies include Anchor Charters (707-964-5440; www.anchorcharterboats.com), All Aboard Adventures (707-964-1881; allaboardadventures.com), *Rumblefish* (707-964-3000), and Telstar Charters (707-964-8770; www.gooceanfishing.com).

DINNER **Old Coast Hotel,** 101 North Franklin St., Fort Bragg; (707) 961-4488; http://oldcoasthotel.com. Red-checked tablecloths give no hint of the sophisticated menu and big wine list; oysters, jambalaya, 20 pastas, fresh fish in imaginative sauces, house-smoked ribs. Warm and cozy on a cold night; live jazz on weekends.

LODGING The **Lodge at Noyo River,** 500 Casa del Noyo Dr., off North Harbor Drive above Noyo Harbor, Fort Bragg; (707) 964-8045; www.thelodgeatnoyoriver

.com. On a forested bluff above Noyo Harbor, the lodge is a California Craftsman mansion with warmly romantic inn rooms and an annex with large suites. In 1868 Scandinavian boat builders handcrafted this unique home of prime redwood. It is furnished with comfortable antiques, Oriental rugs, and vintage art and photos. Full breakfasts and evening wine are served in the sunny dining room overlooking the harbor or on the outdoor deck. Annex suites are spacious, with private decks, harbor views, fireplaces, huge soaking tubs, and sitting areas. With harbor or garden views, inn rooms vary in size and amenities; some have claw-foot or soaking tubs and sitting areas. If you are a light sleeper, ask for a room away from the barking sea lions.

DAY 4 / MORNING

BREAKFAST The **Lodge at Noyo River.** Stroll the gardens and take the short path to the harbor to watch the fishing fleet head out into the morning mist.

Before heading back to the Bay Area, stop in at **For the Shell of It,** 344 North Main St. in Fort Bragg, to shop for shells and shell jewelry, shell posters, folk art, and all things shellish (707-961-0461).

A beautiful three-story, all-redwood home built before the turn of the 20th century, the **Guest House** is a museum filled with photos and artifacts of local history and antique logging equipment, and it has a lovely garden (343 North Main St.; 707-964-4251). Check out the **(Union Lumber) Company Store** at Main and Redwood, an indoor shopping center containing several boutiques and galleries. At the Fort Bragg Depot are a clutch of small shops, including **Fuchsiarama,** a gifts and fabulous fuchsias store; the main Fuchsiarama location is 2 miles north, a lush and beautiful five-acre environment for fuchsias and fantasy gifts; you can also picnic here (23201 North Highway 1; 707-964-0429).

To stretch your legs before you head home, head for **Glass Beach** at the foot of Elm Street, where the sand is sprinkled with pebbles of glass and china that have been tumbled and smoothed in the sea. **Glass Beach Jewelry and Museum** showcases stunning jewelry created from surf-tumbled sea glass foraged from Glass Beach (17801 North Highway 1, 1.1 miles south of town; www .glassbeachjewelry.com).

North of town past the first bridge, **Pudding Creek** has a beach play area and tidepools. Eight miles north of Fort Bragg, Ten Mile River Beach is acres of salt marsh and wetlands at the mouth of the Noyo River, inhabited by nesting birds and ducks; a 4.5-mile dune stretch of sand extends south from the river.

Returning to San Francisco, head south on CA 128 inland, connecting with US 101 South to the Golden Gate Bridge.

There's More

Park. **MacKerricher State Park,** 3 miles north of Fort Bragg off Highway 1; (707) 964-9112; www.parks.ca.gov. Eight miles of beach and dunes, with tidepools at the southern end of the park. Two freshwater lakes are stocked with trout. Horseback-riding, mountain-biking, and hiking trails throughout bluffs, headlands, dunes, forests, and wetlands. Laguna Point is a prime spot for whale-watching, and harbor seals are seen here. The boardwalk affords wheelchair and stroller access from the southwest corner of the parking lot. Developed campsites and RV sites for up to 35-foot vehicles, fire rings, restrooms. Stretching the entire 8-mile length of the park, the paved Haul Road, a former logging road, is a fabulous jogging, biking, and walking route that crosses beautiful sand dunes and has ocean views.

Winery. **Pacific Star Winery,** 12 miles north of Fort Bragg; (707) 964-1155; www.pacificstarwinery.com. Sheep and horses share a windy clifftop with a rustic redwood-and-stone winery where barrels stand in the salt air—a practice winery owner Sally Ottoson claims contributes to the character of the wines. Among unusual varieties produced are dark, earthy Charbonos; hearty Zinfandels, Chardonnays, and more. Bring a picnic and enjoy the crashing waves and the ocean views. You can also taste these wines at Depot Mall in downtown Fort Bragg.

Special Tours. **Skunk Train,** Laurel Street Depot at Main Street, Fort Bragg; (866) 45-SKUNK; www.skunktrain.com. Hauling logs to sawmills in the 1880s, the California and Western Railroad's historic diesel and steam Skunk Trains carry tourists on half-day trips alongside Pudding Creek and the Noyo River through redwood forests, crossing thirty bridges and trestles over river gulches, passing idyllic glades and meadows. Sit inside or wander in and out of open-air cars and enjoy the natural sights and the fresh air. At the halfway point, the train stops to fill up on water, and passengers can stretch their legs, have picnics, and buy souvenirs, hot dogs, homemade cookies, wild organic apple juice, even cappuccino and Mendocino Sunrises—champagne and wild apple juice with fresh mint! Make reservations for summer weekends.

Special Events . . . .

JANUARY
Crab and Wine Days, Mendocino; (866-goMendo; www.gomendo .com). Crab cruises and whale-watching trips, cooking demonstrations, wine and crab tasting, carnival, winemaker dinners, crab feed and crab cake cookoff, and more. *Coastal Living* magazine named this one of the Top 10 Seafood and Wine events in the world.

MARCH

Fort Bragg and Mendocino Whale Festivals; (800) 961-6300; www .mendowhale.com. Chowder and micro beer tasting; food, wine and crafts, doll show, live music, classic car show, boat displays.

APRIL THROUGH JUNE

Wild rhododendrons erupt into pink, white, and red blossoms Apr through June at Kruse Rhododendron State Reserve; (707) 847-3286.

JULY

Mendocino Music Festival, P.O. Box 1808, Mendocino 95460; (707) 937-2044; www.mendocinomusic.com. Classical and jazz, Big Band, chamber music, blues, folk; concerts, lectures and recitals.

World's Largest Salmon Barbecue, Fort Bragg; (707) 964-6030; www.salmonrestoration.com.

AUGUST

Art in the Gardens, Fort Bragg; (707) 964-4352; www.garden bythesea.org. Showcasing more than 60 artists and artisans, live music, wine, and food at the Botanical Gardens.

Art in the Redwoods, Gualala Arts Center; (707) 884-1138; www .gualalaarts.org. For nearly 50 years, a huge display of fine art, fine crafts, food and drink, and live music including the Kronos Quartet.

SEPTEMBER

Winesong! Buy your tickets early for this annual wine tasting and auction fund-raiser. California wineries and restaurants set up tasting booths throughout the beautiful Mendocino Coast Botanical Gardens in Fort Bragg, and live music is played throughout; (707) 961-4909; www.winesong.org.

Paul Bunyan Days, Fort Bragg; (707) 964-3356; www.paulbunyan days.com. Parade, arts and crafts, entertainment, games, food, wine, and beer, ugly dog contest.

NOVEMBER
Wine and Mushroom Festival. Join chefs on forest trails and learn how to spot and prepare edible wild mushrooms. Brothel, Bar and Boarding House historical walking tours; food fair; wild-mushroom/ wine dinners; (866-goMendo; www.gomendo.com).

DECEMBER
Candlelight Tours of Bed-and-Breakfast Inns, Fort Bragg, Little River, Albion, Mendocino; (707) 964-1228; www.mendocinoinntour.com.

Other Recommended Restaurants and Lodgings . . . .

ALBION
Albion River Inn, Highway 1, 6 miles south of Mendocino, P.O. Box 100, Albion 95410; (707) 937-1919; www.albionriverinn.com. Overlooking the rugged coastline, oceanfront rooms with spectacu- lar views, fireplaces, spas, contemporary decor; full breakfast, pri- vate headland path, lush gardens. The clifftop restaurant is one of the best on the coast, serving fresh seafood such as lime and ginger grilled prawns and Cajun oysters; more than 100 California wines.

ELK
Zebo at the Elk Cove Inn and Spa, Highway 1; (800) 275-2967; www.elkcoveinn.com. Right on the ocean, rustic bistro menu with

housemade pasta, seafood, inventive dishes using local ingredients; every wine offered by the glass. Dinners Fri through Mon. Deluxe accommodations, full-service spa with ocean view lounge.

FORT BRAGG

Beach House Inn, 100 Pudding Creek; (888) 559-9992; www .beachinn.com. Overlooking the water, with spa tubs for two, fireplaces, private balconies; surrounded by lovely wetlands at the mouth of Pudding Creek.

Egghead Restaurant, 326 North Main St.; (707) 964-5005. Sit in a comfy booth in a Wizard of Oz environment, complete with yellow brick road, and enjoy big, big omelets, burgers, salads, and sandwiches; breakfast and lunch.

Emerald Dolphin Inn, 211 South Main St.; (707) 964-6699 or (866) 964-6699; www.emeralddolphin.com. A new three-diamond-rated place within short walking distance to beach and town attractions, electric fireplaces, large Jacuzzi tubs, refrigerators, Wi-Fi, continental breakfast; adjacent to mini golf course.

Grey Whale Inn, 615 North Main St.; (707) 964-0640 or (800) 382-7244; www.greywhaleinn.com. This three-story, 1915 landmark has spacious rooms, with high windows looking to the sea or inward through the trees to town. Walk right out the back door along the waterfront on the Old Coast Road. Rooms have sitting areas with armchairs, deep tubs, some fireplaces, and lots of books. Breakfast is a big buffet.

Herons by the Sea, 32096 N. Harbor Dr. in Noyo Harbor; (707) 962-0680. Dynamite tacos, fish and chips, pasta, crab cakes, chowder with an ocean view.

Mendo Bistro, 301 Main St. upstairs in the Company Store; (707) 964-4974; www.mendobistro.com. For dinner nightly, local seafood (best crab cakes on the coast), homemade pasta, steak, veggie items, reasonably priced, hearty comfort food and a lively local's crowd.

Mendocino Cookie Company, in the Company Store, 301 North Main St.; (707) 964-0282. Fresh double chocolate chip cookies, homemade muffins, scones, pastries; ice-cream cones, smoothies and shakes.

North Coast Brewing Company, 455 North Main St.; (707) 964-BREW; www.northcoastbrewing.com. Exotic beers, ales, stouts, local fresh fish, ribs, Mendocino mud cake. If your innards are in good shape, try the Old Rasputin Russian Imperial Stout, the Route 66 chili, and the Cajun black beans and rice. Free tours of the brewery across the street.

Piaci Pub and Pizzeria, 120 West Redwood Ave., Fort Bragg; (707) 961-1133; www.piacipizza.com. Crispy, thin-crust pizza with traditional and inventive toppings; calzones, and panini. Large variety of craft-brewed beers and local wines.

Surf Motel and Gardens, 1220 S Main St.; (800) 339-5361; www.surfmotelfortbragg.com. Two-queen rooms with microwaves and fridges, and two-room suites with kitchens. Grounds are lush with native plants; breakfast and Wi-Fi are free.

LITTLE RIVER
Little River Inn, 7751 Highway 1; (707) 937-5942 or (888) 466-5683; www.littleriverinn.com. Built in the 1850s, a white wedding cake of a house that's expanded to become a sizable resort with one

of the best restaurants in the area, a nine-hole golf course in the redwoods, and tennis. The bar is a favorite locals' meeting place. Some rooms have porches overlooking a beautiful beach and bay. On the menu may be rack of lamb marinated in Cabernet, polenta with porcini mushroom sauce, and warm olallieberry cobbler. Ask about golf/room packages. A day spa offers complete salon, beauty, and body treatments.

Mallory House, 7751 North Highway 1; (888) 466-5683; www .littleriverinn.com. Newly opened, owned by the Little River Inn, on a bluff with sea views framed by coastal pines. Three suites in an 1890 farmhouse, and an adjacent Cape Cod-style cottage, among the largest, most private, and most commodious accommodations on the coast. Seals cavort in Buckhorn Cove, below. Hot tubs, Jacuzzis, fireplaces. For breakfast, crab cakes Benedict, huckleberry scones, olallieberry cobbler.

MENDOCINO
Agate Cove Inn Bed and Breakfast, 11201 Lansing St.; (800) 527-3111; www.agatecove.com. Right in town, beautifully furnished garden cottages with fireplaces, private decks, and ocean views. Breakfast by the fireplace in the dining room with a wonderful sea view. Bluff House and Bluff Cottage on the bluff are new, with a private gazebo on the point and an ocean view hot tub on the deck. The house has a master suite, kitchen and dining area, sunroom, living room with wide ocean views, laundry room and a second bathroom, with an ocean view loft and a second bedroom upstairs. The French doors of the studio cottage open out to an ocean view deck with a hot tub; mini kitchen and fireplace.

Brewery Gulch Inn, 9401 Coast Highway 1 North; (800) 578-4454; www.brewerygulchinn.com. A grand, Arts and Crafts-style lodge constructed with salvaged redwood. Grounds feature a heritage apple orchard, olive grove, trout pond, and mushroom forest. A pleasant trail winds through the property.

Dennen's Victorian Farmhouse, off Highway 1, 2 miles south of town; (800) 264-4723; www.victorianfarmhouse.com. A charming garden inn with 11 rooms and suites and a cottage; featherbeds, period antiques, spa tubs, fireplaces; full breakfast, concierge service.

Glendeven Inn and Gallery, 1.5 miles south of Mendocino on Highway 1, P.O. Box 282, Mendocino 95460; (800) 822-4536; www.glendeven.com. Antiques and eclectic art decorate rooms and suites in a gray-and-white farmhouse; big breakfasts. Walking path to the sea, gardens. Next door is a gallery of contemporary handcrafted furniture, art, jewelry.

Joshua Grindle Inn, 44800 Little Lake Rd.; (707) 937-4143 or (800) 474-6353; www.joshgrin.com. One of the oldest homes in town, a ca. 1880 beauty overlooking the town. Four-diamond-rated, spacious New England-style rooms in the main house and very private accommodations in the water tower and the "chicken coop." Bountiful breakfast at the old harvest table.

Mendocino Hotel, 45080 Main St.; (707) 937-0511 or (800) 548-0513; www.mendocinohotel.com. As classic Victorian hotel full of antiques, artifacts, and atmosphere. Smallish hotel rooms are charming, with ocean or town views. Some with fireplaces and four-posters, the luxurious cottage suites float in glorious gardens, with down comforters and pampering amenities. The dinner restaurant serves top-notch California cuisine and American comfort food; think about grilled game hen, double-baked Brie with roasted garlic, and the signature French onion soup. The blooming Garden Room, brightened by skylights and ocean-view windows, is open for brunch and lunch at marble-topped tables, with a cafe bar menu in late afternoon. Notice the stunning stained-glass ceiling and the 200-year-old Dutch fireplace.

955 Ukiah Street Restaurant, 955 Ukiah St.; (707) 937-1955; www.955restaurant.com. In a rescued water tower, this is one of the best restaurants in town. Think about duck cannelloni, pork loin with port sauce, blackberry toasted-hazelnut ice cream, and strawberry-rhubarb pie. The upper dining area has an ocean view.

The Ravens, Stanford Inn by the Sea, Highway 1/Comptche-Ukiah Road; (707) 937-5615; www.ravensrestaurant.com. The only fine-dining restaurant on the coast serving totally vegetarian food. Even carnivores like the creative specialties, such as Caribbean jerk-rubbed tempeh with plantains and pistachio-crusted tofu with grilled veggies. Breakfast and dinner in a pretty setting just over the bridge from Mendocino.

Sea Rock Inn, 11101 Lansing St.; (800) 906-0926; www.searock .com. One-half mile south of Mendocino in a wild garden, country cottages with kitchens; expanded continental breakfast.

Stevenswood Lodge, 8211 Highway 1, 2 miles south of Mendocino; (707) 937-1237 or (800) 421-2810; www.stevenswood .com. Surrounded by Van Damme State Park in a lovely forest setting with a sculpture garden and a dazzling collection of contemporary art. Four-diamond rated, the suites are simple and lovely, with handcrafted furniture and some ocean views, fireplaces, Wi-Fi, espresso machines, refrigerators. Onsite are a full-service spa (also available to the public), sauna, private outdoor whirlpools; dog-friendly. Gourmet restaurant serves breakfast/brunch and dinner.

For More Information . . . .

Mendocino Area State Parks, (707) 937-5804; www.mendoparks .mcn.org. Information about camping, day use, and interpretive programs. For campsite reservations call (800) 444-7275.

Mendocino Coast Reservations, 45084 Little Lake St., Mendocino 95460; (800) 262-7801; www.mendocinovacations.com. In the Mendocino/Fort Bragg area, rental cottages and homes, some family- and pet-friendly, some with hot tubs and ocean views.

Mendocino Coast Chamber of Commerce, 217 S. Main St., Fort Bragg 95437; (707) 961-6300; www.mendocinocoast.com.

Advice: Driving can be hazardous on the twists and turns of Highway 1, and it's not recommended that you attempt it after dark or during storms. Farm animals and deer in the road can be a scary, and maybe deadly, surprise as you're coming around a blind curve.

NORTHBOUND ESCAPE *Eight*
Marin Waterfront
SAUSALITO AND TIBURON / 1 NIGHT

On the north side of the Golden Gate, Marin County is a "banana belt," sunny and warm all summer when San Francisco is socked in with fog. It's nice to get away for a couple of quiet days in Marin's small, seaside towns.

> Sea views
> Waterfront cafes
> Hilltop walks
> Wildlife sanctuaries
> Island idyll
> Boutique shopping

Sausalito tumbles down steep, forested hillsides to the edge of the bay. Sophisticated shops, sea-view restaurants, and marinas lined with yachts and funky houseboats share postcard views of the San Francisco skyline.

A residential community of vintage mansions and luxury condos, Tiburon occupies a spectacular peninsula surrounded by the quiet waters of Richardson Bay, where kayakers paddle and sailboarders fly about. Raccoon Straits, a narrow, windswept channel carefully navigated by sailboats and ferries, runs between Tiburon and Angel Island, which is a state park.

Shopping, walks in the salty air, and fine dining are primary activities on this trip, with a Mount Tamalpais side trip on the way home.

DAY 1 / MORNING

Take a ferry to Sausalito. Or, in your car, immediately to the north of the Golden Gate Bridge, take the Alexander Avenue exit, descending down into Sausalito. Alexander becomes Bridgeway, the main street.

Downtown Sausalito is a National Historic Landmark District and a long-established haven for artists, writers, and craftspeople. The annual **Sausalito Art Festival** attracts 50,000 people over Labor Day weekend. In midtown, where a hundred or so shops and restaurants are concentrated, is a small city park with palm trees and huge stone elephants with streetlights on their heads, leftovers from San Francisco's 1915 Exposition. Behind the park, ferries come and go to San Francisco and Tiburon.

Now, hit the Bridgeway shops and galleries! **Petri's** beautiful, big store holds a museum-like collection of art glass, the largest and most spectacular array I've seen (675 Bridgeway; 415-332-2225; www.petrisgallery.com); look for the jellyfish. A two-story tasting room and art gallery, **Bacchus and Venus Wine Tasting and Art Gallery** is a multifaceted destination (769 Bridgeway; 415-331-2001; www

.bacchusandvenus.com). Try the daily "flights" of premium California wines, and buy bottles to take away. Browse the array of Wine Country art and Sausalito seascapes, wine-related art and giftware. Aloha-shirt collectors head for **Odyssey** at 673 Bridgeway (415-331-8677). A phenomenon in the art world in the decade or so, sleek Zimbabwean Shona stone sculpture is featured at Spirits in Stone, along with fabulous jewelry, African masks, and bronze sculptures (585 Bridgeway; 415-332-2388; www.spiritsinstone.com). If you are interested in sports, entertainment, and historic figures, stop in at the **Mark Reuben Gallery** to see black-and-white photos of legendary stars and athletes (34 Princess St., off Bridgeway; 415-332-8815; www.markreubengallery.com). Don't fail to stop in at **Tapia Art Gallery,** an institution for many years, where you can usually see the owners/artists painting their seascapes and landscapes in oil, and floral watercolors (52 Princess St., a block off Bridgeway; 415-332-6177). Down the block from Tapia in an alleyway, **Out of Hand** showcases the fine works of local artists, from ceramics, jewelry, clothing, and myriad decorative accessories (30 Princess Ct.; 415-331-1300).

At 100 Bay St. at the entrance to the yacht harbor, the **Harbor Shop** sells sun hats and baseball caps; Sausalito-branded, nice sweatshirts and jackets; nautically-inspired gifts and model boats; a little coffee corner overlooks the yachts (415-331-6008; www .harborshop.com).

Just north of midtown, the **Heathware Ceramics Outlet,** 400 Gate 5 Rd. off Bridgeway (415-332-3732), is worth a stop for seconds from a famous producer of stoneware.

Heading north on Bridgeway, watch for the sign for **Bay Model,** 2100 Bridgeway at Spring Street (415-332-3871), a one-and-a-half-acre, hydraulic working scale model of the San Francisco Bay Delta, a fascinating research tool used by the U.S. Army Corps of Engineers. The natural and cultural history of the bay is traced in exhibits—wetlands, wildlife, shipwrecks, antique equipment.

From the Bay Model, a 3.8-mile flat, paved path between Sausalito and Mill Valley, called the **Sausalito Bikeway,** makes a nice bike ride or walk (from Bridgeway and Wateree Street in Sausalito to Tennessee Avenue and Shoreline Highway in Mill Valley). You will pass the edge of Richardson Bay and Bothin Marsh Open Space Preserve, where shorebirds reside; a heliport; the famous Sausalito houseboats; and an old shipyard.

Nearby at **Open Water Rowing,** off Bridgeway at 85 Liberty Ship Way (415-332-1091; www.owrc.com), take a kayaking lesson on Richardson Bay. All ages find it easy to learn, and it's a great way to get a gull's-eye view of wildlife on the bay. Along the Sausalito shoreline in this area is a series of yacht harbors, marinas, and houseboat moorings.

At the end of Liberty Ship Way near the marina, **Schoonmaker Beach** is a little patch of palm-fringed sand, and good spot for launching kayaks. Here also is **Le Garage,** a charming indoor/outdoor French bistro—duck confit, Kobe beef burger, shiitake mushroom soup, fresh seafood, weekend brunch (85 Liberty Ship Way; 415-332-5625; www.legaragebistrosausalito.com).

Stop in at the **Arques School of Wooden Boatbuilding** off Harbor Drive between noon and 1 p.m. most days to see custom boats and the woodworking, casting, and bronzing going on (415-331-7134; www.arqueschl.org).

Drive south out of town to US 101 to the Tiburon exit, taking Tiburon Boulevard south along Richardson's Bay to **Tiburon.**

LUNCH Sam's Anchor Cafe, 27 Main St., Tiburon; (415) 435-4527; www.samscafe.com. One of several harborfront restaurants with views of the San Francisco skyline. Ferries, yachts, and seagulls slide by; time slides by, too, as you sip a beer on the sunny deck and tuck into clam chowder, fresh crab, and fish of all kinds. Casual, with a frisky bar crowd. Weekend brunches are a reason to spend the day at Sam's.

If you plan to be here on the opening day of yacht season in April, arrive early for a good seat at Sam's or grab enough space for a picnic blanket on the lawns beside the bay. Decorated to the max, hundreds of pleasure craft are blessed; then they sail or motor back and forth while landlubbers engage in vernal behavior, like kite flying.

AFTERNOON

Prior to the 1920s, Tiburon was a lagoon lined with houseboats, called arks. When the lagoon was filled in 1940, the arks were placed on pilings. Today, curvy, tree-lined **Ark Row,** at the west end of Main, is a charming shopping street.

Windsor Vineyards, 72 Main (415-435-3113; www.windsor vineyards.com), will ship gift boxes of wine with your name on the bottles.

The Attic is a collector's dream of vintage video games, comic books, baseball cards, and other finds (96 Main St.; 415-435-0351). At **RJ Sax Apparel,** Aloha shirts, crazy celeb-theme ties, decorated flip-flops, wild and crazy umbrellas and parasols, and gifts for your nuttiest friends (30 Main St., 800-709-4449; http://rjsax.com). Next door, if you love Tommy Bahama, get to **Junella's Tommy Bahama** (32 Main St., 415-435-4752) to browse the entire Tommy Bahama line of furniture, linens, lamps, and decorative accessories—so tropicale!

Even if toting home a stone Buddha isn't what you had in mind, if you love Asian things you won't want to miss **Opia Home and Garden Gallery,** to see wind chimes, jewelry, wall and garden art, and vibrant prints of paintings by a world-famous Chinese master, Jie-Wei Zhou (82 Main St.; 415-435-2511, www.opiahome .com). A brand new gourmet store downtown at 10 Main St., **May**

Madison is selling top quality cookware, cutlery, and accessories for foodies and gourmands (415-435-270; http://maymadison.com).

On the west side of Ark Row, at 52 Beach Rd. on an inlet of the bay, **China Cabin** is a delightful fragment from a sidewheel steamer that plied the trade routes between San Francisco and the Orient in the late 1800s. The saloon was salvaged when the ship burned, and it served as a home for decades before becoming a maritime museum furnished with period antiques and elaborate gold-leaf ornamentation. Call for a seasonal schedule (415-435-5633).

There are a number of historic buildings in Tiburon. You can get a walking-tour brochure from the Tiburon Peninsula Chamber of Commerce (415-435-5633).

From downtown Tiburon to the north end of Richardson Bay is a beautiful waterfront walk, 2 miles long, on a flat, paved path; there are benches along the way and a huge lawn for Frisbee tossing and sunbathing. The path is popular with joggers, in-line skaters, bikers, and tykes on trikes. At the north end of the path is the **Richardson Bay Audubon Center and Wildlife Sanctuary,** (376 Greenwood Beach Rd.; 415-388-2524; www.tiburonaudubon.org), where thousands of sea- and shorebirds, accompanied by harbor seals in wintertime, inhabit a 900-acre preserve. A self-guided nature trail and a bookstore are adjacent to **Lyford House,** a lemon-yellow landmark Victorian open to the public.

Reachable by a short ferry ride from Main Street and a ferry ride from San Francisco (www.angelislandferry.com), **Angel Island State Park** is just offshore (415-435-1915; www.angelisland.org). Popular activities here are walking and biking the breezy island paths and roads to get a gull's-eye view of three bridges and the bay. Once a Miwok hunting ground, then a cattle ranch, a U.S. Army base, and a prisoner of war camp, Angel Island has a unique past, and you will see several historical sites. Take a narrated tour in an open-air tram.

Thirteen miles of hiking trails and 8 miles of mountain-biking roads crisscross the island. Mountain bikes are available to rent, and you can take guided Segway tours (415-897-0715). Less energetic visitors will enjoy sitting on the deck of the cafe with an espresso and a light lunch, watching sailboats and freighters glide by. A few environmental campsites are available (800-444-7275). No dogs, skateboards, or in-line skates are allowed on Angel Island.

The Angel Island-Tiburon Ferry offers a Sunset Cruise on weekends where you bring your own picnic dinner and enjoy cruising the bay in the early evening.

DINNER   **Guaymas,** 5 Main, Tiburon; (415) 435-6300. Spectacular waterfront location; nouvelle Southwest/Mexican food; lively bar and outdoor terrace.

LODGING   Lodge at **Tiburon,** 1651 Tiburon Blvd.; (415) 435-3133 or (866) 823-4669; www.thelodgeattiburon.com. A newly renovated, 102-room downtown hotel done up in contemporary-style Craftsman decor; located within a short walk from the ferry. Has the latest high-tech amenities, refrigerators, and great beds; suites have sitting areas and sofabeds. Small, sunny pool terrace; rooftop terrace lounge with food service, outdoor fireplaces. The indoor/outdoor Tiburon Grill with a bar serves quite good "contemporary grill cuisine." Tiburon has been long overdue for a nice hotel like this, from which you can walk all over town and along the waterfront.

DAY 2 / MORNING

BREAKFAST   **Sweden House,** 35 Main, Tiburon; (415) 435-9767. On a bayside deck with the denizens of Tiburon; pastries, Swedish pancakes topped with fresh berries, egg dishes; breakfast and lunch.

From the east end of Main Street, take Paradise Drive around the west side of the Tiburon Peninsula, a narrow, winding road through forestlands on the edge of the bay. After 1 mile, before Westward Drive, watch for the **Nature Conservancy Uplands Nature Preserve,** also known as the **Ring Mountain Preserve,** 3152 Paradise Dr. (415-435-6465), a 377-acre piece of ridgetop wilderness with walking trails and wonderful views. It's less than a 1-mile walk to the summit on a trail edged with knee-high native grasses dotted with wildflowers in spring. On the hilltop you'll have a 360-degree view of San Francisco Bay, Mount Tam, Marin County, and the East Bay hills.

LUNCH   **Buckeye Roadhouse,** 15 Shoreline Hwy., adjacent to US 101 on the south end of Mill Valley; (415-331-2600; www.buckeyeroadhouse.com). A winding garden path lures you into a historic Bavarian-style lodge right off the freeway, warm and inviting with a fireplace, cushy booths, and Big Band-era music. The food is anything but Bavarian: California cuisine and American comfort food, light-hearted ethnic specialties. Open from lunch straight through the evening.

AFTERNOON

From the Buckeye take the Panoramic Highway north, winding several miles up on the east side of **Mount Tamalpais State Park** (415-388-2070). You can't miss Mount Tam—it's the 2,500-foot mountain peak that you can see from everywhere in Marin. Park at the Pan Toll Ranger Station and Visitor Center, get a trail map, and walk a bit on one of several hiking trails that start here; the shortest one is the **Twenty-Minute Verna Dunshea Trail,** which circles the peak. Views are beyond description, and it's often sunny up here when it's foggy everywhere below. Mount Tam's natural wonders are legion—canyons, forests, streams and meadows, waterfalls, and wildflowers—and offer opportunities for wild-and-woolly mountain biking or easy downhill walking.

Perhaps you'll want to stop for a sunset cocktail on the deck at **Mountain Home Inn,** if you have a designated driver for the trip back to San Francisco. Or stay overnight here. Eleven cozy rooms have French doors or big windows; some have fireplaces and Jacuzzi tubs (810 Panoramic Hwy., 415-381-9000, www.mtnhomeinn.com).

There's More . . . .

Boating and Bay Tours. **Captain Case Powerboat and Waterbike Rental,** Schoonmaker Point Marina off Bridgeway, 85 Liberty Ship Way, Sausalito; (415) 331-0444. Boston whalers, tours on the bay, sunset cruises, water taxis, high-tech water bikes to play with on calm Richardson Bay.

Commodore Seaplanes, from the north end of Sausalito; (415) 332-4843; www.seaplane.com. San Francisco Bay aerial tours, sunset champagne flights.

Sea Trek, Schoonmaker Point, Sausalito; (415) 332-8790; www.seatrekkayak.com. Guided kayak tours of the bay, classes, sunset and full-moon paddles.

Ferries. Tiburon, Sausalito, and Larkspur are accessible by oceangoing ferry: Angel Island Ferry (415-435-2131; www.angel islandferry.com); Blue and Gold Fleet (415-705-8200; www.blue andgoldfleet.com).

Enjoying the Outdoors. **China Camp State Park,** San Rafael; (415) 456-0766. North of San Rafael, take the Civic Center exit off US 101 to North San Pedro Road, heading east. A breezy water-front park on San Pablo Bay, with beach, hiking trails, a small museum, and primitive camping. Sailboarding is a big deal from May through Oct.

Marin Headlands, take the Alexander Avenue exit off Highway 1, the first exit north of the Golden Gate Bridge; (415-331-1540; www.nps.gov/goga). Part of the Golden Gate National Recreation Area with wild open spaces and miraculous views. Hiking trails above the Golden Gate are breezy and bracing. Stop at the visitor center at Field and Bunker Streets for maps to hiking, biking, and equestrian trails and beaches. Besides the Marin Mammal Center (listed below), the main attractions are Rodeo Beach, Rodeo Lagoon, Muir Beach, and the Point Bonita Lighthouse. The lighthouse is perched on a bit of rock at the entrance to the Golden Gate, with incredible views and a (slightly) swaying footbridge over crashing waves; walk down and back on your own and get the history from the ranger in the tiny visitor center, or opt for the guided walk, which takes (it seems) forever. Precipitous clifftop trails near here are not for little kids. The best time to explore Muir Beach is at low tide, when hundreds of sea stars and vividly colored sea anemones are revealed.

Muir Woods National Monument, 3 miles north of Highway 1 on Muir Woods Road; (415) 388-7059; www.nps.gov/muwo. A precious pocket of redwoods, some over a thousand years old and 260 feet high, live in an isolated canyon 12 miles north of the Golden Gate Bridge. Trails wander through an idyllic mixed forest of Douglas fir, big-leaf maple, oak, laurel, red alder, and buckeye—glorious in the autumn. The easiest trail loops from the Visitor Center to Cathedral Grove, a 1-mile, one-hour walk if you stop to read the nature signs and enjoy Redwood Creek; wide, paved and wheelchair and stroller accessible. Mid-week is best, as weekends and summertime are busy with visitors from around the world. No bikes, picnics, or pets. A gift shop shows the works of more than 150 local artisans, and a snack bar.

Stinson Beach Park, Highway 1 and Panoramic Highway; (415) 868-0942. Many Marin beaches are unsafe for swimming and surfing due to undertows and currents; 3-mile-long Stinson is an exception. There are picnic tables, barbecues, restrooms; a snack bar and lifeguards in summer; dogs are allowed in one area only. Rent surf boards, kayaks, and bikes at Stinson Beach Surf and Kayak, (3605 Highway 1, 415-868-2739).

Have breakfast, lunch, or dinner at the **Stinson Beach Grill** (3465 Shoreline Hwy., Stinson Beach; 415-868-2002). Fresh seafood, barbecued oysters, pasta, Southwest cuisine, and 50 varieties of beer.

Wildlife. **Marine Mammal Center in the Marin Headlands;** (415) 289-7325. A rare opportunity to see rescued marine mammals at this hospital for orphaned, sick, and injured seals, sea lions, dolphins, otters, and whales from California's 900-mile coast, from 10-pound newborn harbor seals to 600-pound sea lions. During some months, there are few animals on view; call ahead.

Special Events . . . .

APRIL
Opening Day of Yacht Season, Tiburon and Sausalito waterfront; (415) 435-4771. Pleasure craft decorated and blessed; a beautiful and exceedingly high-spirited day on the bay. Bring a picnic and lounge on the waterfront lawns.

MAY
Tiburon Wine Festival, Tiburon Point Plaza, Tiburon; (415) 435-5623; http://tiburonwinefestival.homestead.com. Outdoors along the plaza lake, 65 wineries and 20 or so restaurants offer tastes while guests enjoy live entertainment. The waterfront location and fine food and wine make this a very popular weekend event that always sells out.

JUNE
Italian Street Painting Festival, downtown San Rafael; (415) 457-4878; www.youthinarts.org. Artists of all abilities use vibrant chalks to create more than 200 stunning works on the sidewalks; live entertainment and food. One of the largest events in the world of this type.

SEPTEMBER
Sausalito Art Festival; (415) 332-3555. A gigantic event, one of the best, and said to be one of the largest art fairs in the country, attracting top-notch artists and thousands of visitors; live entertainment and food.

DECEMBER
Lighted Yacht Parade, Sausalito waterfront and yacht harbor; (415) 331-7262; www.syconline.org.

Other Recommended Restaurants and Lodgings . . . .

CORTE MADERA
Corte Madera Inn, 56 Madera Blvd.; (800) 777-9670; www.best western.com. Nice, busy motel overlooking gardens and lawns, with swimming and wading pools, a laundry, playground, and a good coffee shop. Continental breakfast is free, and so is the shuttle to the San Francisco ferry. Can't beat this combo anywhere in Marin. Next-door is an upscale shopping center, and Max's Café, a popular comfort food headquarters (www.maxsworld.com).

LARKSPUR
Tavern at Lark Creek, 234 Magnolia Ave.; (415) 924-7767. In a ca. 1888 Victorian (formerly the Lark Creek Inn), casual, yet upscale, with period oak tables beneath a giant skylight, and food service

in the cozy bar. Wood oven-roasted local poultry and beef; fresh seafood, burgers and sandwiches, artisanal cheeses and produce. Next-door, a charming sister restaurant, the Yankee Pier Larkspur serves New England-style, sustainable seafood, fresh oysters, and all things fish, a very casual, fun place (www.yankeepier.com).

SAN ANSELMO

Marinitas, 218 Sir Francis Drake Blvd.; (415) 454-8900; www .marinitas.net. One of Marin's newest and hippest, a cavernous yet warm space done up in a Latin American-inspired theme, open until midnight. Fabulous fish tacos, pork and black bean stew, queso fundido, lamb shanks braised Guadalajara style, wines from Argentina and Chile. Lively bar: cocktails focus on liquors of Central and South America, Mexican brews.

SAUSALITO

Cavallo Point, The Lodge at the Golden Gate, at Fort Baker at the northeast base of the Golden Gate Bridge, (415) 339-4700; www .cavallopoint.com. An environmentally sustainable, new luxury hotel with the Michelin starred Murray Circle restaurant, the Farley Bar, a cooking school and the Healing Arts Center & Spa. Sixty-eight historic and 74 contemporary rooms and suites, all with stunning views. Leather armchairs and ottomans, fireplaces, window seats, beautiful contemporary furnishings and decor. Eleven treatment rooms in the full-service spa, heated outdoor pool and Tea Bar. When booking, ask about what groups may be in residence, as this is a popular venue for corporate and non-profit group retreats and events. Also, discuss room choice, as some are on the second or third floors with no elevators.

Fish, 350 Harbor Dr., Sausalito; (415) 331-3474; www.331fish .com. On a patio at the waterfront, sit at picnic tables for fish and chips, chowder, sustainably-produced seafood, pasta, fish tacos, peanut butter and jelly, root beer floats. Very fun, very casual.

Hotel Sausalito, 16 El Portal; (415) 332-0700; www.hotelsausalito .com. As if on the French Riviera, this small, charming boutique hotel is across from the waterfront park and the ferry. Lovely pastel colors in rooms that vary in size and price, with armoires, wrought-iron beds, a small patio; some streetside rooms are noisy.

The Inn Above Tide, 30 El Portal next to the ferry dock, Sausalito; (800) 893-8433; www.innabovetide.com. Twenty-nine luxurious suites with water views, fireplaces, soaking tubs, most with private decks; breakfast and wine hour. No pets; in-room massage available. Impossible to beat the location, the luxury, the service, and the comfort.

Kitti's Place, 3001 Bridgeway; (415) 331-0390. In a small strip mall, a casual, homey atmosphere, Pan-Asian comfort food extraordinaire, from homemade soup to salads and entrees; great sandwiches (try the portobello). Breakfast, lunch, and early dinner. Next-door to the very good Tommy's Wok (www.tommyswok.us).

Poggio Trattoria, 777 Bridgeway; (415) 332-7771, www.poggio trattoria.com. An upscale Northern Italian trattoria open all day and evening, with sidewalk tables. Rustic pasta, spinach ricotta gnocchi, cannelloni, spit-roasted meats and poultry; wood-fired pizza, fresh seafood.

Scoma's, 588 Bridgeway; (415) 332-9551. On the water at the south end of town, in a baby-blue clapboard building; some, not all, tables have good views—sit outside if you can. Dependably great seafood, especially the daily specials.

TIBURON

Waters Edge, 25 Main St.; (415) 789-5999; www.marinhotels.com. In a town with few accommodations, simple, very nice contemporary rooms next to the ferry dock, with skylights, private balconies, featherbeds, some fireplaces, and waterfront views. Complimentary continental breakfast.

For More Information . . . .

Marin County Visitors Bureau, 1 Mitchell Blvd., San Rafael 94903; (415) 925-2060 or (866) 925-2060; www.visitmarin.org.

Sausalito Visitors Center, kiosk next to the ferry landing and also at the Ice House, 780 Bridgeway at Bay; (415) 332-0505, (415) 331-1093; www.sausalito.org. At the Ice House, the local historical society sells books and maps, maintains a small history museum and offers guided walks.

Tiburon Peninsula Chamber of Commerce, 96 Main St., Tiburon 94920; (415) 435-5633; www.tiburonchamber.org.

NORTHBOUND ESCAPE *Nine*
Point Reyes and Inverness
THE NATIONAL SEASHORE / 2 NIGHTS

- Natural seashore
- Beachcombing
- Bird-watching
- Wildflower walks
- Oyster farms
- Inns by the sea

More than a few weekends are needed to discover the many joys of the Point Reyes National Seashore, comprising 71,000 miraculous acres on the edge of the continent: two fingerlike peninsulas pointing jaggedly into the Pacific; the long, shallow biodiversity of Tomales Bay; the big curve of Drakes Bay, where the English explorer Sir Francis Drake set foot in 1579; and oyster farms, clamming beaches, tidepools, and wildlife sanctuaries.

Separated from the mainland by the San Andreas Fault, the unique location of the peninsula gives rise to several distinct habitats. More than 45 percent of the bird species in North America have been sighted here.

From February through early summer, the meadows and marine terraces of Point Reyes are blanketed with California poppies, dark blue lupine, pale baby blue eyes, Indian paintbrush, and a few varieties of wildflowers existing only here. Dominating the landscape is the green-black Douglas fir forest of Inverness Ridge, running northwest to southeast alongside the San Andreas earthquake fault. The summit of Mount Wittenberg, at 1,407 feet, is reachable in an afternoon's climb.

Subject to summer fogs and winter drizzles, Point Reyes is a favorite destination not only for those who love a sunny day at the beach but also for intrepid outdoor types who follow cool-weather nature hikes with cozy evenings by a fireplace in a vintage bed-and-breakfast inn.

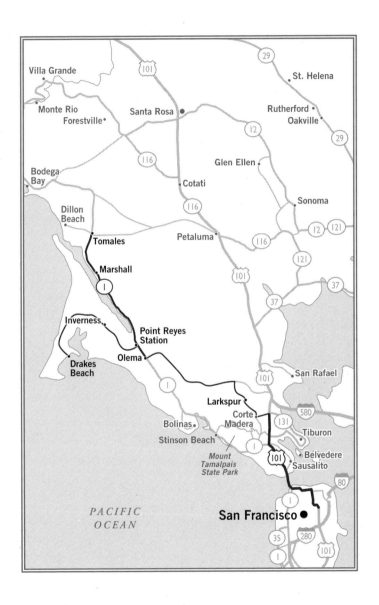

Villa Grande

Monte Rio
Forestville

Santa Rosa

St. Helena

Rutherford
Oakville

29

Bodega
Bay

116

Glen Ellen

Dillon
Beach

Cotati

Sonoma

116

Tomales

Petaluma

116

12 121

Marshall

1

101

121

Inverness

Point Reyes
Station

37

Drakes
Beach

Olema

1

101

San Rafael

580

Larkspur

Corte
Madera

131

Bolinas

Tiburon

Stinson Beach

1

Belvedere
Sausalito

Mount
Tamalpais
State Park

101

80

PACIFIC
OCEAN

San Francisco

1

35 280

1 101

DAY 1 / MORNING

....

Take US 101 north to the Tamalpais-Paradise Drive exit, 15 minutes north of the Golden Gate Bridge. Exit right and take the overpass to your left over the freeway. Turn left on Redwood Avenue then right on Corte Madera Boulevard, which becomes Magnolia Avenue.

BREAKFAST   Pull up to a pasticceria straight from San Marco Square with Italian mahogany, marble inlay, and a hand-painted mural. **Emporio Rulli** (464 Magnolia Ave., Larkspur; 415-924-7478; www.rulli.com) has traditional breads, pastries, hand-dipped chocolates, and more than nine house-roasted coffee blends. You can assemble an excellent picnic by choosing from the daily selection of panini (Italian sandwiches).

Continue driving north on Magnolia Avenue, then turn left onto Sir Francis Drake Boulevard. Proceed west 45 minutes on the winding, two-lane road to the **Point Reyes National Seashore Visitor Center** at **Olema** (415-663-1092; www.nps.gov/pore).

Exhibits, guidebooks, and trail maps at the Point Reyes Visitor Center will help orient you to the many destinations within the National Seashore. According to the day's weather, you may choose beachcombing and sunbathing (or fogbathing), backpacking to overnight sites, or easy walks or bike rides on meadowland paths, or challenging hikes. One of the most popular of the more than 150 miles of hiking, biking, and horseback riding trails is the 8-mile, round-trip **Bear Valley Trail** through forest tunnels, along creeks, and through meadows, ending on a bluff 50 feet above the sea.

At the end of Limantour Road, **Limantour Beach** is a long stretch of windswept sand that is good for surf fishing and sunbathing. Look for the Muddy Hollow Trail for an easy 1-mile bird-watching and wildflower walk.

Bird-watching is excellent in the 500-acre **Limantour Estero Reserve,** west of Limantour Beach. You get to **Drakes Estero,** a much larger saltwater lagoon, from Sir Francis Drake Boulevard on the west side. This rocky intertidal area is a giant tidepool and bird sanctuary, rich with such wildlife as anemones, sea stars, crabs, and even rays and leopard sharks.

LUNCH   **Picnic** on the beach or in a trailside meadow.

AFTERNOON

Energetic hikers can make the steep but short ascent on Sky Trail to the summit of Mount Wittenberg; beach bums will choose from many coastal access trails. The long sandy stretch of Point Reyes Beach is accessible in two places by car.

Short, easy walks near the visitor center include **Kule Loklo,** the Miwok Village, where an ancient Indian site has been re-created, and the **Woodpecker Trail,** a self-guided nature walk leading to the park rangers' Morgan horse ranch and a Morgan horse museum. Horses are bred and trained here on a hundred beautiful acres for the use of the National Park rangers in this park and in Zion and Hawaii Volcanoes National Parks.

The **Earthquake Trail,** less than a mile in length, is where you'll see photos of the effects of the 1906 earthquake and signs explaining earth movement.

DINNER   **Station House Cafe,** Main Street, Point Reyes Station; (415) 663-1515. In a historic red building on Main Street for nearly three decades; good food and fun; breakfast, lunch, and dinner in the casual dining room or on the garden patio, with live weekend entertainment and weekday free happy hour hors d'oeuvres. Homemade breads, free-range poultry and meats; the harvest from an on-site organic garden and a plethora of local products go into a contemporary comfort food menu, from pot roast and duck breast with cherry sauce to lots of fresh seafood; don't miss the pecan pie.

Kick up your heels to live country music and the jukebox, cozy up to the wood stove, and have a Lagunitas IPA or a Boont Amber Ale at the **Old Western Saloon** on Main Street (415-663-1661).

LODGING   **Point Reyes Seashore Lodge,** 10021 Highway 1, Olema; (415) 663-9000 or (800) 404-LODGE; www.ptreyesseashorelodge.com. Near Point Reyes, a castlelike re-creation of a large Victorian inn on the exterior, modern California Craftsman-style inside, sweeping lawns above a creek and woods. Twenty-two rooms and suites with featherbeds, down comforters, bay windows, fireplaces, and Jacuzzi tubs, generous breakfast. The staff will arrange bike, kayak, and horse rentals. Onsite, the Farm House Restaurant Bar and Deli features organic ingredients, comfort food and lots of local seafood (www.olemafarmhouse.com).

DAY 2 / MORNING

BREAKFAST   At the **Point Reyes Seashore Lodge.**

Give your hiking legs a break and spend the morning shopping and cafe lounging in the town of **Point Reyes Station.** Many one-hundred-year-old buildings remain on the main street of this narrow-gauge railroad town founded in the 1800s. The train depot is now the post office, the Fire Engine House a community center. Dairy ranches and commercial oyster companies fuel the rural economy.

Black Mountain Artisans, on Main Street (415-663-9130), is a co-op gallery of fine woven rugs, sweaters, and tapestries, plus jewelry and art. At **Susan Hayes Handwovens,** slip into luscious silk and chenille jackets and vests, jewelry and gifts (80 Fourth St.; 415-663-8057, www.susanhayeshandwovens.com). Equestrians will go into **Cabaline Saddle Shop,** on Main Street (415-663-8303, www.cabaline.com), for English and western saddlery and clothing, shoes, hats, jewelry, travel essentials, gifts, toys and books. Also on Main is **Toby's Feed Barn** (415-663-1223)—fresh flowers, plants, produce, T-shirts, body and bath items, souvenirs, and hay for your horse. In front of Toby's every Sat, June through Oct, a farmers' market takes place. Vendors sell local produce and flowers, wool, poultry and meats, olive oil, preserves, and more.

This and several other specialty vendors are in the barnlike **Tomales Bay Foods** at Fourth and B Streets, an airy emporium of luscious hot and cold take-out foods, organic produce, flowers, artworks, and homemade ice cream. At Tomales Bay Foods on weekends there are often wine, seafood and cooking demonstrations, and tastings of award-winning cheeses from the town's famous **Cowgirl Creamery** (415-663-9335, www.cowgirlcreamery.com). While here and on local restaurant menus, look for the world-famous "Point Reyes Blue" cheese (www.pointreyescheese.com).

Marin County's only kite store is a great one, at Third and B Streets, **Into the Blue.** You will find dual-line, stunt, and acrobatic kites, as well as parafoils, boomerangs, and Frisbees (415-663-1147).

LUNCH   From Point Reyes drive north on Highway 1 along the shoreline of Tomales Bay 10 miles to Marshall to **Hog Island Oyster Company,** where you can bring a picnic, purchase oysters plucked fresh from their nearby beds, and eat them raw or grill them on the barbecue (20215 Highway 1; 415-663-9218; www.hogislandoysters.com).

AFTERNOON

Five miles farther north, the mini town of **Tomales** is a 2-block-long headquarters for crabbing, clamming, and surf fishing. At low tide in winter, catch a clammer's barge from here out to the flatlands around Hog Island in the bay. Hog Island and nearby Duck Island are private wildlife sanctuaries frequented by harbor seals.

Bicyclists and picnickers love to stop at the **Tomales Bakery,** Thurs through Sun, for European-style breads and pastries, pies, amazing calzones, focaccia with exotic toppings, and croissants, all made with local ingredients by a noted chef (27000 Highway 1; 415-878-2429).

On your way back from Tomales to Point Reyes, then around to Inverness, take a walk or swim in the quiet waters of **Heart's Desire Beach** in **Tomales Bay State Park** off Sir Francis Drake Boulevard on Pierce Point Road; (415) 669-1140. Backed by a dramatic stand of first-growth Bishop pine, the wind-protected, easily accessible beach on the bay is the mildest environment in the area for swimming, sailboarding, kayaking, and clam digging. There are picnic tables, 6 miles of easy to moderate trails, and a few hike-in or bike-in campsites.

A resort village since 1889, **Inverness,** population 1,000, is a day-tripper's rest stop and a community of country cottages on steep wooded slopes at the northern end of **Inverness Ridge,** overlooking Tomales Bay. There are seafood cafes, bed-and-breakfast inns, a small marina, and not much else but eye-popping scenery.

Discovered by Spanish explorers in the 1600s, **Tomales Bay** is 13 miles long, 1 mile wide, and very shallow, with acres of mudflats and salt- and freshwater marshes. Commercial oyster farms line the western shore. More than a hundred species of resident and migrating water birds are the reason you'll see anorak-clad, binocular-braced bird-watchers at every pullout on Highway 1. Perch, flounder, sand dabs, and crabs are catchable by small boat.

Rent a kayak and paddle around the bay, where you will likely see bat rays, jellyfish, and ospreys and seal, among other wildlife. Rent kayaks and wet suits and get instructions at **Blue Waters Kayaking** (12938 Sir Francis Drake Blvd., Inverness, and in the village of Marshall; 415-669-2600; www.bwkayak.com). **Point Reyes Outdoors** is another good company that rents boats, and offers classes and guided tours of Drakes Estero and Tomales Bay (11401 State Route 1, Point Reyes Station; (415) 663-8192; www.pointreyesoutdoors.com).

DINNER **Manka's Inverness Restaurant,** 30 Calendar Way, Inverness; (415) 669-1034. A 1917 fishing lodge nestled under the pines; game and fresh fish grilled in an open fireplace, house-cured meat and poultry, home-grown produce; comfortably cozy, candlelit atmosphere; notable chefs; reservations essential. Accommodations here are in a country-luxe lodge in Adirondack style with log beds, Arts and Crafts furnishings, fireplaces, and Ralph Lauren linens; plus a rose-covered cottage.

LODGING **Nick's Cove and Cottages,** 23240 Highway 1, Marshall; (866) 63-NICKS; www.nickscove.com. On Tomales Bay, just the sweetest lineup of comfy cottages you'll ever see, and a private dock. Each cottage is divinely different, romantic and spacious—and pricey. The waterfront restaurant here is wildly popular and famous for fresh seafood and local ingredients.

DAY 3 / MORNING

BREAKFAST At **Nick's Cove.**

Drive north on Sir Francis Drake Boulevard to the Pierce Point Road; take a right and park in the upper parking lot at **McClure**

Beach. It's a 9-mile round-trip around **Tomales Point** and along the coastline. Spring wildflowers float in the meadows; whales spout Dec through Feb. A herd of elk lives in the grassy fields of **Pierce Ranch** on the tip of the peninsula. These windswept moors remind some visitors of Scotland.

McClure Beach is wide, sandy, backed by high cliffs, and dotted with rocks and great tidepools. Bluffs framed by groves of Bishop pine look like Japanese woodcut prints; these pines are found only in a few isolated locations on the California coast.

Point Reyes Lighthouse, at the end of Sir Francis Drake Boulevard, 15 miles south of Inverness, is reachable by 400 steps leading downhill from a high bluff. Below the dramatic cliffs are miles of beaches accessible from Sir Francis Drake Boulevard; exposed to the full force of storms and pounding surf, they are unsafe for swimming or surfing. The headlands, tidepools, sea stacks, lagoons, wave-carved caves, and rocky promontories are alive with birds—endangered brown pelicans, cormorants, surf scooters, sandpipers, grebes, terns—and sea life such as giant anemones and sea palms, urchins, fish, and even the occasional great white shark offshore of Tomales Point. During whale-watching season, December through spring, a shuttle bus may be operating between the lighthouse and **Drakes Beach.** Some 20,000 California gray whales travel the Pacific coastline going south to breed in Mexican waters and then return with their calves to the Arctic.

At the 7-mile-long crescent of Drakes Beach are a visitor center and picnic tables, and

The Drakes Beach Café, a tiny, cozy eatery at the water's edge, with outdoor tables and a telescope for whale watching.

From Sir Francis Drake Boulevard near the lighthouse, take the turnoff to Chimney Rock to the most spectacular wildflower walk in the park, an easy, 1.5-mile route.

LUNCH **Barnaby's by the Bay,** 12938 Sir Francis Drake Blvd., 1 mile north of Inverness at the Golden Hind Inn; (415) 669-1114. Two decks overlooking a marina; fresh fish, salads, barbecued oysters and chicken, and ribs from the applewood smoker; jazz on weekends; you'll be tempted to stay here for the rest of the day.

Head back to the Bay Area.

There's More . . . .

Bolinas. Just north of Stinson Beach off Highway 1, Olema–Bolinas Road; (415) 499-6387. A rustic 19th-century village near beautiful **Bolinas Lagoon,** where salt marsh, mudflats, and calm sea waters harbor thousands of birds and ducks, and a mile of shallow tidepools (415-868-9244; www.egret.org). Agate Beach is a small county park. Four miles northwest of Bolinas on Mesa Road, a short nature trail leads to the **Point Reyes Bird Observatory,** where you can observe bird banding (415-868-1221). This is the Palomarin Trailhead, which leads to four freshwater lakes and to Double Point Bay; 3 miles from the trailhead, watch for Bass Lake, a secret swimming spot. Have lunch, dinner, or Sunday brunch at the surfboard-decorated **Bolinas Coast Café** (46 Wharf Rd., Bolinas; 415-868-2298; www.bolinascafe.com). On the menu are locally produced veggies, seafood, dairy products, and meats; try the barbecue oysters and fish and chips.

Stop in at the tiny **Bolinas Museum** (48–50 Wharf Rd.; 415-868-0330) and prowl around the interesting old cemetery off Olema–Bolinas Road.

Horseback Riding. Five Brooks Ranch, 3 miles south of Olema; (415) 663-1570; www.fivebrooks.com. Guided horseback rides, from a one-hour slow trail ride to longer treks up the Inverness ridge, and incredible beach rides.

Wildlife Watching. Jutting 10 miles into the Pacific, the **Point Reyes Peninsula** makes for prime whale-watching, Dec through Apr, when more than 30,000 gray whales pass by. Best viewing spots: around Chimney Rock and the lighthouse. In winter you can see some of 1,000 elephant seals—9 to 16 feet long and up to 5,000 pounds— and their new pups from the lighthouse parking lot, by the lifeboat station, and at a viewing area a quarter-mile walk from the Chimney Rock parking lot.

Special Events . . . .

JULY
Big Time Festival at Kule Loklo, Point Reyes National Seashore (415-464-5140). Traditional Native American (Coast Miwok and Pomo) trade festival, with demonstrations of basketry, flint knapping, clamshell bead making, and more; informational booths, traditional dancers, craft vendors. No dogs or alcoholic beverages.

SEPTEMBER
Sand Sculpture Contest at Drakes Beach, Point Reyes National Seashore (415-464-5140). It's free to create a spectacular sand castle or sculpture, starting at 9 a.m.; judging at noon, prizes at 3:30 p.m.

California Coastal Cleanup Day, Drakes Beach, Point Reyes National Seashore (415-464-5130). An annual event in which 50,000 volunteers appear at more than 700 cleanup sites statewide to conduct what has been hailed by the *Guinness Book of World Records* as "the largest garbage collection." Meet at the Drakes Beach parking lot at 9:30 a.m.

Other Recommended Restaurants and Lodgings . . . .

INVERNESS

Blackthorne Inn, 266 Vallejo; (415) 663-8621; www.blackthorne inn.com. Five charming rooms in a wooded canyon; a treehouse with decks, hot tub, fireman's pole, spiral staircase, glass-sided "eagle's nest," and buffet breakfast.

Dancing Coyote Beach Bed and Breakfast Cottages, P.O. Box 98, Inverness 94937; (415) 669-7200; www.dancingcoyotebeach .com. Four Southwest-style cottages with decks, views, fireplaces, kitchens.

Golden Hind Inn, 12938 Sir Francis Drake Blvd.; (415) 669-1389; www.goldenhindinn.com. A fresh-looking, white-painted, unassuming motel on Tomales Bay, with a small pool and fishing pier. Two-room suites have queens and sofabeds, microwaves, refrigerators, and fireplaces. Next to Barnaby's by the Bay restaurant and Blue Waters Kayaking.

Ten Inverness Way, 10 Inverness Way, Inverness; (415) 669-1648; www.teninvernessway.com. Country-style inn with five rooms filled with quilts, lace curtains, comfort, and light. Common room with big stone fireplace; lovely gardens, hot tub, full breakfast; walk to hiking trails.

OLEMA

Olema Farm House Restaurant and Deli, 10005 Highway 1; (415) 663-1264; www.olemafarmhouse.com. An 1845 stagecoach stop, decked out with antique bottles, Elvis memorabilia, and fun collectibles. The heated garden patio is the place to be. Fish-and-chips, clam chowder, meat loaf, prime rib, roast chicken, oyster stew, Philly cheese steak; lunch and dinner, with breakfast on weekends.

Olema Ranch Campground, 0.25 mile north of Highway 1 and Sir Francis Drake Boulevard, 10155 Highway 1; (415) 663-8106; www.olemaranch.com. On 30 wooded acres, RV facilities, tent sites, forest and meadow setting, gas, store; Wi-Fi, showers, playground, post office, fire rings.

POINT REYES STATION
Bovine Bakery, Highway 1; (415) 663-9420. Lines may be out the door for fresh artisan breads, pastries, muffins, and scones.

Holly Tree Inn and Cottages, 3 Silverhills Rd.; (415) 663-1554. In a magical world of lawns, gardens, and wooded hillsides, four guest rooms, plus cottages with hot tubs and fireplaces. French provincial decor, antiques, fireplaces—French doors open to the meadows.

Osteria Stellina, 11285 Highway 1; (415) 663-9988; www.osteria stellina.com. Opened in late 2008 to rave reviews, with a fast-changing, contemporary Italian-inspired seasonal menu based on local producers; very casual, noisy interior. Fabulous pizza, "beans and greens," braised goat shoulder, cod and potato chowder, best grilled cheese in the world. Save room for homemade ice cream, especially the Meyer lemon ice-cream sandwich.

Point Reyes Vineyard Inn & Winery, 12700 Highway 1; (415) 663-1552 or (800) 516-1011; www.ptreyesvineyardinn.com. A romantic, secluded Mediterranean-style home in a pastoral setting adjacent to a working ranch and winery. Lots of returnees here, to four spacious rooms (including a two-room suite) with vineyard and wetlands views, generous continental breakfast.

Thirty-nine Cypress, 39 Cypress Rd.; (415) 663-1709. With wonderful views of the Point Reyes Peninsula, a redwood country inn with four guest rooms. Private patio, hot tub, antiques, fireplace; breakfast with stay.

For More Information . . . .

Inns of Marin, (800) 887-2880; www.innsofmarin.com. Referral service for several inns and cottages.

Point Reyes Lodging Association, P.O. Box 878, Point Reyes 94956; (415) 663-1872 or (800) 539-1872; www.ptreyes.com. Inns, small hotels, cottages.

Marin County Visitors Bureau, 1 Mitchell Blvd., San Rafael; (415) 925-2060 or (866) 925-2060; www.visitmarin.org.

West Marin Chamber of Commerce, P.O. Box 1045, Point Reyes Station 94956; (415) 663-9232; www.pointreyes.org.

SOUTHBOUND *ESCAPES*

SOUTHBOUND ESCAPE *One*

Santa Cruz
A CALIFORNIA BEACH TOWN / 1 NIGHT

Beaches

Bikes

Butterflies

The Boardwalk

Wineries

Redwoods

Shopping

The resort town of Santa Cruz is famous for more than 29 miles of wide, sandy, warm-water beaches and an old-fashioned waterfront boardwalk with rides and concessions. Here at the top end of Monterey Bay, the climate is mild, surf's up every month of the year, and the attitude is young and healthy, due to a large population of university students and residents who love outdoor recreation.

The town has many fanciful homes in a variety of architectural styles, such as Queen Anne, Gothic Revival, Mission Revival, and California bungalow. Pacific Avenue, the main street, is a tree-shaded boulevard with outdoor cafes and dozens of shops. The University of California at Santa Cruz and Cabrillo College are located here, and the community is culturally oriented, with a large contingent of artists and musicians in residence and a lively annual schedule of arts events and music festivals.

Even if you are not a beach person, there is much in the way of outdoor recreation and sightseeing to enjoy, and not just in summer. Near the city of Santa Cruz and in the **Santa Cruz Mountains** are country roads that meander through ancient redwood groves and along the banks of the San Lorenzo and Santa Cruz Rivers. Walking and biking trails and campgrounds are liberally scattered throughout the region.

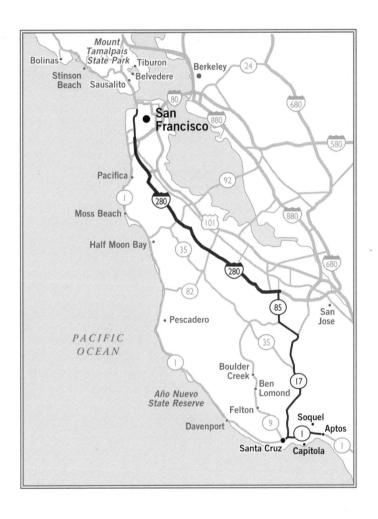

DAY 1 / MORNING

....

Drive south from San Francisco on I–280, south on CA 85 to CA 17 to **Santa Cruz,** about a 90-minute drive, unless it's late Fri afternoon, when it will be a longer trip. As an alternative to the Bay Area's congested highways, the coast route, Highway 1, is longer but far more scenic.

Get right to the ocean views on West Cliff Drive at **Mark Abbott Memorial Lighthouse,** at Lighthouse Point Park overlooking Monterey Bay and the city. Walkers, bikers, joggers, and passengers in baby strollers love the city, sea, and sea-lion views. Go into the lighthouse to see a small surfing museum (831-420-6289); it's free.

Almost every day there are surfers in "Steamers Lane" below. In May the **Longboard Invitational** is held here, and hundreds of surfers from all over the world compete (831-684-1551). The major surf competition, the **O'Neill Coldwater Classic,** is held in the fall (831-479-5648). **Club Ed** at **Cowell Beach** is the place for lessons and board rentals (831-464-0177). **Richard Schmidt School of Surfing,** at 849 Almar Ave., is also well regarded (831-423-0928; www.richardschmidt.com).

Twin Lakes State Beach below East Cliff Drive is where the sailboarders go. There are fire rings here, outdoor showers, and, nearby, wild-bird sanctuaries at **Schwan Lake** (831-429-2850). Prowl around (watching out for poison oak) to see Virginia rail, chickadees, swallows, and belted kingfishers, among dozens more species of birds and waterfowl. You can kayak and canoe on the lake.

The main Santa Cruz beach at the boardwalk and the pier, Cowell Beach (831-420-6014) is the most popular piece of sand on the central coastline for sunning, swimming, and volleyball. The relatively tame waves here are perfect for beginning surfers.

Proceed on West Cliff Drive to Pacific Avenue and downtown Santa Cruz with 4 blocks of boutiques, sidewalk cafes, coffee-houses, and galleries—more than 200 stores in all. In this artists' town, notice the many sidewalk sculptures, and watch for building-size murals on side streets. Browsers love the tree-lined, flower-bedecked boulevard. Book lovers make a beeline to the restored St. George Hotel building at Pacific and Front to **Bookshop Santa Cruz** (831-423-0900), one of the largest independent bookstores in northern California. Scattered throughout are benches, stools, and armchairs, comfortable spots to peruse the books and the huge variety of international magazines and newspapers. There is a cafe in the store, and they serve fresh organic salads, sandwiches, pastas, and chocolate (831-427-9900).

At the corner of Pacific and Cooper, **Pacific Wave** is headquarters for surfboards, skateboards, and all the cool accessories and clothing to go with them (831-458-9283). At **Pacific Edge Indoor Climbing Facility,** try the newest California craze. With the use of safety harnesses, the climbing wall is safe and fun, and you can cool off at the juice bar (104 Bronson; 831-454-9254). River and sea kayaking for all ability levels are also offered by **Adventure Sports** (303 Potrero #15, in the Old Sash Mill; 831-458-3648; www.asudoit.com).

Shen's Gallery (2404 Mission St.; 831-457-4422) is seductive with exotic scents, flute sounds, and Asian antiques and art. It has a large collection of one-of-a-kind tiny ceramic teapots from mainland China, "shard" boxes, and beautiful tea chests. Look for fine, locally produced crafts and art at **Annieglass** (110 Cooper St.; 831-427-4260)—one of the largest showplaces of blown glass and art glass in the state.

In the oldest building downtown, ca. 1850, **LuLu Carpenter's Cafe** has divine pies, salads, and sandwiches, home-baked muffins and scones; Wi-Fi; and a nice courtyard (1545 Pacific; 831-429-9804).

The **Santa Cruz Art League,** nearby at 526 Broadway (831-426-5787), has three galleries and a shop selling fine arts and crafts.

The **Museum of Art and History at the McPherson Center** is a cultural ghetto, encompassing the Art Museum and the History Museum of Santa Cruz County and shops (705 Front St.; 831-429-1964).

LUNCH   **Gabriella's** is a romantic, cozy, much-heralded bistro for lunch and dinner (910 Cedar St., parallels Pacific on the west side; 831-457-1677; www.gabriellacafe.com). In the mood for something spicy? Popular for two decades, El Palomar serves fabulous Mexican food and top-notch margaritas in a stunning dining environment—ask for a booth (1336 Pacific; 831-425-7575).

AFTERNOON

Proceed to the foot of Beach Street for a beach ramble, or go to the **Santa Cruz Beach Boardwalk,** the only beachside amusement park on the West Coast, to indulge in some of three dozen rides, the old-time arcade, the shops, and restaurants (831-423-5590; www.beachboardwalk.com). The classic 1911 carousel and the Giant Dipper coaster are National Historic Landmarks. Replacing the legendary Typhoon ride, the new Sea Swings twirls riders through the sky above the bay. Also new, Desperados is an interactive experience where you sit on a saddle and blast away in a shooting gallery. Many of the kiddie rides allow adults to ride along, such as the Pepsi Convoy, Speedway, Sea Dragons, Freefall, and the Starfish.

Get rid of your spare cash in the Casino Arcade, or just sit on the boardwalk and watch the bikinis and the sailboats glide by. Don't miss **Marini's Candies,** since 1915 on the wharf, for salt water taffy, fresh caramel corn, candy apples, and handmade chocolates and fudge (831-425-7341; www.mariniscandies.com).

Crowds gather here on Main Beach for Fri night band shows in the summer; check the Web site for other free shows, such as the Chinese Acrobats. Now, free Wi-Fi on the boardwalk, too.

Within sight of the boardwalk, **Santa Cruz Municipal Wharf** (831-420-6025) is all about fishing off the pier, shopping in tourist traps, browsing the fresh-fish markets, eating chowder and shrimp cocktail in waterside cafes, and watching the sea lions, the pelicans, and the passing boats. Deep-sea fishing trips and bay cruises depart from the harbor.

On the south side of Santa Cruz, **Santa Cruz Yacht Harbor** (831-475-6161; www.santacruzharbor.org) and its beach are where the locals go to escape the tourists. You can kayak and sail and have a sandwich or a seafood plate at the **Crow's Nest** (2218 East Cliff Dr.; 831-476-4560; www.crowsnest-santacruz.com). The casual, multilevel restaurant has a heated, glassed-in deck overlooking the busy harbor; locals crowd the bar at night.

Drive south 4 miles from the Santa Cruz Wharf on East Cliff Drive to **Capitola Village** (or take the quicker, less-winding route, Highway 1). An oceanside resort since 1861, Capitola remains a quaint artists' colony. Swimmers, waders, and sunbathers flock to **Capitola Beach,** sheltered by two high cliffs. A riparian shelter for birds and ducks, Soquel Creek meanders right through town into the sea. Restaurants with outdoor patios are lined up at beachfront on the Esplanade, and there are a few blocks of boutiques, art galleries, and beachwear shops. Check out the charming **Capitola Museum** in a little red house (831-464-0322). Rent a kayak for a paddle around the quiet cove (831-462-2208), amble along the river trail, or take a blufftop walk on Grand Avenue at sunset.

DINNER   **Shadowbrook Restaurant,** 1750 Wharf Rd., Capitola; (831) 475-1511; www.shadowbrook-capitola.com. Since 1947, likely the most famous and prettiest restaurant in the area. On the banks of Soquel Creek, Shadowbrook is reached by a self-operated cable car down a flower-bedecked hillside or by a winding pathway. In a warren of cozy dining nooks and rooms, most with garden views: signature dishes such as artichoke soup, Dungeness crab-stuffed portobello mushrooms, grilled salmon, slow-roasted prime rib, and lots of fresh seafood; five-course tasting menu, kids' menu, nice bar. Ask about Winemaker Wednesday; Sunday brunch, too.

LODGING **Inn at Depot Hill,** 250 Monterey Ave., Capitola; (831) 462-3376; www.innatdepothill.com. Twelve rooms and suites with fireplaces, featherbeds, marble bathrooms, private garden patios, hot tubs, European traditional furnishings, and antiques. Award-winning luxury and service. Wonderful breakfasts, afternoon wine and hors d'oeuvres, walking distance to Capitola Beach.

DAY 2 / MORNING

BREAKFAST **Zelda's on the Beach,** #203 on the Esplanade at the beach Capitola; (831) 475-4900; www.zeldasonthebeach.com. Sit by the window or on the deck while the early morning sea turns from rosy to silver-blue as it laps Capitola's scruffy old fishing pier. Home-fry scramble, blackened snapper with eggs. Zelda's is a fun hangout any time of day. Live jazz on the weekends.

Capitola Beach and most public beaches in the area are cleaned nightly; even in summer they start out trash-free and pearly white every day.

The shops and galleries near the beach are touristy but fun. **Capitola Dreams** (118 Stockton Ave.; 831-476-5379) has an eye-popping collection of bikinis and wild beachwear. Painted wood gewgaws and jewelry from Thailand are featured at **Oceania** (204 Capitola Ave.; 831-476-6644). An institution for over a decade, **Avalon Visions** specializes in metaphysical books, gifts, and tchotchkes, from Celtic and Tarot items to drums, dream catchers, crystals, Native American and Tibetan gifts, and astrological keepsakes (208A Monterey; 831-464-7245; www.avalonvisions.com). One of the "Mercantile" shops, **Capitola Seashells** offers a huge selection of seashells, plus nautical decor, souvenirs, and beach-going jewelry (115 San Jose Ave.; 831-465-0171). For a hundred stores in an indoor mall, go up the hill to the **Capitola Mall** on 41st Ave.; 831-476-9749; www.shopcapitolamall.com.

Dead on your feet? Retreat to **Bloomsbury Tea Room,** a quaint, cozy English-style tea room where fresh brews and light meals and snacks are served in a 150-year-old carriage house. The feminine, airy garden setting is as sweet as can be. Legendary scones, lemon curd, artichoke soup, hearty sandwiches and salads (911 Capitola Ave.; 831-462-2498; www.bloomsburytearoom.com). **Margarita-ville** in the Esplanade is a lively locals gathering place for drinks, good Mexican food, and live weekend entertainment (831-476-2263; www.margaritavillecapitola.com). Look for the mermaid over the door, and sit on the heated patio above the bay.

On the south end of town, at **New Brighton Beach** (831-464-6330) there is a nice campground, where cypress and pines provide a sense of privacy between campsites.

The next beach south of New Brighton, **Seacliff State Beach** at **Del Mar** has almost 2 miles of shoreline backed by steep sandstone cliffs. A 500-foot wooden pier and the wreck of a concrete ship are roosting spots for birds, and you can fish off the pier. There is a campground and a small visitor center where you can sign up for walking tours to see the fossilized remains of multimillion-year-old sea creatures lodged in the cliffsides (831-685-6442). The paved path here is popular for strollers, wheelchairs, and in-line skates.

Just south of Capitola at **Aptos, Rio Del Mar Beach** is a wide stretch of sand with a jetty and lifeguards. Shopping and restaurants are within walking distance (831-685-6500).

On the north side of Highway 1, just south of Capitola, the village of Aptos is where you'll find **Village Fair Antiques,** behind the Bay View Hotel on Soquel Road (831-688-9883). This is a big antiques collection in a huge old barn, a place for losing track of time. The next village north, Soquel is a one-horse town with more than 20 antiques shops on Soquel Drive.

LUNCH **Cafe Sparrow,** 8040 Soquel Dr., Aptos; (831) 688-6238; www.cafesparrow.com. Across the street from the Bay View Hotel is this charming dining room serving chicken and fresh fish entrees plus seasonal specialties.

AFTERNOON

A cool, green place to take a walk in the highlands near Santa Cruz is the **Forest of Nisene Marks State Park,** a densely forested 10,000-acre wilderness on Aptos Creek (831-763-7063). Popular with runners, bikers, horseback riders, hikers, and picnickers, the park ranges in elevation from 100 to 2,600 feet. Unpaved roads and trails lead to evergreen woods and creekside willows and ferns. Walk-in camping is permitted, as are horseback riding and steelhead fishing in certain areas.

Near the entrance to the park, **Mangels House** bed-and-breakfast is in a wedding-cake-white, ca. 1880 mansion, with six rooms (831-688-7982).

A beautiful beach that makes a nice stop on the way home from Santa Cruz is **Natural Bridges State Beach,** whose entrance is at 2531 West Cliff Dr. at the intersection of West Cliff Drive and Swanton Boulevard (831-423-4609). Named for dramatic sandstone arches, Natural Bridges has tidepools rich with sea life; guided tidepool tours are often conducted. A short boardwalk from the beach parking lot leads through a eucalyptus forest to the **California Monarch Butterfly Preserve.** Depending on the time of year—early Oct through Feb—you'll see hundreds of thousands of butterflies hanging in the trees and moving about in great golden clouds. A 0.75-mile self-guided nature walk begins at the Monarch Trail and heads for Secret Lagoon, where blue herons, mallard ducks, and more freshwater and seagoing birds live.

Seymour Marine Discovery Center, at Long Marine Lab, a University of Santa Cruz research facility near Natural Bridges, is at 100 Shafer Rd. (831-459-3800). On a bluff with spectacular ocean views, the facility focuses on marine research and shows how scientists study, care for, and explore ocean life. Features include interactive exhibits, aquariums, touch tanks, an 85-foot blue whale skeleton, and more, plus a gift shop and bookstore.

On your way back to San Francisco, dawdle in the Santa Cruz Mountains among ancient redwood groves, on sunny riverbanks, and in quiet little resort towns affording peaceful getaway days. Discover rustic boutique wineries, known for their dark Pinots and German varietals. Take a ride on a rollicking steam train, chugging up into redwood country or all the way down to the beach (more on the mountains follows).

Retrace your route back to San Francisco.

There's More . . . .

Parks. **Big Basin Redwoods State Park,** off CA 236 near Boulder Creek in the Santa Cruz Mountains; (800) 444-7275; www.bigbasin .org. Thousand-year-old redwoods, fern canyons, waterfalls, 80 miles of skyline-to-sea trails. The Sea Trail drops from mountain ridges to Waddell State Beach through dense woodlands, along Waddell and Berry Creeks; 11 miles one-way. Bike, horse rentals; campground; store.

Henry Cowell Redwoods State Park, 101 North Big Trees Park Rd., Felton; (831) 335-4598. There are 1,800 acres of stream canyons, meadows, forests, and chaparral-covered ridges along the meandering San Lorenzo River and Eagle Creek. A lovely shaded picnic grove on the river has barbecues and water. Short, easy trails, such as **Redwood Grove Nature Trail** to the **Big Trees Grove** of first-growth redwoods. The redwood-dotted campground in the park has more than a hundred tent and RV sites, for vehicles up to 24 feet, with no hookups (831-438-2396). Stop in at the visitor center for free Wi-Fi, films and kids' programs. **Quail Hollow Ranch County Park,** near Ben Lomond off Graham Hill Road; take East Zayante Road 1.9 miles; (831) 454-7900. A meadowy historic site where easy trails lead to the original ranch house, a pond inhabited by bass and bluegill, a shady picnic area, and a dwarf redwood forest.

Wilder Ranch State Park, 1401 Coast Rd., 2 miles north of Santa Cruz; (831) 426-0505. A 6,000-acre dairy ranch since the 1800s is now a leafy park. Picnic in the apple orchard; see historic displays in the Victorian home and take a guided walk on week-ends; or hike, horseback ride, or bike on your own on miles of trails. The newly restored early 1900s Meder farmhouse is now open, complete with replica furnishings and supplies. From here you can connect to Gray Whale Ranch, a world of grasslands, oak woodland, and mixed conifer forest threaded with trails and fire roads. Just north of the ranch, Four Mile Beach is reachable by a hike down a bluff—a nice spot to lie on the sand.

Boating. **Chardonnay Sailing Charters,** at the harbor, Santa Cruz; (831) 423-1213; www.chardonnay.com. On a 70-foot luxury yacht, whale-watching, brunch cruises, and sunset sails. New: two-hour, eco-tourism cruises of the Monterey Bay National Marine Sanctu-ary, narrated by biologists. Pacific Yachting, 790 Mariner Park Way, Santa Cruz; (831) 423-7245. Day tours.

Historic Site. **Felton Covered Bridge,** on CA 9 near CA 236. Built in 1892, this is the tallest bridge of its kind in the country and one of the few left in the state.

Special Attraction. **Roaring Camp and Big Trees,** just south of Felton on Graham Hill Road in the Santa Cruz Mountains; (831) 335-4484; www.roaringcamp.com. A re-creation of an 1880s logging town, complete with covered bridge, general store, and a wonderful narrow-gauge steam train that you can ride up through forests of giant redwoods to the summit of Bear Mountain on the steepest railroad grade in North America. A second route runs along the San Lorenzo River down to Santa Cruz Beach. A chuck-wagon barbecue serves charcoal-broiled steak and chicken burgers in a forest glade.

Wineries in the Santa Cruz Mountains. The Winegrowers Association Web site shows a map and description of the dozens of wineries and tasting rooms in the mountains and along the coastline (www.scmwa.com).

Byington Winery and Vineyard is on Bear Creek Road, with dizzying views of Monterey Bay from the picnic grounds (408-354-1111).

David Bruce Winery, Bear Creek Road east of Boulder Creek; (408) 354-4214. A gold-medal maker of Pinot Noir and Chardonnay. Open for tasting on the weekends, by appointment during the week.

Hallcrest Vineyards, 379 Felton-Empire Rd.; (831) 335-4441. Specializing in organic Gewürztraminers, Rieslings, Pinot Noir, and grape juices. From the sunny garden deck behind the old cottage, look out over old vines.

Bonny Doon Vineyard, 321 Ingalls St., Santa Cruz; (831) 425-4518; www.bonnydoonvineyard.com. World-famous for biodynamically produced fine wines. In-town tasting room includes the charming Cellar Door Café, which features small plates paired with wines, noon until 9 p.m.; some communal tables for dinners.

Menus focus on local, organic produce and fresh fish. The unique cafe is modeled on the form of a chambered nautilus, constructed of recycled wine barrels and tanks.

Special Events . . . .

MARCH

Jazz on the Wharf, Municipal Wharf, Santa Cruz; (831) 420-5273; www.santacruzwharf.com.

Kayak Surf Festival, Steamer Lane, Santa Cruz; (831) 458-3648; www.asudoit.com. Hundreds of kayak surfers from all over the world compete at the national championships; free kayak clinics.

MAY

Art and Wine Festival, Boulder Creek; (831) 338-7099.

Civil War Battles and Encampment, Roaring Camp; (831) 335-4484. The largest encampment in the United States.

Longboard Invitational, Steamers Lane, Santa Cruz; (831) 684-1551. Hundreds of surfers compete. Watch from Cliff Drive.

JUNE

Woodies on the Wharf, Santa Cruz Municipal Wharf; (831) 420-5273. Two hundred pre-1950s "woodies" line the wharf. Live music, memorabilia and prize drawings, too.

JULY

Art on the Wharf, Santa Cruz Municipal Wharf; (831) 420-5273. Dozens of artists display original paintings, photography and other works outdoors, with live jazz and kids' activities.

AUGUST

Cabrillo Festival of Contemporary Music, concerts held throughout the area; (831) 426-6966; www.cabrillomusic.org. An internationally acclaimed two-week musical extravaganza.

SEPTEMBER

Capitola Begonia Festival, Capitola; (831-476-3566; www.begonia festival.com). Residents vie for awards for their spectacular waterborne floats that are maneuvered perilously down Soquel Creek into town; you've never seen a watery parade like this one.

DECEMBER

Lighted Boat Parade, Santa Cruz Yacht Harbor; (831) 457-6161.

Other Recommended Restaurants and Lodgings . . . .

APTOS

Seascape Beach Resort Monterey Bay, 1 Seascape Resort Dr. off San Andreas, 10 miles south of Santa Cruz; (800) 929-7727; www.seascaperesort.com. On a bluff overlooking miles of beach, upscale, comfortable studios, suites, and condos for up to eight people, with balconies or patios, sofa sleepers, fully equipped kitchens, fireplaces, ocean views. This is a full-service resort with a nice sea-view restaurant, supervised activities for kids, golf packages, and extras like in-suite massage and "Beach Fires to Go"—you are driven down to the beach, where a fire is built for you, "s'mores" are provided, and you are picked up later, after a romantic evening on the beach. The resort offers access to an adjacent golf course and sports club with lighted tennis courts, an Olympic-size pool, and fitness center.

CAPITOLA
Gayle's Bakery and Rosticceria, 504 Bay Ave., on the corner of Bay and Capitola Avenues; (831) 462-1127. Homemade pasta, salad, pizza, sandwiches, spit-roasted meats. The bakery is famous for pies, cheesecake, breads, and pastries.

Monarch Cove Inn, 620 El Salto Dr.; (831) 464-1295. In a luxurious garden overlooking Monterey Bay, beautifully furnished Victorian guest rooms, cottages, and apartments. Continental breakfast.

Paradise Beach Grille, 215 Esplanade; (831) 476-4900. A casual cafe with a jukebox and charcoal grill. The menu, printed every day, includes a huge variety of fresh seafood.

SANTA CRUZ
Beach Street Cafe, corner of Beach and Cliff Streets across from the boardwalk; (831) 426-7621; www.beachstreetcafe.com. The walls are covered with prints by Maxfield Parrish, a famous pre-Art Deco artist. Bistro food, espresso.

Casablanca, 101 Main St.; (831) 426-9063; www.casablanca-santacruz.com. Overlooking beach and boardwalk, elegant, candlelit, fresh seafood, notable wine list, wine-tasting dinners. Some of the very nice 33 ocean-view rooms here have fireplaces, kitchens, balconies, or terraces.

Dream Inn, 175 West Cliff Dr.; (866) 774-7735; www.dreaminnsanta cruz.com. Newly owned and operated by the great boutique hotel chain, Joie de Vivre, 165 beachfront rooms and suites, all with ocean views and private balconies or patios; adjacent to the Beach Boardwalk. Fresh, retro-chic-style decor, beachfront pool deck, pool bar and beach access. Sea views and fresh seafood from the on-site Aquarius restaurant, which features American cuisine made with local, organic and sustainable products (http://aquariussantacruz.com).

Pacific Blue Inn, 636 Pacific Ave. downtown; (831) 600-8880; www.pacificblueinn.com. A striking new, bright blue and white, nine-room boutique hotel that is one of the most eco-conscious around. Quiet courtyard, free bike use, complimentary breakfast; simple, bright, sleek king rooms.

Soif, 105 Walnut Ave.; (831) 423-2020, www.soifwine.com. A trendy new wine and tapas bar and wine merchant, with wine flights each evening and 50 wines by the glass. Small plates of sophisticated, contemporary, and traditional Spanish-, Italian-, and Asian-inspired appetizers for snacks or light meals. Special weekend tastings and live music. Open late on weekends.

Villa Vista, 2-2800 East Cliff Dr.; (408) 866-2626; www.villavista .com. Two perfectly wonderful condo units with living rooms, each with three master bedrooms with baths, gourmet kitchen, sea-view patio, home entertainment center, and laundry facilities. Great for several couples or a large family.

West Cliff Inn, 174 West Cliff Dr., Santa Cruz 95060; (831) 457-2200 or (800) 979-0910; www.westcliffinn.com. On a bluff above Monterey Bay, a ca. 1877 mansion is now one of the 12 lovely Three Sisters inns. The stately, three-story Italianate Victorian is outfitted in fresh blues and whites; 10 rooms have fireplaces, Wi-Fi and iPod players, ocean views; some have private decks, hot tubs. Gourmet breakfast and afternoon wine and hors d'oeuvres.

Zachary's, 849 Pacific Ave.; (831) 427-0646. Voted "Best Breakfast in Santa Cruz"; sourdough pancakes, scones, corn bread, and more. Breakfast, lunch, brunch.

For More Information . . . .

Santa Cruz Mountains Winegrowers, 7605 Old Dominion Ct., Suite A, Santa Cruz 95063; (831) 685-VINE; www.scmwa.com. Free brochure and map locating many wineries. Ask about the special advantages of the Passport Program.

Santa Cruz Visitor Information Center, 3 blocks from Highways 1 and 17; 1211 Ocean St., Santa Cruz 95060; (831) 425-1234 or (800) 833-3494; www.santacruzca.org. Get a Bicycle Adventure Kit, a free Traveler's Guide and a free Birding and Wildlife Watching Kit with maps of birding and wildlife spots and itineraries. Visitors can now book Santa Cruz County hotels, travel packages and rental cars online or by calling (877) 220-8155; www.santacruzcounty. travel.

Capitola Chamber of Commerce, 716-G Capitola Ave., Capitola 95010; (831) 475-6522.

SOUTHBOUND ESCAPE *Two*

Half Moon Bay

HARBOR LIGHTS, TIDEPOOL TREASURE / 2 NIGHTS

The small Victorian town of Half Moon Bay and the beaches and harbors nearby hold several days' worth of discoveries. Accessibility to the San Francisco Bay Area, good weather, sea air, and the out-

> Beaches, bikes, hikes, fishing
> Wellness retreat
> Art and antiques
> Flower marts, veggie farms

door fun to be had here are what create bumper-to-bumper traffic at times on summer weekends. Weekdays and off-season are the times to come, although you can get pleasantly lost and alone in the redwoods or on the beach any day of the year.

Besides commercial ocean fishing, the important endeavor in Half Moon Bay is flower and vegetable growing. The annual Pumpkin and Art Festival and Great Pumpkin Parade in Oct draw hundreds of thousands of revelers and their children.

Within huge greenhouses and in the fields around them, flowers are grown for shipment all over the world, and you can buy plants and flowers—and Christmas trees—at several places along the highways. May through Dec on Saturdays, the Coastside Market brings it all together with three dozen vendors of locally grown vegetables, fruits, flowers, gourmet cheeses, herbs, honey, breads, and pies, accompanied by live music and arts and crafts displays (Kelly Avenue and Cabrillo Highway; www.coastsidefarmersmarket.org).

A stroll through the town of Half Moon Bay turns up Western saloons, country stores, fancy boutiques, galleries, and hundred-year-old hotels and homes, many on the National Register of Historic Places.

On the north end of town in Princeton near Pillar Point Harbor is a new atrium mall of about two dozen shops and cafes, many

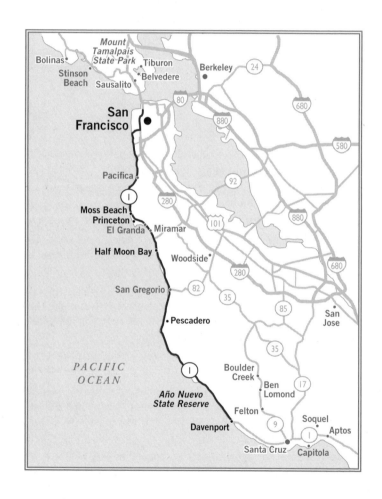

locally owned, anchored by the luxurious Ocean Hotel. The harbor is a good place to escape the tourist mania. You can watch fishing boats and yachts go in and out of the marina, fish for flounder and rockfish from the wharf, or go shelling on the little beach west of the jetty. South along the coast, within an hour of Half Moon Bay, beaches, nature preserves, and two tiny old villages await the visitor.

DAY 1 / MORNING

Drive south from San Francisco on Highway 1, along the Pacific Coast through Pacifica to **Moss Beach,** an hour's drive. This estimated time does not account for heavy weekend and holiday traffic.

The **Fitzgerald Marine Reserve in Moss Beach** (650-728-3584; www.fitzgeraldreserve.org) is a good place to stretch your legs. A walking trail loops through meadows and along a bluff above some of the richest tidepools on the Pacific Coast. At low tide, a kaleidoscope of sponges, sea anemones, starfish, crabs, mollusks, and fish emerges. With a special fishing license, you can take abalone and some rockfish. For the best tidepooling, call ahead to find out when the low tides are scheduled.

The best place to stay in Moss Beach is the **Seal Cove Inn,** a big yellow mansion in an English garden on the edge of the Marine Reserve (650-728-4114; www.sealcoveinn.com). The inn is a classic, with spacious, luxurious public rooms and guest rooms, all with garden views, wood-burning fireplaces, and traditional furnishings.

Drive south to **Pillar Point Harbor** at Princeton-by-the-Sea, a picturesque harbor busy with a fleet of more than 200 fishing boats and yachts. Here you can walk on trails to beaches and marshlands on both the north and south sides of the harbor. Pillar Point Marsh is a favorite bird-watching site; nearly 20 percent of all North American bird species have been sighted here.

From Dec through Apr, whale-watching boats depart from the wharf. You are almost guaranteed to see California gray whales on their 4,000-mile migration from the Arctic to Baja. **Riptide Sportfishing and Whale Watching** (888-747-8433; www.riptide.net), **Captain John's** (650-728-3377), and **Huck Finn Sportfishing** (650-726-7133) are charter companies based at the harbor that offer regular whale-watching and fishing expeditions.

Just south of the harbor, Surfer's Beach is popular not only for surfing but for ocean kayaking, boogie boarding, sailboarding, and Jet Skiing. Surfers from around the world compete annually at "Mavericks" off Pillar Point, where massive waves breaking over a rocky reef up the ante; some say these are the biggest waves in the world. For the daily surf report, call or stop in at the **Cowboy Surf Shop** (2830 Cabrillo Hwy.; 650-726-0654; www.cowboysurfshop.com). A new shop, the **Surf Factory,** has opened in the new Harbor Village center, selling trendy clothes, shoes, sunglasses, and all things surfing (650-726-1476; www.hmbboardshop.com).

Two fish markets at the harbor sell a huge variety of fresh and locally caught seafood. There are several small cafes and bars frequented by locals who wouldn't be caught dead in the trendy downtown establishments of nearby Half Moon Bay.

LUNCH   **Half Moon Bay Brewing Company,** 390 Capistrano Rd., Princeton By-the-Sea; (650) 728-2739, www.hmbbrewingco.com. Weekenders and locals congregate under the outdoor heaters around the fire pits and at the horseshoe bar inside to sip Mavericks Amber Ale and nutty Pillar Point Pale Ale, which are brewed onsite (call ahead for a brewery tour). Live jazz and blues bands kick off lively Fri and Sat evenings. Top-notch fish-and-chips, chowders, an extensive seafood menu, and hearty pub food.

AFTERNOON

Save at least a half day for browsing Main Street in Half Moon Bay, a few blocks of buildings built early in the 20th century that are now inhabited by upscale, country-chic shops, cafes, and galleries. Armed with a walking tour map (available at the Visitor Bureau kiosk at Main and Kelly), history buffs look for the oldest house in town—a plain and sturdy, blue and white bed-and-breakfast inn at 324 Main St. The Zaballa House was built in 1859 by Estanislao Zaballa, prosperous owner of a large Spanish land grant, a general store, and a saloon. Around the corner at 615 Mill St. in an expanded 1900-era cottage, claw-foot tubs, featherbeds, and Victorian-era antiques are among the fancy trappings of the Mill Rose Inn. Another turn-of-the-20th-century landmark, the San Benito House at 356 Main St. is an antiques-filled restaurant and inn where a collection of early coastside paintings and photographs lines the walls.

At 604 Main St., in a terra-cotta-colored enclave called **La Piazza,** are several shops and a popular bakery that serves coffee drinks and pastries in a streetside cafe (**Moonside Bakery;** 650-726-9070; www.moonsidebakery.com).

Quail Run (412 Main; 650-726-0312) is a nature-oriented emporium with elaborate bird mansions for the feathered few and butterfly gardens for kids. On display at **Galleria Luna** are spectacular art glass, wearable art, and the works of American and International artists such as master impressionists Jean Henry and Royo, abstract artist R. Cook, Hessam Abrishanni and Goli Mahalatti (300 Main St., 650-726-8932, www.gallerialuna.com).

Gallery M is said to be the west coast's premier woodworking gallery, with furniture, lamps, clocks, gifts, and accessories from more than 100 woodworkers (328 Main St.; 650-726-7167; www.gallerym.net). A marine and wildlife shop, the **Harbor Seal Company,** sells unusual sea- and bird-life toys, puzzles, soft animals, educational toys, books, and games (406 Main St.; 650-726-7418; http://harborsealcompany.com).

One of the oldest established businesses in town, **Cunha's** (448 Main St.; 650-726-4071) is a grocery with a large deli, its own line of homemade packaged gourmet foods, and upstairs are Western boots, hats, souvenirs, hardware, and T-shirts. On the corner across from Cunha's, the city has set up a nice picnic table area.

At the north end of Main, **The Tinnery** is another indoor mall crammed with small shops and cafes, including a sushi bar, a coffee cafe, a card shop, and a gallery.

DINNER **Cetrella,** 845 Main St., Half Moon Bay; (650) 726-4090; www.cetrella.com. In a warm bistro setting with fireplaces, rustic Mediterranean cuisine, seafood, tapas; meats and poultry roasted in a wood-burning oven; cheese cave, exhibition kitchen; live music in the cozy bar.

LODGING **Beach House Inn,** 4100 North Cabrillo Hwy., Half Moon Bay; (650) 712-0220; www.beach-house.com. Above a small beach, spacious, commodious suites with sea views from private balconies or patios, kitchenettes, sofabeds, fireplaces, soaking tubs, luxurious bath amenities, and cozy flannel robes; new spa venue for couples. Heated lap pool, lavish continental breakfast, evening wine and cheese.

DAY 2 / MORNING

BREAKFAST **Main Street Grill,** 435 Main at Kelly, Half Moon Bay; (650) 726-5300. Cajun sausage, artichoke omelets, and homemade waffles and muffins. Also good for lunch: grilled sandwiches, thick milk shakes, microbrewed beers, and a jukebox.

South from Half Moon Bay along Highway 1 are a string of beaches, wildlife preserves, and two tiny historic towns. It's 15 miles to the

Pescadero State Beach, one of the prettiest, duniest, tidepooliest places you could spend an afternoon (650-726-6238). On the inland side of Highway 1, **Pescadero Marsh** is 588 acres of uplands and wetlands, an important stop on the Pacific Flyway. More than 200 species of waterfowl and shorebirds make this a must-see for avid birders. Great blue herons nest in the blue gum eucalyptus trees, egrets walk stiffly in the shallow waters, northern harriers glide above, and marsh wrens follow you around.

It's 2 miles from Highway 1 on Pescadero Road to **Pescadero,** a block or so of clapboard buildings and steepled churches, ca. 1850. Peek into the few antiques boutiques and stop at **Arcangeli Grocery/Norm's Market,** where the irresistible aroma of warm artichoke and garlic/cheese bread wafts out the door; some of the 24 kinds of bread are "halfbaked"—for you to take home, stow in the freezer, and bake later (650-879-0147; www.normsmarket.com).

A half mile beyond the town on Pescadero Creek Road, park under the giant oak and get out your camera at **Phipps Ranch** (650-879-0787), a combination produce market, farm, plant nursery, and menagerie of exotic birds and farm animals. There are fancy chickens, big fat pigs, a variety of bunnies, and antique farm equipment. You can pick your own berries or buy them at the produce stand.

A real sleeper of a park and campground, **Butano State Park** off Pescadero Road is a lush piece of the earth, with magnificent redwood groves freshened by creeks and fern glades (2 miles past Pescadero, turn right onto Cloverdale Road; travel 5 miles to park entrance; 800-444-7275). From small, pretty campsites, you can walk streamside paths or take a challenging mountain hike on an 11-mile loop to the **Año Nuevo Island** lookout.

Back on the highway, proceed south; it's 22 miles to **Davenport,** where you'll have lunch. On the way is the ca. 1870, 10-story-tall **Pigeon Point Lighthouse,** open for tours on weekends

(650-879-2120). The hostel here offers inexpensive private and shared rooms and marvelous views (www.norcalhostels.org). Just north of the lighthouse are beautiful beaches, tidepools, and wildflower meadows.

Proceed to the village of Davenport for lunch (36 miles south of Half Moon Bay).

LUNCH   **Davenport Roadhouse at the Cash Store,** on Highway 1, Davenport (831-426-8801; www.davenportroadhouse.com). Tuck into truffle fries, duck confit, spring rolls, crab cakes, pulled pork, wood-grilled salmon, and big sandwiches and salads (breakfast, lunch, dinner, and happy hour specials, take-out items, bakery, and a full bar; can be crowded on weekends). In the store are artisan-made jewelry, soaps, honey, food products, books, postcards, wearable art, and guidebooks. Upstairs is a casually comfy bed-and-breakfast. Across Highway 1 from the restaurant are a short walking path on the bluffs and a nice beach.

AFTERNOON

Returning north 9 miles, stop at **Año Nuevo State Reserve,** which may turn out to be the highlight of your trip on the central coast (650-879-0227 or 800-444-4445; www.anonuevo.org). On 1,200 acres of dunes and beaches, the largest group of elephant seals in the world come to breed from Dec through Apr. A 0.5-mile walk through grassy dunes brings you to an unforgettable sight: dozens of two-ton animals lounging, arguing, maybe mating, cavorting in the sea, and wiggling around on the beach. As many as 2,500 seals spend their honeymoons here, and there's lots of other wildlife to see, too. During the mating season it is necessary to reserve spaces in guided interpretive tours (800-444-7275). At other times you can wander around on your own but are not allowed to come too close to the animals. No pets.

DINNER **Duarte's Tavern,** 202 Stage Rd., Pescadero; (650) 879-0464. Crowded on sunny weekends but worth the wait, Duarte's has for more than 50 years been a family restaurant serving cioppino, seafood specialties with a Portuguese accent, artichoke soup and fresh artichokes with garlic aioli, deep-fried calamari, cracked crab, abalone sandwiches, shrimp cakes, and olallieberry pie. Local ranchers belly up to the Old West-style bar. Daily breakfast, lunch, and dinner.

LODGING Beach House Inn.

DAY 3 / MORNING

BREAKFAST **Half Moon Bay Coffee Company,** 20A Stone Pine Rd. at the north end of Main Street, Half Moon Bay; (650) 726-3664. A casual place busy with locals and tourists digging into homemade pies and pastries, pancakes, burgers, sandwiches, and simple, hearty entrees. Breakfast, lunch, and dinner.

Buy a kite at **Lunar Wind Inventions** in town, and head for 3 miles of sand at **Half Moon Bay State Beach** just south of town; to get there, go west on Kelly Avenue (650-726-8820). At Francis Beach, the most popular of the three beaches here, are developed RV and tent campsites, cold showers, barbecues, picnic sites, and the ranger station. (If the campground is full, try the nice Pelican Point RV Park on Miramontes Point Road; 650-726-9100.) Water temperature is chilly, even in summer, and the surf can be treacherous, so plan to dip your toes and play on the sand.

Before you leave town, drive 3 miles east on CA 92 and keep a sharp eye out for the right turn into Half Moon Bay Nursery (11691 San Mateo Rd.; 650-726-5392). This is a rambling, gorgeous kingdom of blooming garden and house plants, from orchids and ferns to thousands of geraniums, herbs, azaleas, camellias, climbing vines, hanging baskets, and seasonal bulbs—a veritable flower show. In wintertime, it's cozy in the main greenhouse by the woodstove.

LUNCH On your way back to San Francisco on Highway 1, have lunch at the **Moss Beach Distillery** (Beach and Ocean, Moss Beach; 650-728-5595), said to be haunted by the Blue Lady, who wanders the nearby cliffs where she died mysteriously in the 1930s. On a spectacular hilltop overlooking a cove, with an outdoor patio and indoor dining room and bar with sea views, Moss Beach Distillery serves luscious fresh local seafood for lunch, dinner, and weekend brunch. Best place for a cocktail: in a double rocker, covered with the provided blankets, above the crashing waves of Seal Cove.

There's More . . . .

Entertainment. **Bach Dancing and Dynamite Society,** P.O. Box 302, El Granada 94018, at Miramar Beach, 2.5 miles north of Half Moon Bay; (650) 726-4143; www.bachddsoc.org. Sunday big-name jazz and classical concerts with catered lunches and dinners; purchase tickets in advance.

Hiking. **Bean Hollow Trail,** 18 miles south of Half Moon Bay on Highway 1 (park at Pebble Beach or Bean Hollow State Beach); (650) 879-0832. A 2-mile bluff trail crossing six bridges. You'll see the legendary gemlike pebbles at Pebble Beach (it's forbidden to gather them), harbor seals on the offshore rocks, unique limestone formations, and sheets of blooming seaside plants such as lupines and primroses. Restrooms.

Burleigh Murray State Park, Mills Creek Ranch Road off Higgins Purissima Road, a mile south of Half Moon Bay; (650) 726-8820. Century-old dairy barn, said to be the only one of its kind remaining in the state. Past the barn, a pretty creekside trail ambles for about a mile.

Coastside Trail. Running along the bluffs, from Mirada Road in Miramar and to Kelly Avenue on the south end of town (parking here), the flat, easy Coastside Trail promises walkers and bikers more than 3 miles of sea views, bird-watching, and beaches.

Purissima Creek Redwoods, Higgins Purissima Road, a mile south of Half Moon Bay; (650) 691-1200. On the western slope of the Santa Cruz Mountains, a redwood preserve with hiking, biking, and equestrian trails, some wheelchair-accessible trails. Wildflowers, ferny creeks, giant redwoods, maples, and alders.

Rentals. **Bicyclery,** 432 Main St., Half Moon Bay; (650) 726-6000. Rentals, accessories, service.

Half Moon Bay Kayaking Company, Two Johnson Pier, Pillar Point Harbor; (650) 773-6101; www.hmbkayak.com. Rent single, double, or triple kayaks to cruise the harbor, the coastline and beyond among harbor seals, seabirds, and other marine sanctuary wildlife, either on your own or on a guided trip; nearly anyone can do it, even with kids aboard; instruction provided.

Golf. **Half Moon Bay Golf Links,** 2000 Fairway Dr. off Highway 1, Half Moon Bay; (650) 726-4438. Stunning ocean views from every hole, steady breezes, tight fairways, and few trees call for the irons on the Arthur Hills-designed Ocean Course, which *Golf Magazine* called "a rip-roaring experience." Mere mortals head for Arnold Palmer's Old Course, a lovely parkland layout with a few ocean holes. The clubhouse, including the casual restaurant, has been expanded and remodeled.

Coastal Attraction. **Point Montara Lighthouse,** Highway 1 at Sixteenth Street, Montara; (650) 728-7177. A short, chunky lighthouse on a high bluff, the 1875 Point Montara Fog Signal and Light Station is open to the public.

Horseback Riding. **Sea Horse and Friendly Acres Horse Ranches,** Highway 1 at Half Moon Bay; (650) 726-2362; www.horserentals .com/seahorse.html. Ride on your own or guided rides on the beach and trails; hayrides; picnic area. Beginners and first-timers are welcome.

Special Events . . . .

JANUARY

Mavericks Surf Contest, an annual surfing competition on wintertime's monumental waves, some 50 feet tall or more; www.mavericks surf.com. Surfers come from around the world, and thousands gather to watch from the shoreline at Pillar Point Harbor. The event is scheduled on a 24-hour alert, according to when the waves are expected to be highest, and it may be anytime from Dec through Mar. Register online for the alert, so you can either enjoy the show, or avoid the crowds.

APRIL

Pacific Coast Dream Machines Show, Half Moon Bay Airport; www.miramarevents.com. Two thousand driving, flying, and working machines from the 20th and 21st centuries. Cool cars, fire engines, motorcycles, trucks, antique engines and tractors, an airship, competitions, and displays and performances of historic military aircraft.

JUNE

Vintner's Festival, at more than 50 wineries on both sides of the Santa Cruz Mountains and on the coast, first two weekends in the month. New releases, barrel tastings, food, live music, chef demos, art displays, and more (831-685-8463; www.scmwa.com).

JULY
Tour des Fleurs. Guided tours of many nurseries and greenhouses, wineries, and farms that are not ordinarily open to the public; (650) 726-8380; www.halfmoonbaychamber.org.

AUGUST
Pescadero Arts and Fun Festival, Pescadero. Old-fashioned country fair, local artists, live entertainment, local food and wine, kids area; free admission; www.pescaderoartsandfunfestival.com.

OCTOBER
Pumpkin and Art Festival, Half Moon Bay; (650) 726-9652; www .miramarevents.com. Great Pumpkin Parade, live entertainment, pumpkin carving, pie-eating, biggest pumpkin contest, a haunted house, and more than 250 vendors. Meet locals at the pancake breakfast and the Halloween costume competition. Come early to avoid the huge crowds.

DECEMBER
Harbor Lighting Ceremony, Pillar Point Harbor; (650) 726-5202. Boat owners compete with lighted and decorated boats.

Other Recommended Restaurants and Lodgings. . . .

HALF MOON BAY
Best Western Half Moon Bay Lodge, 2400 South Cabrillo Hwy./ Highway 1; (800) 710-0778; www.halfmoonbaylodge.com. Spacious rooms with small patios or balconies overlooking gardens; some fireplaces. Large swimming pool, sheltered outdoor Jacuzzi.

Cafe Gibraltar, 425 Avenue Alhambra, 5 miles north of town; (650) 560-9039. Highest Zagat rating for any restaurant on the San

Mateo coast and an award-winning wine list. Authentic Mediterranean cuisine with an ocean view; fresh seafood and wood-oven
roasted local organic lamb, poultry; mezza platters, slow-braised
baby back ribs, sea bass baked in a clay pot. Try to get one of the
comfy, romantic, pillow-lined booths.

Cameron's Restaurant and Inn, 1410 South Cabrillo Hwy.; (415)
726-5705; www.cameronsinn.com. Just south of town, European
brews on tap, darts and games, pub food and pizza; double-decker
bus/smoking lounge; kids' game room, volleyball, and a warm welcome make this a popular English pub. Simple hotel rooms upstairs.
Look for the red phone booth!

Oceano Hotel and Spa, 280 Capistrano Rd., Half Moon Bay; (888)
623-2661; www.oceanohalfmoonbay.com. A new upscale hotel
in a shopping mall on the harbor has spacious king and double
rooms, and extended-stay villas with loft bedrooms, kitchens, fireplaces and living/dining areas. Luxurious throughout, right on the
water, with fitness venue, day spa, restaurant and bar, in-room
dining.

Old Thyme Inn, 779 Main St.; (650) 726-1616; www.oldthymeinn
.com. A Queen Anne Victorian in an English garden on the quiet end
of Main. Four-posters, fireplaces, whirlpool tubs, full breakfast.

The Ritz-Carlton, Half Moon Bay, 1 Miramontes Point Rd.; (650)
712-7000 or (800) 241-3333; www.ritzcarlton.com. A grand, 19th-
century style, 261-room, ultra-luxurious, recently renovated seaside
lodge on a scenic bluff with two top-rated golf courses, romantic
restaurants, tennis and indoor swimming pool. Most guest rooms
have panoramic views; some have fireplaces, window seats, and
balconies; separate deluxe guest cottages. Fifth-floor guests enjoy

a private, seaview lounge with concierge and all-day and evening food and beverage service. Newly renovated full-service spa and spa suites, Roman bath, sauna, steam; new menu of pumpkin- and lavender-infused treatments, and "Ocean Mist Stones Massage." In the lobby, the paneled library, and the conservatory, there are dazzling views and museum-quality artwork, tapestries, and antiques. Take tea in the Tea Salon, complete with finger sandwiches, petits fours, and scones. Mediterranean dishes and fresh seafood at semi formal Navio restaurant; ENO wine bar.

Sam's Chowder House, 4210 North Cabrillo Hwy.; (650) 712-0245; www.samschowderhouse.com. By the harbor overlooking the sea, every seat has a view. Fresh fabulous New England-style seafood, lobster rolls, linguini and clams, seafood spaghetti and risotto, cioppino, Dungeness crab; live music on weekends.

San Benito House, 356 Main St.; (650) 726-3425; www.sanbenito house.com. English garden, inexpensive bed-and-breakfast rooms with antiques and brass beds. Incorporating Sofia's Premier Steakhouse and the San Benito Deli.

MIRAMAR

Cypress Inn, 407 Mirada Rd.; (650) 726-6002; www.cypressinn .com. On 5 miles of beach, eight contemporary-design, luxury rooms and suites; sumptuous breakfasts and afternoon wine. Fireplaces, private decks, sea views, skylights, in-house massage therapist!

Miramar Beach Restaurant, 131 Mirada Rd., 2.5 miles north of Half Moon Bay; (650) 726-9053; http://miramarbeach.com. Lunch, dinner, and weekend brunch across the street from Miramar Beach, fresh seafood specialties, lively bar crowd, occasional live music.

PESCADERO

Costanoa Lodge and Camp, 2001 Rossi Rd., Pescadero; (650) 879-1100; www.costanoa.com. Surrounded by beautiful park-lands, upscale camping in luxury tents, cabins, and lodge rooms, plus RV and tent sites. Light breakfast, spa and sauna, bikes to rent, well-stocked general store with gourmet and deli foods to take out or eat at picnic tables. You can hike into pristine wilderness right from the camp.

For More Information . . . .

Half Moon Bay Coastside Chamber of Commerce, 520 Kelly Ave., Half Moon Bay 94019; (650) 726-8380; www.halfmoonbaycham ber.org.

SOUTHBOUND ESCAPE *Three*
Monterey and Big Sur
SPANISH HISTORY, WILD COASTLINE / 3 NIGHTS

In the late 1700s Spanish explorers arrived in force on the Monterey Peninsula, making it headquarters for their huge Baja and Alta California domains, and Father Junípero Serra built one of his largest and most beautiful missions. Then Mexico took a turn as occupier of Monterey for more than 20 years.

Museums, mansions, mountains
Beachcombing
A golfer's dream
Shopping, biking, hiking
Chowder and cioppino

This rich Hispanic heritage remains in the thick-walled adobes and Spanish colonial haciendas of Monterey. Beneath the gnarled old olive trees, in courtyard gardens planted by the early conquistadors, and beside spectacular Monterey Bay are the upscale shops, world-class restaurants, and museums that draw visitors today. Add more than 20 championship golf courses, and more than a weekend is called for on the Monterey Peninsula.

In stark contrast to the historic neighborhoods and sophisticated atmosphere of present-day Monterey, Big Sur is a sparsely developed stretch of wilderness running 90 miles south to San Simeon, a series of cliffs and river valleys hemmed in by a high mountain range on one side and a largely inaccessible seacoast. A longtime resident of Big Sur, author Henry Miller, said of the area, "It is a region where extremes meet, a region where one is always conscious of weather, of space, of grandeur, and of eloquent silence."

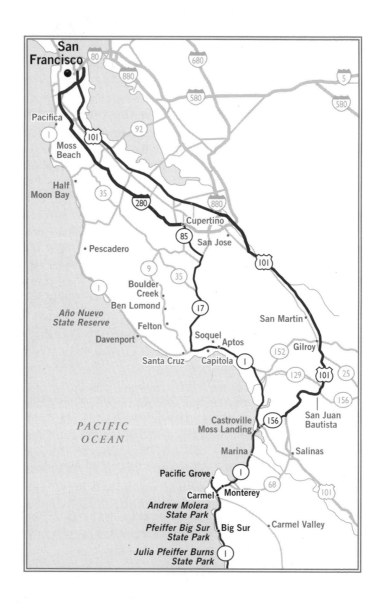

DAY 1 / MORNING

Drive south from San Francisco on I–280, taking CA 85 south to CA 17 south to Monterey, about a two-hour drive. Take the Monterey exit; head west and turn onto Del Monte Boulevard. Pick up a walking tour map at the **Monterey County Visitor Center** (765 Wave St., Monterey; 800-555-6290; www.seemonterey.org) and spend a couple of hours strolling in and out of the historic buildings and garden courtyards on the Monterey State Historic Park **"Path of History,"** a 2-mile walk that includes the grassy knolls of **Colton Hall,** at Pacific and Jefferson, a museum in an old school. Notice the small plastered-adobe homes in back of Colton Hall, some of the first built in California. Admission to most buildings is free; guided tours cost a few dollars per person (831-649-7118).

Part of the park complex, **Cooper Store,** on Polk Street, sells antique toys, postcards, and souvenirs. Go through the store to the museums and gardens behind; a spectacular cypress towers overhead. In the heart of the Historic District is the **Monterey Peninsula Museum of Art,** with a fine collection of Western and Asian art and photography (559 Pacific St.; 831-372-5477; www.monterey art.org).

The **Maritime Museum of Monterey** at the waterfront focuses on the Monterey Peninsula's long seagoing history (5 Custom House Plaza; 831-375-2553; www.montereyhistory.org). Priceless marine artifacts include the 16-foot-tall, 10,000-pound lens that once operated atop the Point Sur Lighthouse. When you are ready to get off your feet for 20 minutes, take in the historical film here—it's free.

LUNCH   **Abalonetti's Seafood Trattoria,** 57 Old Fisherman's Wharf, Monterey; (831) 373-1851. Sit indoors or on the wharf; calamari, Italian antipasto, pizza, seafood pasta; for 40 years one of the best fish cafes on the wharf.

AFTERNOON

....

Old Fisherman's Wharf (831-649-6544; www.montereywharf.com) still smells of salt spray and caramel corn. Fishing boats bob in the harbor, seagulls squawk and wheel overhead, and sea breezes blow between slightly seedy boardwalk cafes and tourist shops.

Walk along the waterfront **Monterey Bay Coastal Trail** that runs from the wharf all the way along Cannery Row and around Pacific Grove, a distance of 5 miles, if you care to walk that far—or bike that far (rent a bike or a pedaling vehicle that seats four). On the way, pelicans, barking sea lions, and sea otters vie for your attention. Along the trail are drinking fountains, benches, picnic sites, and bike racks. The trail runs north along the shoreline for a total of 29 miles, from Pebble Beach to Castroville (www.mprpd.org).

DINNER **Fishwife Seafood Restaurant,** 1996½ Sunset Dr., Pacific Grove; (831) 375-7150; www.fishwife.com. Casual, popular, reasonably priced cafe at Asilomar Beach with sunset views. Wide variety of fresh fish, Cajun blackened snapper, salmon Alfredo, Key lime pie; reservations a must. Lunch, dinner, Sunday brunch.

LODGING **Monterey Bay Inn,** 242 Cannery Row, Monterey; (800) 424-6242; www.montereybayinn.com. Unassuming on the outside, a very nice four-diamond inn in an unbeatable location at the south end of Cannery Row, with bay or harbor views and the sound of the surf from 47 guest rooms. Big glass doors lead to private balconies, where binoculars are provided for viewing sea life and boating activity. King featherbeds and plush linens; armchair sitting areas, not one but two coffeepots, high-tech amenities; rooftop, bay-view hot tub; complimentary continental breakfast. Nice, big bathrooms with double sinks and long tubs. Ask about aquarium, dinner, massage, and other packages. It's a short walk to the aquarium, walking trails, and most sights of Monterey; steps from the beach, a popular "put-in" location for scuba divers. The inn has dive lockers, showers, and a sauna on the ground floor; the Monterey Bay Dive Center is across the street.

DAY 2 / MORNING

BREAKFAST	Monterey Bay Inn.

A blockbuster attraction on the Central Coast is the **Monterey Bay Aquarium,** one of the largest—and some say the best—aquariums in the world. For more than 20 years in a spectacular location on Cannery Row at the edge of Monterey Bay, the aquarium is worth a day and some planning (886 Cannery Row; 831-648-4800; www .montereybayaquarium.org). In an architectural masterpiece, some 700 species of sea creatures, and 250,000 animals and plants reside here in giant tanks. The three-story Kelp Forest is the world's tallest aquarium exhibit, so huge that it feels as if you're swimming around in there with the sharks and the schools of silvery fish. The Monterey Bay exhibit is 90 feet long, full of fascinating reef life. Playful sea otters and bat rays have their own watery homes, and it's fun to watch them during feeding time. There are frequent live videos from a research submarine prowling Monterey Bay, as deep as 3,000 feet.

A new attraction is The Secret Lives of Seahorses in four multimedia galleries, one of the nation's largest collections of these mysterious animals. Recently completed was a $4 million transformation of the popular Splash Zone, an interactive, simulated marine-environment venue for kids and toddlers. A million gallons of seawater behind the largest window on the planet, the Outer Bay contains 10-foot-tall, 1.5-ton sunfish, pelagic stingrays, green sea turtles as big as dining room tables, vast schools of yellowfin tuna, and species of sharks too big for other aquariums. The Drifters gallery is the largest-scale jellyfish exhibit in the world, where otherworldly music and a dreamlike design for the jellies venue transfix viewers before the pulsing, drifting, rainbow-hued beings. Ocean's Edge comprises a rocky shore gallery and a walk-through tunnel where waves crash over your head, plus a large aviary, giant octopus and hands-on venues. Mission to the Deep features high-definition video of robots that explore the deep sea, a hands-on experience of using high-tech tools to explore a whale skeleton, map undersea mountains, and discover alien life forms. Aquarium Adventures programs for kids include a scuba experience, Science Under Sail cruises, kayaking, and whale-watching.

To avoid lines at the entrance in summer and on weekends, buy tickets in advance and arrive early; the Web site shows packages, daily and special events, tours, and feeding times. Consider signing up for a morning behind-the-scenes tour. A day, even a half day, at the aquarium is an intense, stimulating experience. Take the time to wander out onto the terraces to rest and take in the sights and sounds of the Monterey Bay waters, and plan to have snacks and a meal here. Within the building, the upscale **Portola Cafe** and Restaurant serves fresh seafood, pasta, appetizers, full bar service and use of Zeiss binoculars (reservations 831-648-4870); and there is the Oyster Bar and a self-service cafe (pizza, pasta, Mexican food, clam chowder in a sourdough bowl, sandwiches, and salads), all with fabulous bay views. On summer weekend nights, you can listen to live jazz, stroll through the galleries with a glass of wine, have a light meal from the espresso cart and enjoy dinner at Portola.

One of the most biodiverse marine environments in the world, Monterey Peninsula waters attract divers from all over the world to the **Monterey Bay National Marine Sanctuary,** encompassing 4,000 nautical square miles of kelp forests and rocky reefs inhabited by a miraculous variety of creatures such as leopard shark, bright nudibranchs, and hundreds more species, plus the ever-present otters, dolphins, and whales. *Scuba Diving* magazine chose Monterey Bay as the "Favorite Shore Dive in the U.S.," and the bay has also been in the top five "Favorite Beginner's Dive Destinations." The **Monterey Bay Dive Center** is a PADI (Professional Association of Diving Instructors) dive center where you can rent equipment, take a guided dive tour, and arrange to get certified as a diver (225 Cannery Row; 831-656-0454; www.montereybaydivecenter.com).

LUNCH   **Montrio Bistro**, 414 Calle Principal, Monterey; (831) 648-8880; www.montrio.com. Euro-American urban bistro in a 1910 landmark firehouse. From the display kitchen come Dungeness crab cakes, grilled salmon with fennel ratatouille, and homemade pasta; from the wood-burning rotisserie come rosemary and garlic chicken, plus Black Angus rib eye. The wine list received an award of excellence by *Wine Spectator.* If you can't get a reservation, you can eat in the pleasant cocktail lounge.

AFTERNOON

Stroll about and shop on **Cannery Row** and on Wave Street, just above. At one time just a few blocks of weathered cannery buildings with funky shops and cafes, the waterfront promenade is now rampant with elegance and élan. Steinbeck and sardines were replaced by upscale boutiques and fancy hotels. The seals, otters, and sailing yachts of Monterey Bay remain.

    Cannery Row Antique Mall is more than 20,000 square feet of the antiques and collectibles of 150 dealers (471 Wave St., 831-655-0264; www.canneryrowantiquemall.com). At 700 Cannery Row is a complex of almost three dozen shops and galleries, plus a wax museum, a winery, and cafes. Located here is **A Taste of Monterey,** where you can enjoy a panoramic view of Monterey Bay, wine and food tasting, exhibits, and a multimedia show about the region (831-646-5446; www.tastemonterey.com). What is a day by the bay without a kite? You will find lots of vivid and unique kites, flags, banners, windsocks, and toys at **Windborne Kites** (711 Cannery Row, 831-645-9072). Shoppers and cafe-sitters are drawn to the sophisticated eateries and boutiques on 2 blocks of old Alvarado Street, downtown between Del Monte Avenue and Jefferson Street. Locals head for **Rosine's** for home-style breakfasts, lunches, and dinners, six-layer cakes, pasta, and burgers (434 Alvarado; 831-375-1400; www.rosinesmonterey.com). Wood-fired pizza, an antipasti bar, oak-grilled sandwiches and contemporary Italian food draws a crowd to the bistro, **Tutto Buono** at 469 Alvarado (831-372-1880). The Old Monterey Farmers' Market is held on Alvarado on Tues (831-655-8070).

Drive to the Spanish Bay entrance to the **17-Mile Drive** at Asilomar near the Fishwife restaurant; you'll pay a fee that's well worth it, even on a foggy day, (831-649-8500; www.pebblebeach .com). Ghostly cypress forests and red lichen-painted rocks frame the many vista points. Stop and explore the beautiful beaches and many tidepools; walk or jog on the winding waterfront path. If you're a golfer, this is a chance to see three of the most famous and most difficult courses in the world.

DINNER   **Sardine Factory,** 701 Wave St.; (831) 373-3775; www .sardinefactory.com. For nearly four decades above Cannery Row; elegant, award-winning dining in the ornate Captain's Room, a 19th-century drawing room with a fireplace and candlelight; or in the glass-enclosed garden Conservatory. Choose from a huge menu of seafood, from Dungeness crab cakes to cioppino; herb-crusted ahi to sand dabs; lobster, wild salmon, and prime steaks. Dress up for this special occasional restaurant, and expect perfect service; a smashing wine list and superb food in a town world-famous for its restaurants. The lounge is a hot gathering spot, with an extensive bar menu and live entertainment most evenings; stop here for drinks and appetizers or for a casual dinner. Ask about getting a peek at the medieval-style wine cellar.

LODGING   Monterey Bay Inn.

DAY 3 / MORNING

BREAKFAST   Monterey Bay Inn continental breakfast. Or enjoy buckwheat pancakes or huge omelets at the **Old Monterey Cafe,** voted "Best Breakfast" in the county (489 Alvarado St.; 831-646-1021; www.cafemonterey.com).

Drive south on Highway 1 to Big Sur, about 30 miles on a two-lane, winding mountain road. The brooding shoulders of the **Santa Lucia Mountains** loom to the left, and to the right it's a sheer 1,000-foot drop to a rocky, mostly inaccessible coastline pierced by the small valleys of the Big and Little Sur Rivers. Several river and forest parks are here in the **Los Padres National Forest** (805) 968-6640), where you'll also find good campgrounds and walking and hiking trails. Big Sur is a banana belt, with higher temperatures than Carmel and Monterey, getting more inches of rain but also more sunny days.

You'll cross the **Bixby Creek Bridge,** also known as the Rainbow Bridge, a 260-foot-high single-spanner constructed in 1932. Stop at the Point Sur Lighthouse to whale-watch and take photos, or take a three-hour guided tour, a one-mile distance rising 360 feet in elevation (19 miles south of Rio Road in Carmel; 831-625-4419; www.pointsur.org). Built in 1887-89, this is the only complete Victorian lighthouse open to the public in the state, and it is still used by ships at sea. At **Andrew Molera State Park** (831-667-2315), the **Big Sur River** flows down from the Santa Lucias through this 4,700-acre park, falling into the sea at a long sandy beach. One of many hiking trails runs along the river, through a eucalyptus grove where monarch butterflies spend the winter, to the river's mouth, where you can see a great variety of sea- and shorebirds. For trail maps and information, write in advance to the USDA Forest Service, 406 South Mildred, King City 93930 (831-385-5434). The park is headquarters for the **Ventana Wilderness Society Big Sur Cultural and Natural History Center** where you can watch bird-banding, learn about condors, and see exhibits (831-624-1201; http://ventanaws.org)

One of the most unforgettable ways to see Big Sur is on horse-back. **Molera Horseback Tours** offers daily two-hour rides, each featuring a different perspective, such as the beach, redwood groves, mountain ridges, and sunset excursions (800-942-5486; http://molerahorsebacktours.com).

LUNCH **Nepenthe,** Highway 1 just south of Ventana Inn, Big Sur; (831) 667-2345; www.nepenthebigsur.com. The stone patios of the restaurant are perched on a magical promontory at the edge of the continent, with a bird's-eye view of a long shoreline. Just offshore are natural arches and sea stacks, rocky remnants of an ancient coastline. Try the ambrosia burger or the fresh fish.

AFTERNOON

Drive through **Big Sur Valley,** not a town, really, but a handful of river resorts and campgrounds on both sides of the highway. **Pfeiffer Big Sur State Park** (831-667-2315) is another place to hike, picnic, and fish in the Big Sur River. Docent-led nature walks are given in summer; one trail leads to **Pfeiffer Falls,** in a fern canyon. From the falls, climb the Valley View Trail for zowie views of the lighthouse and the Big Sur Valley gorge.

Just inside the entrance to the park, the casual restaurant at **Big Sur Lodge** overlooks the river. Cottage-style lodge rooms here are in big demand during vacation season, and have been for more than 75 years (831-667-3100; www.bigsurlodge.com). The nearby **Post Ranch Inn** (P.O. Box 219, Big Sur 93920; 831-667-2200; www.postranchinn.com) is a luxurious, visually stunning inn with fireplaces, spa tubs, a renowned restaurant, and complete privacy for guests.

Ten miles farther down the coast, **Julia Pfeiffer Burns State Park** is 2,400 acres of undeveloped wilderness. Trails along McWay Creek lead to a waterfall that plunges into the ocean (831-667-2315). The Partington Creek Trail goes through a canyon and a 100-foot-long rock tunnel to Partington Cove beach, where sea otters play in the kelp beds offshore. A popular walk in the woods is the **Pine Ridge Trail,** right off Highway 1 at Big Sur Station Visitor Center, just south of Julia Pfeiffer Burns State Park. Wild iris and columbine bloom in shady redwood glens and fern grottoes, and if you can make it 7 miles, there are swimming holes at the Big Sur River and a hot springs another 3 miles farther on. Get a topographical map and check trail conditions at the visitor center.

(If you decide to continue to southern California, take note that the two-lane Big Sur highway south from here to San Simeon crosses 30 bridges over deep canyons and stream-cut valleys—breathtaking scenery—and is unrelentingly curvy. About halfway to San Simeon, **Jade Cove** is actually a string of coves, where Monterey jade is found at low tide and following storms. It's a 0.25-mile walk down to the cove from the highway, where you are allowed to collect what will fit into your pockets.)

DINNER   **Ventana Inn and Spa,** 30 miles south of Carmel on Highway 1, Big Sur; (800) 628-6500; www.ventanainn.com. After dark, the walk up lighted outdoor stairs through a forest is a romantic beginning to a romantic evening in the four-star restaurant, which serves lunch and dinner. Indoors, a warm, woodsy atmosphere; outdoors, a stone patio floating high above the sea.

LODGING **Ventana Inn and Spa.** One of the fabulous Joie de Vivre properties, a rustic country-luxe, quiet resort on a hillside between the sea and mountain ridges, a compound of several pine buildings, each with canyon or ocean views. High-ceilinged, wood—paneled luxury suites with fireplaces and a feeling of isolation. Decor is of stone, wood, soft earth-toned fabrics.

There are two heated lap pools, Japanese hot baths, sauna, and massages on your own completely private deck. Indulge yourself in the full-service spa with wraps, scrubs, massages, and exotic, soothing therapies in a glorious natural setting. The elaborate afternoon wine and cheese buffet is in the main lounge. Wild gardens abloom with native flowers and vines; oceans of clematis and jasmine pour over balconies; tree ferns create shady glades. Call ahead for a monthly listing of scheduled special events, from guided naturalist hikes to history, literary, and gardening lectures and musical performances.

DAY 4 / MORNING

BREAKFAST At the Ventana Inn. Enjoy the big breakfast buffet in the sunny dining lounge, outside on a choice of several garden patios, or in your room. Fresh berries, melons, tropical fruits; homemade coffee cakes, croissants, muffins, yogurt, granola.

After a morning exploring the meadow and mountainside trails that start at Ventana Inn, head back to the Bay Area.

There's More . . . .

Golf. **Golf Monterey,** www.golfmonterey.net. Voted "World's #1 Golf Destination" by *Golf Digest*, the peninsula is world-famous for the spectacular, seaside **Pebble Beach Golf Links.** Although a round at Pebble comes with a several-hundred-dollar price tag, there are numerous other top notch courses open to the public.

Bayonet & Black Horse, 1 McClure Way, Seaside; (831) 899-7271; www.bayonetblackhorse.com.

Del Monte Golf Course, 1300 Sylvan Rd., Monterey; (831) 373-2700. Oldest course west of the Mississippi, lovely, reasonable rates.

Laguna Seca Golf Course, 10520 York Rd. off CA 68, Monterey; (831) 373-3701. A Robert Trent Jones beauty from the 1970s.

The Links at Spanish Bay, 17-Mile Dr., Pebble Beach; (800) 654-9300; www.pebblebeach.com. One of the "Greatest Resort Courses" and "Best Golf Resorts in America." All but four of the holes flank the sea, close to true Scottish links.

Pacific Grove Links, 77 Asilomar Blvd., Pacific Grove; (831) 648-5777; www.ci.pg.ca.us/golf.

Pebble Beach Golf Links, 17-Mile Dr., Pebble Beach; (800) 654-9300. Legendary site of U.S. Opens, PGA Championships, and the AT&T Pro-Am, riding the headlands over Stillwater Cove as it has since 1919. Swirling winds and misty hazes, long tee shots over gaping crevasses, and tiny greens create a golfing challenge equaled by few courses in the world.

Peter Hay Golf Course, 17-Mile Dr., Pebble Beach; (831) 622-8723; www.pebblebeach.com. Nine-hole executive course across the street from Pebble Beach Golf Links, reasonable green fees, great for kids and beginners.

Poppy Hills Golf Course, 3200 Lopez Rd., 17-Mile Dr., Pebble Beach; (831) 625-2035; www.poppyhillsgolf.com.

Spyglass Hill Golf Course, Stevenson Drive and Spyglass Hill, Pebble Beach; (800) 654-9300; www.pebblebeach.com. Semi private, ranked #11 on "America's 100 Greatest Public Courses" list by *Golf Digest.*

Races. **Mazda Raceway Laguna Seca,** (800) 327-7322; www
.mazdaraceway.com. Grand Prix auto and motorcycle races bring
out huge crowds at the raceway, just north of Monterey. Come for
the excitement at annual MotoGP, historic car, Grand Am, American Le Mans, and other races. Plan way ahead, and ask about hotel
packages.

Rentals and Tours. **Adventures by the Sea,** 299 Cannery Row,
Monterey; (831) 372-1807; www.adventuresbythesea.com. Rent
mopeds, bikes, kayaks, sign on for a guided bike tour of the
17-Mile Dr.

    Bay Bikes, 585 Cannery Row, Monterey; 831-655-2453; www
.baybikes.com. Rental bikes, surreys and trailers; guided tours.

    Monterey Bay Kayaks, 693 Del Monte Ave., Monterey; (800)
649-5357; www.montereybaykayaks.com. Rentals, tours of Monterey
Bay and Elkhorn Slough, classes.

Wildlife Viewing. **Point Lobos State Reserve,** 2.5 miles south of
Carmel on Highway 1; (831) 624-8413. A rocky point surrounded
by a protected marine environment; otters, whales, harbor seals,
sea lions; scuba diving; spectacular landscape; picnicking, walking, photo snapping (more on Pt. Lobos in the Carmel chapter).

    Monterey Bay Whale Watch, 84 Fisherman's Wharf, Monterey;
(831) 375-4658; www.montereybaywhalewatch.com. Three-hour
winter and spring cruises to see gray whales and dolphins.

Special Events . . . .

FEBRUARY

AT&T Pebble Beach National Pro-Am; (800) 541-9091; www.attpb
golf.com. On one of the most spectacular seaside golf courses in

the world, a legendary golf tournament attracting movie stars, PGA pros, and huge crowds.

MAY

Cooking for Solutions, Monterey Bay Aquarium; (831) 648-4800; www.mbayaq.org. Two days of events focusing on sustainable seafood—where to get it, what to buy, how to cook it. Celebrity chefs from around the world, wine gurus, and other luminaries present cooking demonstrations, seminars, guided farm and vineyard tours, and the incredible food/wine/special presentations "gala" in the aquarium, where the sea life exhibitions are backdrops for food and wine from area restaurants and wineries. The Saturday information fair is free with aquarium admission.

JUNE

Monterey Bay Blues Festival; (831) 394-2652; www.monterey blues.com. On three stages for three days, nearly 50 blues and R&B acts, featuring the likes of the Neville Brothers, Dr. John, Ruth Brown, and Billy Preston.

JULY

California Rodeo Salinas. Pro bull riding, bareback bronco, barrel racing, ridin', ropin' and more rodeo events, two parades with hundreds of horses and costumed riders, Country Western concert (800-771-8807; www.carodeo.com).

Carmel Bach Festival, P.O. Box 575, Carmel 93921; (831) 624-1521; www.bachfestival.org. For more than seven decades, renowned performing artists from around the world, orchestral and choral works, vocal and chamber concerts, recitals, master classes, lectures and informal talks, and family events.

AUGUST

Concours d'Elegance, Pebble Beach; (831) 622-1700; www.pebble beachconcours.net. Pre- and postwar Marques and contemporary marvels of the automobile world, in the stunning setting of Pebble Beach. Wear your glad rags.

SEPTEMBER

Monterey Jazz Festival; (831) 373-3366; www.montereyjazzfes tival.org. At the oldest continuous jazz fest in the world, more than 500 performers, many internationally famous, on seven stages.

Cherry's Jubilee; (831-759-1836; www.svmh.com). Set up lawn chairs and sit back for the free "Show 'n Shine" cruise of more than 1,000 classic cars through Cannery Row, Pacific Grove and downtown Monterey, the kick-off of a three-day event.

OCTOBER

Butterfly Parade and Bazaar, Pacific Grove. School bands and children in butterfly costumes welcome the monarchs' return to their winter home in Pacific Grove, a charming hometown event. Oct to Feb, see thousands of butterflies massing in the trees at the Monarch Grove Sanctuary (www.pgmuseum.org).

Monterey Wine Festival; (800) 422-0251; www.montereywine.com. Held at the aquarium and at a luxury hotel, the oldest and one of the largest wine fests. Auction, food and cooking demonstrations, special tastings, seminars, live entertainment.

NOVEMBER

Great Wine Escape Weekend; (831) 375-9400; www.monterey wines.org. Special winery tours and open houses, winemaker dinners, discounts.

DECEMBER

Parade of Lights, Pacific Grove; (831) 373-3304. Holiday floats, marching bands, dance teams, equestrian groups, and Santa Claus. After the parade, stores are open and carolers entertain.

Other Recommended Restaurants and Lodgings. . . .

BIG SUR

Big Sur River Inn and Restaurant, Pheneger Creek; (800) 548-3610; www.bigsurriverinn.com. Eighteen rooms and family suites with balconies overlooking the river; simple, rustic accommodations. Restaurant and bar, swimming pool, general store, near state parks. Stop in for lunch and the Sunday-afternoon live concerts on the lawn above the river.

Rocky Point, 10 miles south of Carmel on Highway 1; (831) 624-2933; www.rocky-point.com. Spectacular views of the coast from the dining room and the terrace make breakfast, lunch, and dinner memorable experiences. Try the enchiladas, the crab salad, or one of the fabulous steaks.

MONTEREY

Hotel Pacific, 300 Pacific St.; (831) 373-5700 or (800) 554-5542; www.coastalhotel.com. Contemporary Spanish-hacienda suites with fireplaces, down comforters, private patio or balcony; continental breakfast, afternoon tea; fountains, hot tubs, and gardens.

Andril Cottages, 569 Asilomar Blvd., Pacific Grove; (831) 375-0994; www.andrilcottages.com. Retro casitas in a parklike setting 2 blocks from the beach, barbecues, lawns, wood-burning fireplaces, full kitchens, reasonable rates.

Best Western Victorian Inn, 487 Foam St.; (800) 232-4141; www.victorianinn.com. Sixty-eight charming rooms and suites, marble fireplaces, private balconies or patios, some with living rooms and kitchenettes, hot tub; breakfast buffet and afternoon refreshments; walking distance to Cannery Row and the Wharf.

InterContinental—The Clement Monterey, 750 Cannery Row; (831) 375-4500; www.intercontinental.com/montereyic. Brand new on Cannery Row adjacent to the aquarium, a 208-room, urban-chic-style luxury hotel. In the rooms and suites, fireplaces, balconies, the latest high-tech amenities and sea views. Full-service spa, Kids' Club day care. Every seat in the glamorous C Restaurant and Bar has an ocean view; the open-air Pacific View Courtyard for drinks, appetizers and small plates by the outdoor fire pits.

Monterey Plaza Hotel and Spa, 400 Cannery Row; (831) 646-1706); www.montereyplazahotel.com. A four-star, luxury hotel with top-notch restaurants, in a bayside setting with sea views from nearly every public space and from more than half of the 290 rooms (without sea views, some rooms overlook the street, busy Cannery Row). European-style full-service spa. In a lovely setting by the bay, the Duck Club Grill specializes in seafood and regional cuisine. Schooner's Bistro on the Bay, with an open-air bar and terrace, is for casual meals and snacks. Open to the public, big-name summer jazz concerts are held on the outdoor decks of the hotel.

Old Monterey Inn, 500 Martin St.; (831) 375-8284; www.old montereyinn.com. Four-diamond rated, a vine-covered, 1929 Tudor mansion with patios abloom with wisteria, aromatic jasmine, and hundreds of hanging baskets and pots. Understated European country-house decor, fireplaces, elegant extras, extraordinary service. Two honeymoon cottages. Full breakfast by the fire in the elegant dining room.

Spindrift Inn, 652 Cannery Row; (800) 841-1879; www.spindrift inn.com. On the water, 41 luxury rooms, half with ocean views, all with wood-burning fireplaces, down comforters, window seats or private balconies; complimentary breakfast and afternoon wine and cheese.

Tarpy's Roadhouse, CA 68 and Canyon Del Rey near the Monterey airport; (831) 647-1444; www.tarpys.com. A 1920s ranch house with stone walls trailing vines on the outside, covered with art on the inside; large wine cave; garden courtyard dining; updated versions of old-fashioned comfort foods such as polenta with wild mushrooms, Cajun prawns, fresh local seafood, grilled meats, honey mustard rabbit with apples and thyme.

PACIFIC GROVE
Asilomar Conference Center, 800 Asilomar Ave.; (831) 642-4242; www.visitasilomar.com. Unknown to most tourists, this secluded, rustic, historic conference resort hides in a pine-and-oak forest above beautiful Asilomar State Beach. When space is available, individuals and families rent rooms and suites in 32 rustic buildings at reasonable rates that include a bountiful breakfast buffet in a bright, pleasant dining room (dinner available, too, and you can just stop in here for a meal). There is a heated pool, volleyball, a game room, some fireplaces, some kitchens, and easy accessibility

to the wonderful tidepools and the wide, sandy beach; unsuitable for swimming. A mile-long, seaview boardwalk meanders through dunes and wildflowery clifftops. Take a guided history walk with a park ranger (831-372-4076).

Fandango, 223 Seventeenth St., Pacific Grove; (831) 372-3456; www.fandangorestaurant.com. By the fire in the dining room, on the glass-domed terrace, or on the garden patio, European country-style cuisine in a Mediterranean setting. Wood-burning grill, pasta, paella, seafood, cassoulet. Signature dishes are rack of lamb Provençal and Velouté Bongo Bongo Soup. Full bar, exceptional wine list; lunch, brunch, and dinner.

Green Gables and Grand View Inns, 555 and 557 Ocean View Blvd.; (831) 372-4341; www.pginns.com. Side-by-side Queen Anne Victorians with bay views from 25 rooms and cottages; exquisite period interiors, fireplaces, bicycles; elaborate breakfasts and afternoon teas. Walk to Cannery Row.

Lighthouse Lodge and Suites, 1150 Lighthouse Ave.; (831) 655-2111; www.lhls.com. On Point Pinos, with a heated pool; 31 suites with ocean views, fireplaces, Jacuzzi tubs; full breakfast, afternoon refreshments. Complimentary poolside afternoon barbecues. Casual and quite reasonably priced.

Passionfish Grill, 701 Lighthouse Ave.; (831) 655-3311; www.passionfish.net. Line-caught local fish, slow-roasted meats, organic vegetables and salad greens from local farmers.

For More Information . . . .

Big Sur Chamber of Commerce, P.O. Box 87, Big Sur 93920; (831) 667-2100; www.bigsurcalifornia.org.

Cannery Row; www.canneryrow.com. The myriad pleasures of historic and commercial Cannery Row, from accommodations, shopping, dining, outdoor recreation to events, historic sites, and more. Sign up to receive information on special packages.

Monterey County Convention & Visitors Bureau, 765 Wave St., Monterey; (800) 555-6290; www.montereyinfo.org or www.see monterey.org.

Pacific Grove Chamber of Commerce, P.O. Box 167, Pacific Grove 93950; (831) 373-3304.

SOUTHBOUND ESCAPE *Four*

Carmel Sunshine and Shopping

HOME ON THE RANCH, ARTS AND BOUTIQUE MECCA /
2 NIGHTS

Cowboy days

Tennis, golf, horseback rides

Beach walks

Serra's mission

Boutique binge

Art galleries

The Carmel River ambles over the valley floor between two mountain ranges through horse farms, ranch resorts, and meadows liberally sprinkled with spreading oaks. Just a few miles from the Pacific coast, but a world away, the tawny climate of Carmel Valley is warm and dry. Your choices are golf, horseback riding, hiking, biking, tennis, or lying in the sun by a swimming pool.

Once settled in the peace and quiet of the valley, you may find it difficult to leave, but you will enjoy forays to the ocean beaches and to the artists' colony and shopping mecca of Carmel, a square-mile village of rustic country cottages and shingled beach houses in an idyllic forest setting. Carmel's winding lanes are shaded with ancient oaks and cypress, and everyone in town, it seems, is an avid gardener. Hanging baskets and blooming window boxes are everywhere.

Shopping at the hundreds of boutiques and art galleries is the main activity of visitors to Carmel. Originally a Bohemian artists' and writers' colony, the town has more than one hundred art and photography galleries.

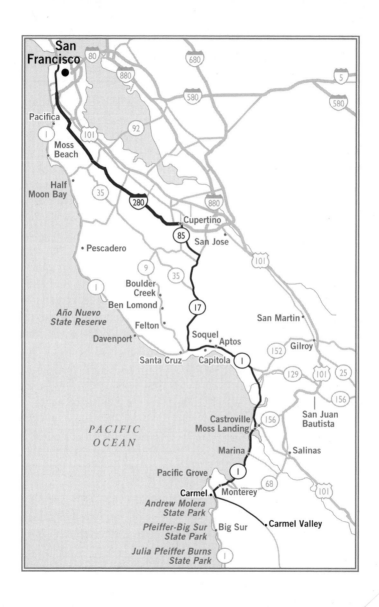

DAY 1 / MORNING

Drive south from San Francisco on I–280, south on CA 85, then CA 17 south to Santa Cruz. From Santa Cruz follow Highway 1 south to Carmel Valley Road, turning east; the trip will take about three hours. You will find a large shopping and restaurant center at the intersection, and along the 12-mile route through the countryside to **Carmel Valley Village** are plant nurseries, a state park, a few winery tasting rooms, and large resorts.

About 3 miles east of Highway 1, in a beautiful setting between the foothills and a green hillside, the **Earthbound Farm Stand,** for 25 years has been laden with organic fresh and dried fruits, herbs and vegetables, flowers, artisanal cheeses, prepared picnic foods, and homemade bakery goods. Even if buying produce is not on your agenda, stop for a cold drink or a snack, and to shop for gifts. Wander the Kids' Garden, the cut-your-own herb garden, and the aromatherapy labyrinth; call ahead to join harvest walks and chef-led tours through 60 acres of garden, and to participate in garlic braiding, crafts workshops, and more events and classes (7250 Carmel Valley Rd.; 831-625-6219; www.ebfarm.com). This unique farm is now America's largest grower of certified organic produce.

Before you reach the village, **Chateau Julien Wine Estate,** a winery with French flair, will welcome you to a soaring, peak-roofed, stone-floored Great Hall, where a blaze in the fireplace lights up the stained-glass windows (8940 Carmel Valley Rd.; 831-624-2600; www.chateaujulien.com). Within the 15-inch-thick stone walls of the "chair" house, crisp "sur lie" Chardonnays and zesty Merlots and Cabernets age in oak barrels.

Annual art and music festivals are held in the lush gardens and the courtyard. The 5-day "Dine in De-Vine" gala involves classic cars, dinners in the vineyards, and more special events. One of seven appellations composing Monterey County's diverse wine country, the Carmel Valley Viticultural Area favors the growing of Bordeaux-style varietals, in particular, Cabernet Sauvignon. Among a grouping of wineries in Carmel Valley Village, **Heller Estate Organic Vineyards** commands attention with a 15-foot-high bronze sculpture entitled *Dancing Partners,* at the entrance to a flamboyant sculpture garden (69 West Carmel Valley Rd.; 831-659-6220; www.hellerestate.com). The winery's motto: "Magical Wines That Dance on Your Palate."

The valley's cattle ranching heritage is recalled at Running Iron Restaurant and Saloon, the oldest continuously operating eating place in these parts, opened in the 1940s (24 East Carmel Valley Rd.; 831-659-4633). Cowboy boots and spurs hang from the ceiling, ranch hands belly up to the bar, and steaks and south-of-the-border specialties are on the menu for local ranchers, winemakers, and tourists.

LUNCH   **Bon Appetit**, 7 Delfino Place, Carmel Valley Village; (831) 659-3559. Sit outdoors under an umbrella, watch the passing scene of the village, and enjoy bouillabaisse, paella, mesquite-grilled fresh fish, gourmet pizzas, and a notable wine list. Another top choice, in a sweet garden cottage, the **Village Fish House** is famous for seafood sizzled over an oak-burning grill, crab ravioli, grilled oysters, cioppino, and more fresh harvest from the sea, which is just a few miles away (19 East Carmel Valley; 831-659-4671; http://villagefishhouse.com).

AFTERNOON

Stretch your legs on some of the 5,000 acres at **Garland Ranch Regional Park** with a hike, stroll, or bike ride along the **Carmel River,** across the forested hillsides, and up on the high ridges overlooking the valley (831-372-3196). An easy, flat 1-mile walk is the Lupine Loop in the lower meadow, a pleasant, wildflowery route in winter and spring, but hot and dry in summertime and fall, unless it has recently rained. The Waterfall Trail is lush with ferns, rushing streams, and beautiful falls that run winter through spring. Other trails take you to breezy hilltop meadows and ponds where birds and ducks reside.

Just a few steps from the parking lot, picnic sites beside the river are pleasant. John Steinbeck wrote in *Cannery Row,* "The Carmel [River] crackles among round boulders, wanders lazily under sycamores, spills into pools, drops in against banks where crayfish live . . . frogs blink from its banks and the deep ferns grow beside it. . . . It's everything a river should be."

Plan to arrive at your valley lodgings early enough to enjoy a late afternoon swim or a game of tennis or perhaps golf.

DINNER **Marinus** at Bernardus Lodge, 415 Carmel Valley Rd., Carmel Valley; (831) 658-3500 or (888) 648-9463. Amble by the jazz combo in the lobby, settle into a gold velvet banquette by the 12-foot-wide stone fireplace, and sip a glass of smoky-cherry Bernardus Cabernet while contemplating the menu. Signature dishes include portobello soup, yellowfin tuna tartare, and lobsterlike, local "spot" prawns. *Wine Spectator* gives the wine list a Grand Award.

LODGING **Bernardus Lodge**, 415 Carmel Valley Rd., Carmel Valley; (831) 658-3400; www.bernardus.com. You are greeted with—what else?—a glass of Bernardus wine at this posh Mediterranean-style retreat in a stunning mountain setting. The four-star lodge feels like a big villa, with shady arbors and gardens, thick walls and stone terraces, a big swimming pool, tennis, bocce, and a croquet lawn. Spacious, cozy rooms have fireplaces, sofas and chairs, two-person tubs, and featherbeds with silky, imported linens. French doors open onto sunny balconies with mountain views. Special services are many, including twice-daily room freshening and nightly wine and cheese in your room. A full-service spa and fitness venue.

DAY 2 / MORNING

BREAKFAST   Bernardus Lodge.

Head west on Carmel Valley Road then just south on Highway 1
to the **Mission San Carlos Borromeo de Carmelo,** one of the most
impressive in California's chain of missions (831-624-1274; www
.carmelmission.org). Star-shaped stained-glass windows, cool col-
onnades, and beautiful courtyard gardens and fountains make this
a place to linger. A warren of thick-walled rooms, restored from
original mission buildings, holds a magnificent museum collection of early Indian, religious, and historical California artifacts.
Inside, the cathedral, cool and silent even on the hottest days, is
sienna, burnt umber, and gold, with soaring ceilings and heavy
wooden pews.

Continue on Rio Road 2 blocks to Santa Lucia; turn left and
follow this street to the waterfront, bearing left to the north end of
Carmel River State Beach (831-649-2836), adjacent to **Monastery
Beach** and the **Carmel River Bird Sanctuary.** Frequented by a wide
variety of waterfowl and shorebirds, these two beaches are visited
by fewer people than Carmel Beach. Wander over the dunes that
form a "plug" for the Carmel River most of the year. Pick up driftwood and shells, or make a 4-mile round-trip run or walk. You may
see scuba divers getting ready to descend into the kelp forests of
the **Carmel Bay Ecological Reserve** offshore.

Monastery Beach is fine for picnicking, but heavy surf can
make it unsafe for swimmers.

Four miles south of Carmel on Highway 1 is **Point Lobos State
Reserve,** named for the offshore rocks called Punta de los Lobos
Marinos (Point of the Sea Wolves), where sea lions lie about (831-
624-8413). A rocky, forested point surrounded by a protected
marine environment, the park's spectacular landscape includes

several miles of trails, pebbled beaches, and one of only two naturally occurring stands of Monterey cypress (the other is at Pebble Beach). In the late 1800s, Robert Louis Stevenson called it the *"most beautiful meeting of land and sea on earth."*

From 6 miles of coastline, whales, harbor seals, and otters are often seen, as well as storms of pelicans, gulls, and cormorants. In the meadows mule deer tiptoe through purple needlegrass and wild lilac. Point Lobos is completely protected—the land, the marine life on the beach and in the tidepools, and the flora and fauna underwater. Not a thing may be removed or disturbed, dogs are not allowed, and visitors are required to stay on hiking trails or beaches. An easy half-hour walk to Headland Cove accesses Sea Lion Point, where sea lions bark and you can see the otters. Come early on weekends, when guided interpretive walks are conducted by park rangers.

LUNCH **Rio Grill** in the Crossroads shopping center at Carmel Valley Road and Highway 1 (831-625-5436; www.riogrill.com). Southwestern-style decor and award-winning food, voted "Best Restaurant in Monterey County," make this a top choice. A wood-burning grill and an oak-wood smoker produce fresh fish, meat, and poultry specialties.

AFTERNOON

In the Crossroads center are several apparel and gifts stores, a bookstore, a European furniture shop; Woodies of Carmel, a Hawaiian and auto-themed shop; jewelry, a coffee shop, a bistro, a Chinese restaurant, a wine shop, and more (www.crossroadsshoppingvillage .com). Adjacent to the Crossroads, **The Barnyard** (831-624-8886; www.thebarnyard.com) is a rambling complex of 50 shops and restaurants in barnlike buildings. In every nook and cranny are riots of blooming native perennials; thousands of flowers, shrubs, and trees; and oceans of bougainvillea, rivers of begonias, and streams of California poppies.

Among the many Barnyard shops is a dollhouse museum, a metalsmithing studio, upscale apparel stores, beauty and health salons, and a chocolatier. Restaurants in the Barnyard include a pizzeria, a Japanese open-hearth grill, a steakhouse, a bistro and a Mexican place. The weekly Carmel Farmers' Market is held here, an annual art and wine festival, and other events.

DINNER Mission Ranch Restaurant, 26270 Dolores St. on the south end of Carmel; (831) 625-9040; www.missionranchcarmel.com. Overlooking the Carmel River with views of the bay and Point Lobos, Mission Ranch is a place where cowboys and cowgirls kick back and eat steak, local fresh fish, and California cuisine in upscale, casual surroundings.

LODGING Carmel Mission Ranch, 26270 Dolores St., Carmel; (831) 624-6436. Plush, pricey rooms here are in charming former ranch buildings; some have fireplaces, living rooms, and memorabilia from Clint Eastwood's movies (he owns the place).

DAY 3 / MORNING

BREAKFAST Rub elbows with the locals at **Katy's Place** (downtown Carmel, Mission Street between Fifth and Sixth; 831-624-0199; www.katysplacecarmel.com), and dig into platters of French toast, eggs, and cottage fries like Grandma used to make.

Lace up your walking shoes, warm up your credit cards, and set off for a day of shopping and gallery hopping. On San Carlos between Fifth and Sixth is the visitor bureau, upstairs in the Eastwood

Building, where you can pick up a walking-tour map and schedule of events (831-624-2522). Also in the building, **GJ's Wild West** sells everything Western, from boots and belts to gorgeous leather jackets, and home decor (800-613-2762; www.americanwestern wear.com).

If you're a jazz fan, look for **The Jazz and Blues Company Store,** which is also a gallery and jazz club, at Fifth and San Carlos next to the Hog's Breath Inn (831-624-6432; www.thejazzandblues company.com). Touted as the "world's only all-jazz store," it's the official Monterey Jazz Festival merchandise headquarters, selling an amazing array of new and vintage records and CDs, art, apparel, posters, books, memorabilia, instruments, and more.

If time is short, stroll down one side of Ocean Avenue and up the other. With time on your hands, wander the side streets, the courtyards, and alleyways. Even those allergic to shopping will enjoy the mix of architecture, everything from English country cottage to California Mission style.

A few notable places to visit: the **Carmel Art Association** at Dolores between Fifth and Sixth (831-624-6176; www.carmelart .org), a cooperative with a wide-ranging collection of the works of top artists; the **Weston Gallery** at Sixth and Dolores (831-624-4453; www.westongallery.com), where three generations of famous photographers are represented; the **Mischievous Rabbit** (Lincoln between Ocean and Seventh; 831-624-6854), a warren of Peter Rabbit-inspired treasures—hand-painted baby clothing, rabbit videos and books, carrot surprises.

Careful browsers discover gardens and shops in more than 60 courtyards; a short courtyard-tour map is available at the visitors bureau. Look for the winding path to the serene **Secret Garden,** on Dolores between Fifth and Sixth, to see unique statuary, a bevy of blooming baskets, and wind chimes; and, incorporating the Pilgrim's Way Bookstore (831-624-4955).

LUNCH — Porta Bella, Ocean between Lincoln and Monte Verde, Carmel; (831) 624-4395. Inventive Mediterranean cuisine in the flower-bedecked Court of the Golden Bough, in the charming cottage, or on the year-round heated garden patio. Lunch, afternoon tea, and dinner. The restaurant loves your dog on the heated patio, presenting your pampered pooch with water in a champagne bucket on a napkin-covered plate.

AFTERNOON

In fact, the whole town is dog-friendly, with many restaurant patios open to leashed pets. Carmel Beach is one of few California beaches to allow four-legged visitors off leash. Co-owned by actress and animal rights activist Doris Day, the elegant **Cypress Inn** welcomes well-behaved pets in your room and on leash in the bar and around the hotel (Lincoln and Seventh Streets; 800-443-7443; www.cypress-inn.com). Nightly doggy biscuit turndown is among the special services. Stop in at Terry's Lounge in the hotel to enjoy live music in the evenings.

A boutique for dogs and cats, **Diggidy Dog** at Mission and Ocean Avenues sells fabulous toys, apparel, gourmet treats, collars, and carriers. In the pet bakery, tempt your pooch with cannoli, biscotti, doughnuts, and cookies (831-625-1585; www.diggidydogcarmel .com). At **Mackie's Parlour Pet Boutique,** Ocean and Monte Verde, pick up a jeweled collar, homemade dog treats, and the board games *Dogopoly* and *Catopoly* (831-626-0600; www.mackiesparlour.com). In the Carmel Plaza shopping center, take your pooch to the Fountain of Woof drinking fountain.

Aviation is the theme at **Wings America,** on the corner of Dolores and Seventh (831-626-9464; www.wingsamerica.com). The collection of aircraft model sculptures and specialty authentic aviation apparel is astonishing; also books, videos, and jewelry.

New and antique art, decoys, and gifts with waterfowl, wildlife, and sporting dog motifs are on display at **The Decoy,** on Sixth between Dolores and Lincoln (831-625-1881).

Golf is on stage at **Golf Arts and Imports** (Dolores and Sixth; 831-625-4488)—part shop, part museum and gallery—in photos and paintings of legendary courses and collectibles and antiques. Look for a second shop at the Lodge at Pebble Beach.

Many of the inns and hotels in Carmel are historic landmarks, such as **La Playa Hotel** at Eighth and Camino Real, a pink Mediterranean mansion built in 1904 (831-624-6476; www.laplayahotel .com). Take a peek at the luscious gardens blooming beneath a canopy of Angel's Trumpet trees. The lobby is a museumlike world of heirloom furnishings and contemporary art. Rooms are upscale traditional, with views of the sea, the gardens, or the village. Cottages are hidden in a pine and cypress grove; each has a kitchen, a fireplace, and a private terrace. With a lovely ocean-view terrace, the **Terrace Grill** here is one of the best restaurants in town for breakfast, lunch, dinner, and brunch (831-624-4010). You can dine until 11 p.m. in the lounge.

Before leaving town, take a late-afternoon walk on **Carmel Beach** at the foot of Ocean Avenue—truly white, powdery sand; truly memorable sunsets. If you spot a stone spire above a stone cottage above the beach, that is the **Robinson Jeffers Tor House and Hawk Tower,** built by hand by the famous poet of the early 20th century. On weekends, you can tour the home, tower, and gardens (26304 Ocean View Ave.; 831-624-1813; www.torhouse.org).

Drive north on Highway 1 to CA 156, connecting with US 101 north to San Francisco.

There's More . . . .

Special Tour. Carmel Walks, P.O. Box 975, Carmel 93921; (831) 642-2700; www.carmelwalks.com. Two-hour guided tours to hidden courtyards and gardens, storybook cottages; inside scoop on the history, the famous artists, writers, and movie stars, and the charms of Carmel, including photographer Edward Weston's photo studio, architectural landmarks by such legendary creators as Frank Lloyd Wright, Greene, Bernard Maybeck and Julia Morgan, and more.

Golf. **Golf Club at Quail Lodge,** 8000 Valley Greens Dr., Carmel Valley; (831) 620-8808; www.quaillodge.com. Recently updated, a Robert Muir Graves beauty in the Carmel Valley. Luckily, you are not required to take a cart, all the better to enjoy the 840 acres of wild countryside and elaborate landscaping.

Rancho Canada Golf Course, Carmel Valley Road, 1 mile from Highway 1; (831) 624-0111. Two 18-hole public courses with mountain backdrop and valley views.

Hiking. **Jacks Peak County Park,** Jacks Peak Road, Monterey on the north side of Carmel Valley; (831) 647-7799. Hike in an enchanted pine forest up the trail to valley views, or take a short trek to a picnic spot.

Mission Trail Park, Carmel. Thirty-five acres of native vegetation, 5 miles of trails. Enter at Mountain View and Crespi, at Eleventh Street and Junípero, or on Rio Road across from the Mission.

Special Events . . . .

MAY

Carmel Art Festival, Carmel; (831) 642-2503; www.carmelartfestival.org. Gallery Walk open house and entertainment; meet the artists at dozens of Carmel galleries; gala party and auction; sculpture in the park; four days of events.

JUNE THROUGH AUGUST
Outdoor Forest Theatre Season, Carmel; (831) 626-1681; www
.foresttheaterguild.org.

JULY
Carmel Bach Festival; (831) 624-2046; www.bachfestival.com.
Internationally acclaimed; two weeks of concerts and classes.

AUGUST
Carmel Valley Fiesta, Carmel Valley Village; (831) 644-6180. Wild-
boar barbecue, street dance, parade, dog and car shows, arts and
food booths, golf tournament, entertainment on outdoor stages.

SEPTEMBER
Carmel Shakespeare Festival; (831) 622-0100.

Sand Castle Building Contest, Carmel Beach; (831) 624-2522.
Architects and amateurs vie for biggest, best, and most outrageous
sand structure.

Other Recommended Restaurants and Lodgings . . . .

CARMEL
The Cottage, Lincoln between Ocean and Seventh; (831) 625-
6260; www.cottagerestaurant.com. Panettone French toast for
breakfast, artichoke soup and chicken stew in a sourdough basket
for lunch, lemon chicken for dinner.

Highlands Inn, Park Hyatt Carmel, 4 miles south of Carmel on
Highway 1; (831) 620-1234; www.highlandsinn.hyatt.com. Since
1917, wonderful accommodations at a full-service, five-star resort
with glorious ocean views. The renowned restaurant, Pacific's Edge,

has spectacular sea views from big windows and a California/French menu to match. Twenty-seven thousand bottles of wine in the cellar. The casual California Market cafe here is a fun place to have lunch on the way to Big Sur—a table on the deck overlooking the coast or indoors by the pot-bellied stove; pasta, salads, sandwiches. Luxurious rooms have wood-burning fireplaces, outdoor decks, or balconies. Suites have Jacuzzi tubs, kitchens, and special amenities like terry robes and large dressing areas. Heated pool, spa.

L'Auberge Carmel, Monte Verde at Seventh Street; (831) 624-8578; www.laubergecarmel.com. A Relais & Chateaux, luxurious European-style inn and restaurant. Twenty spacious, romantic rooms around a garden courtyard have such special features as soaking tubs, hammered-copper sinks, designer linens, comfy seating areas, and original artwork. In the intimate 12-table restaurant, local seafood, meats, and produce, some from the on-site organic garden, become succulent dishes—from braised artichokes to rabbit ragout, venison with sour cherry sauce, and fresh fish of all kinds; not to be missed, the chocolate-banana beignets. Take a peek in the 5,000-bottle, underground wine cellar. Parking can be difficult. This is the highest rated lodging in town, so reserve well ahead.

Vagabond House Inn, Fourth and Dolores; (831) 624-7738; www.vagabondshouseinn.com. Half-timbered English Tudor country inn; blooming courtyard gardens; elegant, traditional decor; continental breakfast.

Village Corner Mediterranean Bistro, Dolores and Sixth; (831) 624-3588. For more than 50 years, inside and on the patio, locals have been meeting here to complain about how Carmel isn't like it used to be. Breakfast, good sandwiches, salads; less expensive than most.

CARMEL VALLEY

Carmel Valley Ranch, 1 Old Ranch Rd.; (866-282-4745; www
.carmelvalleyranch.com. Newly renovated, a sprawling luxury resort
on an oak-studded hillside overlooking a beautiful golf course
and the valley. An outdoor dining and cocktail terrace overlooks a
spectacular pool and gardens. Huge suites are private and quiet,
secluded in the trees. Twelve tennis courts come with a full-time
pro, and the Pete Dye championship golf course is one of the most
challenging on the peninsula; with a clubhouse restaurant. New
owners promise additional enhancements.

Cobblestone Inn, Junipero between Seventh and Eighth; (800) 833-
8836; www.cobblestoneinncarmel.com. A real Carmel charmer in
the English style, with stone fireplaces in each room, antiques,
four-posters, and privacy. Full breakfast on the garden patio and
afternoon tea by the fire. Bicycles; warm, special attention.

Inn at Stonepine, 150 East Carmel Valley Rd.; 800-678-8946;
www.historichotels.org. Old-world elegance at a ca. 1920 country estate, with tennis, horseback riding, a four-hole practice golf
course, sumptuous accommodations in the château or in a guest
house. Impeccable service, privacy, and unparalleled natural surroundings, lodging in elaborate suites. You can take lessons and/
or watch dressage, hunter-jumper, and sulky track activities, and
enjoy carriage rides, hayrides, the formal gardens, and the golf
practice course. Events and weddings take place here, so ask about
those when making your reservations.

Quail Lodge Resort and Golf Club, 8205 Valley Greens Dr.; (831)
624-1581; www.quaillodge.com. Four-diamond rates, an upscale,
full-service resort with a golf course at the foot of the mountains.
Rooms, suites, and villas open into lush gardens; some have

fireplaces. *Travel + Leisure* calls it one of the "Best Small Hotels in the World." The Covey Restaurant here is one of the best on the peninsula, a casually elegant place with views of a lake, gardens, and the hills. Swimming pool, tennis, nearby walks, and a certain relaxed luxury make this a place to hide away for a long weekend.

PEBBLE BEACH

Inn at Spanish Bay, 2700 17-Mile Dr.; (800) 654-9300; www.pebble beach.com. In the lee of the dark, brooding Del Monte cypress forest, the luxurious resort hotel lies a few hundred feet from the shoreline. Contemporary-design rooms and suites, each with private patio or balcony, marble bathrooms, some fireplaces, sitting rooms. One of the top tennis complexes in the country, fitness club, complete spa facilities and beauty treatments, restaurants, and upscale shops. Surrounded by the Links at Spanish Bay, the inn is a mecca for golfers who play here and at nearby Pebble Beach. Fabulous sea views, glamorous blond Art Deco decor, and world-class Euro-Asian cuisine make Roy's at Pebble Beach, at the inn, a special occasion restaurant (831-647-7423).

The Lodge at Pebble Beach, 17-Mile Dr.; (800) 654-9300; www .pebblebeach.com. One of the world's great hostelries, Pebble feels like a private club. Luxury rooms and suites, all quite spacious, most with private balcony, sea or garden views, large dressing and sitting areas, some with fireplaces. Guests may play golf at Pebble Beach Golf Links—California's most famous course—and at nearby Links at Spanish Bay, Spyglass Hill, and Old Del Monte. Pool with sea view, 14 tennis courts, fitness club, equestrian center, several outstanding restaurants and cafes. Spectacular is too small a word to describe Pebble Beach. If ultra-luxe and ultra-privacy what you're seeking, book a suite at Casa Palmero on the first and seconds fairways, with an exclusive main house with living room, library, billiard room, heated outdoor pool, and complimentary evening refreshments in the bar and lounge. (This is where Tiger Woods stays).

Stillwater Bar and Grill, 17-Mile Dr.; (831) 625-8524. At one of the world's great hostelries—the Lodge at Pebble Beach—within view of crashing waves of the Pacific and the notorious 18th hole of the Pebble Beach Golf Links. Fresh seafood is superb in a fresh, contemporary, casual setting; don't miss the grilled abalone appetizer.

For More Information . . . .

Carmel-by-the-Sea Visitors Bureau, San Carlos between Fifth and Sixth, P.O. Box 4444, Carmel 93921; (800) 550-4333; www .carmelcalifornia.com.

Carmel Valley Chamber of Commerce, 13 West Carmel Valley Rd., Carmel Valley 93924; (831) 659-4000; www.carmelvalleychamber .com.

Inns by the Sea; (800) 433-4732; www.innsbythesea.com. Reservation services for several inns.

Monterey Peninsula Golf Packages, P.O. Box 504, Carmel Valley 93924; (800) 214-4653; www.golfmonterey.net.

INDEX

ABOUT THE AUTHOR

Karen Misuraca is a travel, golf and outdoor writer based in Sonoma, in the heart of California's Wine Country. When not exploring the California coast and the San Francisco Bay Area, she writes travel books and contributes articles to a variety of publications.

She is the author of *Backroads of the California Coast, Backroads of the California Wine Country, The 100 Best Golf Resorts of the World, The California Coast, Our San Francisco,* and *Fun With the Family Northern California.* Karen is the founder and editor of BestGolfResortsofTheWorld.com.

She has written about golf in Ireland, ancient cities in Jordan, waterborne safaris in Africa, and adventure travel in Central America and Vietnam. She is accompanied on some of her journeys by her three daughters, a lively contingent of grandchildren, and her husband, Michael Capp, an international broker of architectural products.

Travel Like a Pro

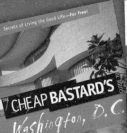

Secrets of Living the Good Life—For Free!

THE CHEAP BASTARD'S
Washington, D.C.

100
BEST
Resorts of the Caribbean

OFF THE BEATEN PATH
WASHINGTON
A GUIDE TO UNIQUE PLACES →

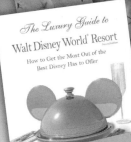

The Luxury Guide to
Walt Disney World Resort
How to Get the Most Out of the
Best Disney Has to Offer

shifra stein's
day trips

from kansas city
fifteenth edition

JOHN HOWELL S III

NINTH EDITION
CHOOSE COSTA RICA
FOR RETIREMENT

fun with the family Texas
hundreds of ideas for day trips with the kids

Tampa

SCENIC DRIVING
COLORADO